# Business Writing

## FOR DUMMIES®

A Wiley Brand

## by Natalie Canavor

D1016058

FOR DUMMIES®
A Wiley Brand

**Business Writing For Dummies®**

Published by: **John Wiley & Sons, Ltd.**, The Atrium, Southern Gate, Chichester, www.wiley.com

This edition first published 2013

© 2013 John Wiley & Sons, Ltd, Chichester, West Sussex.

John Wiley & Sons Ltd, The Atrium, Southern Gate, Chichester, West Sussex, PO19 8SQ, United Kingdom

For details of our global editorial offices, for customer services and for information about how to apply for permission to reuse the copyright material in this book please see our website at www.wiley.com.

The right of the author to be identified as the author of this work has been asserted in accordance with the Copyright, Designs and Patents Act 1988.

Wiley publishes in a variety of print and electronic formats and by print-on-demand. Some material included with standard print versions of this book may not be included in e-books or in print-on-demand. If this book refers to media such as a CD or DVD that is not included in the version you purchased, you may download this material at http://booksupport.wiley.com. For more information about Wiley products, visit www.wiley.com.

Designations used by companies to distinguish their products are often claimed as trademarks. All brand names and product names used in this book are trade names, service marks, trademarks or registered trademarks of their respective owners. The publisher is not associated with any product or vendor mentioned in this book.

For general information on our other products and services, please contact our Customer Care Department within the U.S. at 877-762-2974, outside the U.S. at (001) 317-572-3993, or fax 317-572-4002. For technical support, please visit www.wiley.com/techsupport.

For technical support, please visit www.wiley.com/techsupport.

A catalogue record for this book is available from the British Library.

ISBN 978-1-118-58364-7 (pbk); ISBN 978-1-118-58361-6 (ebk); ISBN 978-1-118-58362-3 (ebk); ISBN 978-1-118-58363-0 (ebk)

Printed in Great Britain by TJ International Ltd, Padstow, Cornwall

10 9 8 7 6 5 4 3 2 1

# Contents at a Glance

*Introduction* ............................................................. *1*

*Part I: Winning with Writing* ............................. *7*

Chapter 1: Make Writing Your Not-So-Secret Weapon ....................... 9

Chapter 2: Planning Your Message: Your Secret Weapon ................ 21

Chapter 3: Making Your Writing Work: The Basics.......................... 47

Chapter 4: Self-Editing: Professional Ways to Improve
Your Own Work........................................................................ 73

Chapter 5: Troubleshooting Your Writing: Fixing
Common Problems ................................................................. 99

*Part II: Putting Your Skills to Work for
Everyday Business Writing* ............................. *123*

Chapter 6: Writing Emails That Get Results...................................... 125

Chapter 7: Creating High Impact Business Correspondence........... 149

*Part III: Writing Business Documents,
Promotional Material and Presentations* .......... *175*

Chapter 8: Building the Biggies: Major Business Documents.......... 177

Chapter 9: Promoting Yourself and Your Organization ................... 201

Chapter 10: Writing for the Spoken Word ........................................ 223

*Part IV: Writing for the Digital Universe* ......... *247*

Chapter 11: Evolving Your Writing for Online Media ...................... 249

Chapter 12: Writing for Websites and Blogs .................................... 269

*Part V: Thinking Global, Writing Global* .......... *297*

Chapter 13: Using English as the Global Language of Business ...... 299

Chapter 14: Adapting Business English to Specific Countries......... 313

*Part VI: The Part of Tens* ................................. *335*

Chapter 15: Ten Ways to Advance Your Career with Writing ......... 337

Chapter 16: Ten Ways to Tweet Strategically.................................... 345

*Index* .................................................................. *353*

# Table of Contents

*Introduction*................................................. 1

  Conventions Used in This Book .............................. 2
  What You Need Not Read ...................................... 2
  Foolish Assumptions ........................................ 2
  How This Book Is Organised ................................. 3
    Part I: Winning with Writing ............................ 3
    Part II: Putting Your Skills to Work for Everyday
      Business Writing ..................................... 4
    Part III: Writing Business Documents, Promotional
      Materials, and Presentations ......................... 4
    Part IV: Writing for the Digital Universe ............... 4
    Part V: Thinking Global, Writing Global ................. 4
    Part VI: The Part of Tens ............................... 5
  Icons Used in This Book .................................... 5
  Where to Go from Here ...................................... 5

*Part I: Winning with Writing* ........................... 7

  **Chapter 1: Make Writing Your Not-So-Secret Weapon . . .9**

    Planning and Structuring Every Message .............. 12
    Applying Audience-Plus-Goal Strategy to Any Business Need ..... 16
      Impressing with email, letters, and
        business documents ............................ 16
      Using stories and value propositions ............ 17
      Writing the spoken word ......................... 17
      Writing online: from website to blog to tweet ... 18
      Globalizing business English .................... 19

  **Chapter 2: Planning Your Message: Your**
  **Secret Weapon** ..........................................21

    Adopting the Plan-Draft-Edit Principle .............. 21
    Fine-Tuning Your Plan: Your Goals and Audience ...... 23
      Defining your goal: Know what you want .......... 23
      Defining your audience: Know your reader ........ 25
      Brainstorming the best content for your purpose ... 29
      Writing to groups and strangers ................. 30
      Imagining your readers .......................... 31

Making People Care ................................................ 33
Connecting instantly with your reader ...................... 33
Focusing on what's-in-it-for-them ........................ 34
Highlighting benefits, not features ............................ 35
Finding the concrete, limiting the abstract .............. 36
Choosing Your Written Voice: Tone ...................................... 38
Being appropriate to the occasion, relationship
and culture .............................................................. 39
Writing as your authentic self ...................................... 40
Being relentlessly respectful ........................................ 41
Smiling when you say it ................................................ 42
Using Relationship-Building Techniques ............................. 43
Personalizing what you write ........................................ 44
Framing messages with 'you' not 'I' .............................. 45

## Chapter 3: Making Your Writing Work: The Basics . . . 47

Stepping into 21st Century Writing Style ............................ 47
Aiming for a clear, simple style .................................... 48
Applying readability guidelines .................................... 49
Matching reading level to audience ................... 50
Assessing readability level ................................... 51
Finding the right rhythm ................................................ 53
Fixing the short and choppy ............................... 54
Fixing the long and complicated ....................... 54
Achieving a conversational tone ................................ 56
Enlivening Your Language ...................................................... 58
Relying on everyday words and phrasing ................. 58
Choosing reader-friendly words .................................. 59
Focusing on the real and concrete ............................. 60
Finding action verbs ...................................................... 62
Crafting comparisons to help readers ....................... 64
Using Reader-Friendly Graphic Techniques ....................... 66
Building in white space .................................................. 67
Toying with type .............................................................. 67
Fonts .......................................................................... 67
Point-size .................................................................. 68
Margins and columns ............................................. 68
Keeping colors simple .................................................... 69
Adding effective graphics ............................................. 70
Breaking space up with sidebars, boxes and lists ..... 70

**Chapter 4: Self-Editing: Professional Ways
to Improve Your Own Work.....................73**

Changing Hats: Going from Writer to Editor ........................ 74
Choosing a way to edit.................................................. 74
Option 1: Marking up print-outs ........................ 75
Option 2: Editing onscreen................................... 75
Option 3: Tracking your changes ...................... 76
Distancing yourself from what you write .................. 77
Reviewing the Big and Small Pictures ............................... 78
Assessing content success............................................ 78
Assessing the effectiveness of your language............ 79
Avoiding telltale up-down-up inflection...................... 81
Looking for repeat word endings................................ 82
The -ing words ....................................................... 83
The -ion words ....................................................... 84
The -ize words......................................................... 85
The -ent, -ly and -ous words............................. 85
Pruning prepositions..................................................... 86
Cutting all non-contributing words ........................... 87
Moving from Passive to Active............................................ 89
Thinking 'action' .............................................................. 90
Trimming 'there is' and 'there are'............................... 91
Cutting the haves and have nots ................................. 92
Using the passive deliberately..................................... 92
Sidestepping Jargon, Clichés and Extra Modifiers .............. 93
Reining in jargon.............................................................. 93
Cooling the clichés .......................................................... 95
Minimizing modifiers...................................................... 95

**Chapter 5: Troubleshooting Your Writing:
Fixing Common Problems .....................99**

Organizing Your Document ................................................... 100
Paragraphing for logic................................................... 100
Building with subheads.................................................. 102
Working with transitions .............................................. 103
Working in lists: Numbers and bulleting ................. 105
Numbered lists................................................. 105
Bulleted lists ...................................................... 106
Catching Common Mistakes ..................................................... 108
Using comma sense........................................................ 109
Using 'however' correctly.............................................. 111
Matching nouns and pronouns ................................... 112
Weighing 'which' vs. 'that'.............................................. 113
Pondering 'who' vs. 'that'................................................ 114

Choosing 'who' vs. 'whom' ........................................ 114
Beginning with 'and' or 'but' .................................. 115
Ending with prepositions........................................... 115
Reviewing and Proofreading: The Final Check.................. 117
Checking the big picture............................................ 117
Proofreading your work............................................. 119
Creating your very own writing improvement
guide ........................................................................ 120

## Part II: Putting Your Skills to Work for Everyday Business Writing ............................ 123

### Chapter 6: Writing Emails That Get Results ......... 125

Fast-Forwarding Your Agenda In-House and
Out-of-House ........................................................... 126
Getting Off to a Great Start ...................................... 128
Writing subject lines that get your message read... 129
Using salutations that suit............................................ 131
Drafting a strong email lead ....................................... 132
Building Messages That Achieve Your Goals..................... 134
Clarifying your own goals............................................. 134
Assessing what matters about your audience......... 136
Determining the best content for emails.................. 138
Structuring Your Middle Ground ............................... 140
Closing Strong ......................................................... 142
Perfecting Your Writing for Email.............................. 143
Monitoring length and breadth ................................ 144
Signalling style .............................................................. 144
Going short: Words, sentences, paragraphs........... 144
Using graphic techniques to promote clarity ......... 145
Add subheads ................................................... 145
Bring in bulleted and numbered lists ............. 146
Consider bold face ........................................... 147
Respect overall graphic impact...................... 147
Using the signature block ............................................ 148

### Chapter 7: Creating High Impact Business Correspondence ............................... 149

Succeeding with Cover Letters ............................. 150
Planning a cover letter.............................................. 151
Opening with pizazz ................................................... 152
Targeting a cover letter's multiple audience ........... 153
Saving something special for cover letters ............. 154

Networking with Letters.......................................................... 157
    Making requests: Informational interviews,
       references and intros ............................................ 157
    Saying thank you................................................................ 160
Writing to Complain............................................................... 163
Crafting Letters of Record ...................................................... 165
Introducing Yourself in Letter Form....................................... 167
Creating Sales Letters............................................................. 169

## Part III: Writing Business Documents, Promotional Material and Presentations........... 175

### Chapter 8: Building the Biggies: Major Business Documents .....................................177

Writing the Executive Summary.......................................... 178
    Giving long documents perspective......................... 179
    Determining what matters........................................ 180
Shaping Successful Reports................................................. 182
    Focusing reader attention ....................................... 183
    Shaping the report..................................................... 185
    Drafting the report..................................................... 186
Fast-tracking Yourself through Proposals....................... 187
    Writing formal proposals.......................................... 187
    Writing informal proposals ...................................... 190
Creating Business Plans....................................................... 193
Writing Tips for All Business Documents............................195
    Finding the right tone............................................... 195
    Putting headlines to work......................................... 196
    Incorporating persuasive techniques ...................... 198

### Chapter 9: Promoting Yourself and Your Organization ..........................201

Finding the Heart of Your Business Message...................... 202
    Searching for true value............................................ 204
    Making your case in business terms ........................ 208
    Stating your personal value...................................... 209
    Representing your department.................................. 210
    Putting your core value message to work................ 211
Finding, Shaping, and Using Stories ................................... 212
    Finding your story ...................................................... 213
    Building your story..................................................... 214
    Story-writing tips ....................................................... 215
    Putting stories to work............................................... 217

Using Value Messages and Stories to Promote ................ 218
Writing better résumés ............................................. 219
Writing online profiles ............................................ 220
Writing email promotions ......................................... 221

**Chapter 10: Writing for the Spoken Word ......... 223**

Elevating Your Elevator Speech ................................... 223
Defining your goal ....................................... 224
Defining your audience ............................... 225
Strategizing your content .......................... 225
Representing your organization and yourself ......... 228
Preparing and Giving Presentations ............................ 229
Planning what to say ................................... 230
Beginning well ................................... 231
Middling well ..................................... 231
Ending well ....................................... 232
Crafting your presentations with writing ......... 232
Integrating visuals ..................................... 233
Standing and delivering ............................. 235
Scripting for Video ................................................ 237
Introducing yourself with video ................... 238
Sharing expertise ....................................... 239
Writing the script ....................................... 240
Scripting Yourself for Practical Purposes .................... 243
Composing talking points for fun and profit ......... 244
Scripting telephone messages that work ............ 245

**Part IV: Writing for the Digital Universe ......... 247**

**Chapter 11: Evolving Your Writing for Online Media ... 249**

Gaining Perspective on Digital Media ......................... 251
Changing significantly – and yet very little .......... 251
Leveraging your digital power ..................... 252
Strategizing Your Digital Media Program ................... 254
Thinking through your online goals .............. 254
Attracting the online audiences you want ......... 256
Turning Scanners into Readers ................................. 258
Adopting a share-it outlook ........................ 258
Clarifying your message ............................. 259
Communicating credibility ......................... 259
Cutting the hype, maxing the evidence ............ 261

Using non-linear strategies...................................... 261
Incorporating interactive strategies......................... 262
Shaping Your Writing for Digital Media ............................. 263
Loosening up..................................................... 264
Keeping it simple ............................................. 264
Keeping it global ............................................. 266
Keeping it short: Tweets and texting ....................... 266

**Chapter 12: Writing for Websites and Blogs ........269**

Shaping Your Words for Websites and Blogs..................... 270
Working on your writing style for websites
and blogs..................................................... 271
Consciously adapt your writing style ............. 271
Keep your copy short, pithy, substance-
focused, and straightforward..................... 271
Choose your keywords early on..................... 271
Use your keywords in headlines, subheads
and body copy ................................... 272
Break copy up into small chunks ................... 272
Minimize scrolling................................. 272
Make every page self-explanatory and
self-contained................................... 272
Go for clear (rather than clever) title
buttons, icons and links........................ 273
Frame everything in you, and we or I ............ 273
Craft conversational, fast-reading copy ........ 273
Building a Traditional Website............................. 273
Defining your goals....................................... 274
Refining your audience ideas ....................... 275
Structuring a basic site............................... 276
Assembling a home page ............................. 278
Company names and taglines ................... 279
The positioning statement ..................... 280
Calling for action........................................ 282
Writing your inside pages............................. 283
About Us ............................................. 283
The Services page................................... 284
The Contact page ................................. 285
Testimonials....................................... 285
Incorporating Graphics and Other Elements ................... 286
Creating Your Own Blog.................................... 288
Planning your blog..................................... 289
Choosing a subject ..................................... 290

Writing for blogs ............................................... 292
    Structure and organization ............................ 292
    Tone ............................................................... 292
    Length ............................................................ 293
    Headlines ....................................................... 293
    Subheads ........................................................ 294
Categories and tagging .................................... 295

# Part V: Thinking Global, Writing Global .......... 297

## Chapter 13: Using English as the Global Language of Business ........................299

Considering Native English in All Its Flavors ..................... 300
Adapting Your Writing for Global English ......................... 302
Writing Messages to Send 'Round the World' ..................... 304
    Monitoring your assumptions .................................... 304
    Connecting with other cultures ................................ 305
    Writing first messages ............................................. 307
        Beginning well ..................................................... 307
        Writing the middle and end ............................. 308
        Maintaining the correspondence ..................... 309
Writing Other Materials .................................................. 309
    Translating promotional materials ........................... 310
    Globalizing your website ......................................... 310
    Reviewing your Internet presence ............................ 312

## Chapter 14: Adapting Business English to Specific Countries ........................313

Writing to China ............................................................ 315
    Practical tips for email and letters ................. 315
    Mistakes to avoid .............................................. 316
    Cultural issues .................................................. 316
Writing to Russia ........................................................... 317
    Practical tips for email and letters ................. 318
    Mistakes to avoid .............................................. 319
    Cultural issues .................................................. 319
Writing to France .......................................................... 320
    Practical tips for email and letters ................. 320
    Mistakes to avoid .............................................. 321
    Cultural issues .................................................. 321

Writing to Japan ............................................................ 322
    Practical tips for email and letters ................... 323
    Mistakes to avoid ............................................. 323
    Cultural issues ................................................. 324
Writing to India .............................................................. 325
    Practical tips for email and letters ................... 325
    Mistakes to avoid ............................................. 326
    Cultural issues ................................................. 326
Writing to Mexico .......................................................... 327
    Practical tips for email and letters ................... 327
    Mistakes to avoid ............................................. 328
    Cultural issues ................................................. 328
Writing to Germany ....................................................... 329
    Practical tips for email and letters ................... 329
    Mistakes to avoid ............................................. 330
    Cultural issues ................................................. 330
Writing to Brazil ............................................................ 331
    Practical tips for email and letters ................... 332
    Mistakes to avoid ............................................. 332
    Cultural issues ................................................. 333

## *Part VI: The Part of Tens* ................................ *335*

### Chapter 15: Ten Ways to Advance Your Career with Writing ......................... 337

Use Everything You Write to Build Your
    Professional Image ................................................ 337
Write a Great Elevator Speech – and Use It ...................... 338
Write a Long-Range Career Plan for Yourself .................... 338
Write an Ad for Your Dream Job ...................................... 339
Go Out of Your Way to Thank People ............................... 339
Take Notes to Control the Conversation ........................... 340
Use Messages to Stay in Touch and Build
    Relationships ......................................................... 340
Write First-Rate Blog Posts, Comments and Tweets ........ 341
Know How to Explain Your Value ..................................... 342
Profile Your Supervisor for a Better Relationship ........... 342

### Chapter 16: Ten Ways to Tweet Strategically ....... 345

Plan Your Twitter Program ............................................. 346
Decide Who You Want to Be ............................................ 346
Take Pains with Your Bio and Photo ................................ 347
Listen to Your Target Audiences ..................................... 347

Aim to Be Useful..................................................................... 348
Avoid Blatant Self-Promotion ............................................. 348
Use Twitter for Surveys and Questions ............................. 349
Write Tweets as the Ultimate Self-Edit Test ...................... 349
Tweet at Optimal Times.......................................................... 350
Treat Twitter as a Serious Job-Hunting Tool..................... 350

*Index*............................................................................ *353*

# Introduction

. . . . . . . . . . . . . . . . . . . . . . . . . . . . . . . . . . . . . . . . . .

*A* funny thing happened on the way to the 21st century. The ability to write well turned into a power tool for success.

Whether you're a manager who wants to rise, an entrepreneur who hopes to do it *your* way, a professional or a specialist of any kind, good writing helps you accomplish your goals.

If you're reading this book, you already know that, but I think you'll be surprised by how many more ways good writing can reward you than you now suspect. Research shows that good writers are hired first and promoted early, particularly in today's growth industries. No surprise there! Companies, non-profits, and government agencies alike must communicate well to survive and thrive. Good writers are increasingly at a premium in every field.

The growing role of writing is a rarely mentioned by-product of the digital revolution. Earlier, decision-makers used slews of people to help them look good in written form, from secretaries who rewrote their memos to public relations staffers to speak for the company. Now, with delivery systems so accessible, few managers are so sheltered. You stand on your own for everyday messaging. And you depend on writing for entrée to a world of nearly overwhelming opportunity.

Today you still need the memos, letters, reports, proposals and articles – plus newer media like websites, blogs, marketing emails, and social media posts. Whenever a new communication venue emerges, the writing challenge grows.

No wonder communication professionals proclaim that 'Content is king'. In this new democratized world where anybody can reach anyone else, you need writing to connect with people and opportunities. The Internet is the biggest consumer of written content that anyone ever imagined – and good content wins.

I wrote this book to give you a high-stakes tool for accomplishing your own goals and dreams. The method here is totally pragmatic. Every idea and technique is ready to use and fully demonstrated. I base everything on my own decades of trial and error as a journalist, magazine editor, corporate communications director, and consultant.

I created writing-for-results workshops during every phase of my career because I noticed how in every setting, people missed their opportunities and undermined themselves with mediocre writing. So every piece of advice in this book has been field tested by business people, public relations professionals, corporate communicators, and non-profit leaders.

This book gives you a complete foundation for good business writing as well as guidelines to instantly improve your own writing. I hope the following chapters inspire you to keep improving what you write, a process I see as an endlessly rewarding quest.

# Conventions Used in This Book

When I introduce a new term, I write it in italics and then define what it means. The only other conventions in this book are that web and email addresses are in monofont and the action part of numbered steps and the key concepts in a list are in **bold**.

# What You Need Not Read

The grey-tinted sidebars contain extra text, such as more detailed information, that's not essential to understanding the section in question. By all means skip these boxes if you prefer, safe in the knowledge that you're not missing out on any essential tips or practical insights.

# Foolish Assumptions

I assume that *you* *a*ssume some or all of the following:

- ✔ Writing well is a talent you're born with – or not
- ✔ Improving poor writing is difficult

✔ Good writing is defined by correct grammar and spelling

✔ Memorising 'the rules' is essential

✔ Expressing complex thought demands complex language

✔ Writing dense copy with long words makes you look more intelligent and educated

✔ Reserving your best skills for 'important' material makes sense

Every one of these assumptions is false. I debunk all of them in this book. For now, the important truth is that _you can write better,_ whether you need basic grounding or are already a good writer and want to become better yet.

This book is about practical business writing. The ideas and techniques are all down to earth and easy to use. Further, as part of my mission, I leave you with ways to recognize whether you're succeeding and if not, how to fix your writing.

# How This Book Is Organised

As the author, naturally I'm happy if you read the whole book in the sequence I created for it and build your skills step by step. However, you can equally choose to dip into chapters and sections as you need them or the spirit moves you. Use the table of contents or index to find what you want and after you're there, you may see options for delving further into subjects elsewhere in the book. Follow up on these as you like.

I organize the book into six parts.

## Part 1: Winning with Writing

This part gives you the whole groundwork for writing everything well. Discover a planning structure that helps you figure out _what_ to say in any writing situation, as well as a set of techniques for _how_ to say it the best possible way. Apply pragmatic strategies for editing and revising your own work that empower you to fine-tune your writing until it succeeds.

## Part II: Putting Your Skills to Work for Everyday Business Writing

Email and letters remain today's communication staples, though supplemented more and more by social media. Both offer extraordinary opportunities to build your business relationships and professional image, while accomplishing your day-to day-goals. This part shows you how to leverage these tools.

## Part III: Writing Business Documents, Promotional Materials, and Presentations

Proposals, reports, and marketing materials are often turning point opportunities, so you need these tools in your arsenal. And you want to know how to script yourself to be a confident, effective presenter, including for that 15-second 'elevator pitch'. This part also shows you how to use your value proposition and storytelling skills to show off your company – and yourself.

## Part IV: Writing for the Digital Universe

Good writing is the cornerstone of new media, which from the communications perspective adds one more set of message delivery systems to the mix. Websites, blogs, and social media are very competitive, requiring your best writing to capture and hold viewers' attention. Find guidelines and ideas for an ever-growing array of new media in this section.

## Part V: Thinking Global, Writing Global

English is the accepted language of international business, but that doesn't mean everyone, everywhere, thinks alike. To connect successfully with your counterparts or new markets in other countries, become aware of differences. This part starts off with tips that apply to writing for all people whose native language is not English (as well as those with limited education) and then goes deeper into eight different cultures.

## Part VI: The Part of Tens

Many readers find this section the most fun section of the *For Dummies* book series. Look here for ten punchy ideas to advance your career with writing and how to tweet strategically.

# Icons Used in This Book

To help you focus on what's most important and move it into memory, look to the icons.

These are practical ideas and techniques you can put to work immediately – and amaze yourself with good results!

This icon keys you in to guidelines and strategies to absorb and use for everything you write.

This icon signals thin ice, don't take the risk! Observe these cautions to avoid endangering your business, image or cause.

Why leave all the work to me? Take these opportunities to try your own hand or apply an idea. Nothing builds your skills like practice – and you may even enjoy it.

# Where to Go from Here

Starting at the beginning gives you a foundation that applies to everything you write. But if you prefer diving right in for help on a specific challenge, by all means do so. The advice may suggest other sections for more depth and you can follow up – or not.

Everyone learns differently. Grown-ups enjoy the advantage of knowing their own learning style. Furthermore, you have your own writing problems to recognize and address. To be most useful, I offer choices – different ways to identify problems and improve everything you write.

Build a personal repertoire of techniques that work for you, then take this toolkit on the road with you. Doing so brings you a more successful journey, new confidence and a lot more fun along the way.

# Part I
# Winning with Writing

getting started with

business writing

# *In this part . . .*

- ✔ Learn the craft of business writing and watch your business reap the benefits.

- ✔ Identify your audience in order to guarantee their attention.

- ✔ Inject enthusiasm into your language to make your writing a cut above the rest.

- ✔ Optimize your organization by assessing your writing's readability.

- ✔ Fine-tune your work to ensure clarity in your message.

# Chapter 1

# Make Writing Your Not-So-Secret Weapon

**In This Chapter**

▶ Rising above the pack with good writing

▶ Accepting that you can write much better than you now do

▶ Applying a planning structure to everything you write

▶ Writing successfully for print, online, and spoken media

▶ Crossing borders with globalized business English

G ood writing can change your life. Does that sound like an extreme, even ridiculous statement? Maybe, but I believe it.

In this digital communication age, most opportunities come to you through writing. You need letters and résumés to get jobs. You need proposals to earn buy-in, marketing material to sell and reports to show what you accomplished – and get promoted.

You need websites, blogs, and social media to reach beyond your geographic territory and personal ability to be wherever you need to be. You may want to script yourself for speeches, video, and even important conversations. And most of all, you need to be part of the everyday global communication fabric of email, texting, and perhaps tweeting.

Good writing is one of the most powerful weapons you can add to your career arsenal. It can make a big difference in the personal side of your life too, enabling you to stand out in a host of competitive situations. To speak from my own experience, I came out ahead in competing for a desirable apartment, obtained refunds when a purchase or service disappointed me, and even avoided a traffic ticket once – all by writing good letters.

Writing is a major tool for achieving what you want. As with every facet of business today, just showing up isn't good enough anymore. The competition is simply too vast to turn out adequate, ordinary writing and hope to succeed.

Consider these statistics:

- ✓ 100 billion business emails sent daily
- ✓ 200 million active Twitter users, 400 million tweets per day sent
- ✓ 634 million websites
- ✓ 200 million blogs

Of course, you're not competing with all of them or reading every one. But people nowadays are extremely selective about what they choose to read because they have so many options. See the sidebar 'Communication in perspective' for an even more expansive view of these trends.

From a writer's viewpoint, you no longer have a captive audience. Getting your messages read is a challenge in itself. Getting them acted upon demands writing that is not only good, but also strategic.

What is *strategic writing?* Simply, planned communication that achieves a set of goals. The good news is that to write strategically you need only add a mindset and set of writing techniques to what you know.

Following are some of the things you already know.

- ✓ **Your subject**: You've invested in your field and knowledgeable about it.
- ✓ **Your audience:** They may be people you work with, colleagues, prospective employers, or a target market.
- ✓ **Your goal:** You know what you want – now and further down the line.

# Communication in perspective

Once upon a time (but less than 600 years ago), writing and reading were the domains of the privileged elite. So was travel, which meant that few people could extend their personal networks beyond the places where they found themselves.

Then came the movable type printing press. Almost overnight many more people could read, learn, and in some cases, circulate their own ideas, research, and thinking far beyond their own locations. Material of course had to be printed and physically distributed in the form of books, magazines, newspapers, and all the rest. For the past five centuries this didn't seem like much of a limit.

But leapfrog to the 21st century. Thanks to digital communication and the Internet, everyone with access to basic systems and equipment can communicate with anyone, anywhere, as instantly as they wish. You're limited only by your imagination and capabilities. Now everyone can be his or her own author, editor, critic, publisher, *and* distributor.

The opportunities for individuals and organizations of every kind are nearly overwhelming.

Here are some of the things you may *not* know yet – that this book shows you:

- ✔ How to capture and retain reader attention
- ✔ How to make people care about your message
- ✔ How to select the right content to make your case
- ✔ How to use writing techniques that make your material persuasive and convincing
- ✔ How to use every single thing you write to build relationships and advance your cause
- ✔ How to sharpen your ear and eye so you can spot your own writing problems and fix them

This chapter highlights the core elements of good business writing and points you in specific directions to solve your most pressing communication challenges. It introduces an audience-plus-goal structure that makes all your writing easier, more effective, and more fun.

# *Planning and Structuring Every Message*

Faced with a blank page and something to accomplish, many people freeze at the first question: where do I start? The answer? Start with what you know – your audience, your goal, and your subject. However, you need to think about all these things more systematically than you ordinarily may.

Your over-arching goal is usually more far-reaching and complex than your immediate reason for writing. And you must analyze your audience in depth to tease out the factors that tell you your best approach. Then you can translate what you know about the subject into content that supports your message.

For example, suppose you want to ask your supervisor for a plum assignment you see on the horizon. You can simply write:

> *Jane, I'd like to present myself as a candidate for the lead role on the Crystal Project. You know my work and qualifications. I'll really appreciate the opportunity, and I'll do a great job. Thanks. – Jake*

This is maybe OK – clear, no obvious errors – but definitely not compelling. All Jane knows from the message is that Jake wants the opportunity and thinks he's qualified.

Jake would fare better if he first looked at his own goals in more depth. Perhaps he wants a chance to:

> *Exercise more responsibility*
>
> *Show off his capabilities and be noticed*
>
> *Expand his know-how in regard to the project's subject*
>
> *Add a management credential to his résumé*

But he also has the longer term to consider. Jake almost certainly will find it useful to:

> *Strengthen his position for future special assignments*
>
> *Remind his boss of his good track record*

*Build his image as a capable, reliable, resourceful, leader*

*Build toward a promotion or higher-level job in his current organization or elsewhere*

From this vantage point, Jake can see the pitch itself as a building block for his overall career ambitions, which calls for a better message than the perfunctory one he dashed off. He must think through the actual assignment demands and how his skills match up. Then there's Jane to consider. What qualifications does she, the decision-maker, most value? What does she care about?

After some thought, Jake may come up with a list like this:

*Job requires: planning skills; ability to meet deadlines; knowledge of XYZ systems; experience in intra-departmental co-ordination; good judgment under pressure*

*Jane values: collaborative teaming; people skills; department reputation; effective presentation. She is weak in systems planning and insecure with technology.*

This bit of brainstorming helps Jake produce a blueprint for persuasive content. His email can briefly cite his proven track record in terms of the job requirements; his ability to deliver results as a team leader; his awareness that success will enhance the department's reputation, and that he'll use his excellent presentation skills to ensure this result.

The weaknesses he pinpointed for Jane give Jake another avenue for presenting himself as the best choice. He can suggest a planning system he'll use to make the most of staff resources and/or a specific way to incorporate new easy-to-use technology. These aspects of his message are very likely to hook Jane's attention.

All Jake's points must be true, needless to say. I don't suggest ever making up credentials but rather that you take the trouble to communicate the best of what is real.

Further, never assume people understand your capabilities or remember your achievements, even if you work closely with the person you're communicating with. *Other people don't have time to put you in perspective. That's why doing it yourself has such power.*

Even if Jake doesn't get the assignment, writing a good memo contributes to his long-range goals of presenting himself as ready, willing, and able to take on new challenges and to be seen as more valuable.

The beauty of using this audience-plus-goal structure to plan your messages, whether they're emails or proposals or anything in between, is how far the effort takes you to the real heart of good writing – real and relevant substance. Writing is not a system for manipulating words nor does it camouflage a lack of thought. Good writing is good thinking presented clearly, concisely, and transparently.

I make you a rash promise: for very centimeter you improve your writing, you improve your thinking along with it.

Chapter 2 gives you an in-depth demonstration of this planning structure and shows you how to translate it into successful messages. While you may pick and choose which sections of the book to read, and draw upon them at need, I encourage you to invest in Chapter 2. It gives you the entire foundation for deciding *what* to say in any circumstance.

The other essential groundwork for successful writing is *how* to say what you want. This is writing's technical side, which I cover in Chapters 3, 4 and 5. If you're afraid that I'll ask you to dig out your old high school textbook or memorize grammar rules, no worries. I provide a set of common-sense techniques so that you can identify problems and then fix them.

One central technique to quickly upgrade anything you write is the *say-it-aloud diagnosis.* When you read your own copy aloud (or whisper it to yourself if you're not alone), you get immediate signals that something isn't working or can work better. You may be forcing your sentences into a sing-song rhythm that denotes awkward construction, unnecessary words, and too-long sentences. You may hear repetitive sounds or inappropriate pauses demanded by poor punctuation. You can easily fix all these problems, and many more, when you use this technique to find clues to better writing.

Chapters 3 through 5 give you a host of down-to-earth strategies for monitoring your own work and improving it. These include computer resources like Word's easy-to-use and much-underutilized Readability Index, which provides helpful guidance for making your writing clear.

No matter where you now see yourself on the writing spectrum, you always have room to improve. Most of the professional writers I know, whether they're journalists, corporate communicators, or public relations specialists, are obsessive with discovering and developing better ways to write. They want to write material that's ever more interesting, persuasive, and engaging.

For people inhabiting any part of the business and non-profit worlds, the rewards of better writing are often immediate. Your emails and letters get the results you want much more often. Your proposals are more seriously considered. People accord you more respect. And you move toward your goals faster.

You also find yourself actively building relationships that benefit you over the long run. If a negative relationship hampers you at work, the structured thinking I show you in Chapter 2 even provides a tool for turning that relationship around.

## Yes, you can write better!

If good writing is a skill that can be acquired – and I say it can! – you may wonder why you don't currently write as well as you'd like. You already learned to write in school, right?

Actually, few people did. Unless you were very lucky and ran across an unusual teacher, the people who taught you to write never worked on practical writing themselves. Unlike the business world, the academic system is not geared to getting things done but rather to thinking about them. Writing for school is mostly aimed at demonstrating your knowledge of what you've been taught, or contributing to the store of human knowledge. Academia traditionally rewards dense, complicated, convoluted writing full of expensive words.

Business writing, on the other hand, always has a goal and is geared toward action. And whatever the goal, it is always best accomplished by being accessible, direct, clear, concrete, and simple. What you write should be conversational as well as engaging and persuasive.

Emulating 19th century writing traditions in your work makes little sense, and striving to produce empty, cliché-ridden 21st century business writing is just a recipe for boring your readers. Even though no one wants to read or believe them, these styles of writing surround us. That's why your good writing gives you a major competitive advantage.

# Applying Audience-Plus-Goal Strategy to Any Business Need

Beginning with Chapter 6, *Business Writing For Dummies* shows you how to use the planning and writing strategies to meet all your writing challenges. I progressively cover the various communication vehicles available to you today.

## Impressing with email, letters, and business documents

Email is the most-used medium for many people and in many ways the most basic, so it's a natural starting point.

Don't underestimate the importance or overall impact of email. This everyday workhorse offers an extraordinary opportunity to build your reputation and image, incrementally. You can actually decide how you want to be perceived: Confident? Creative? Inventive? Responsible? Steady? An idea source? Problem-solver? Make up your own list and write from inside this persona, using what you know and all your best writing techniques.

Audience analysis pays off hugely with email. Understanding the person who reads your message shows you how to ask for what you want, whether you're requesting an opportunity, inviting the reader to a meeting, or pitching for a new piece of equipment. Even further, knowing your audience in depth enables you to anticipate your reader's response and build in answers to objections she's apt to raise.

Framing the right content at the intersection of goal and audience works equally well for business correspondence, networking messages, cover letters, and more, as you find in Chapter 7. You may be surprised to see that the same principles also give you the foundation for long-form materials that often feel like make-or-break opportunities: proposals, reports, and executive summaries – all covered in Chapter 8.

## Using stories and value propositions

Chapter 9 takes you into new territory by showing you how to work with two staples of contemporary communication. One is the *selling proposition* or *core value,* a concise statement used by businesses and non-profits to communicate what distinguishes them from competitors. The second is *storytelling,* the oldest human connector of all.

While the business world embraces both tools widely, they can be difficult to use without direction from professional communicators. But small- and medium-size businesses can profit from both core value statements and stories. The creation process channels productive thinking and defines an organization's true strengths. Working with these concepts, using the structure I present, gives you a more solid basis for all communication.

Less widely recognized is how *individuals* can use value statements. Job-hunting is easier when you can clearly convey your uniqueness. Justifying your position or presenting yourself for more responsibility or promotion, rests on ready-made ground. And in general, when you can speak for yourself – or your department, profession, or company – you possess an asset that translates into personal success.

Chapter 9 gives you practical guidelines to identify both core value and good stories, and shows you how to craft them to deliver magnetic messages.

## Writing the spoken word

Knowing your value and story can help you work magic when you need to deliver your material live, whether in a 15-second 'elevator speech' that introduces you to people you want to know, or as part of a substantial talk or presentation. Chapter 10 shows you how to write for the spoken word.

The same planning process (Chapter 2) works for presentations, just as it does for emails, reports, proposals, and all the rest. Start by understanding your goal – what you want people to do as a result of listening to you – and analyzing your audience. The technical guidelines are similar to those for print, too, just more extreme: aim for even simpler and clearer language based on short, everyday words that you can speak naturally and easily.

Don't be distracted – or let your audience be distracted – by presentation systems such as PowerPoint. Shape your thoughts in writing first, not to suit a limited format, and keep the focus on yourself.

These ideas apply to scripting your own video, too. And for every occasion when you must prepare to think on your feet, use the technique of politicians and CEO's alike: write talking points for yourself.

## *Writing online: from website to blog to tweet*

Digital media seem so revolutionary that people often assume they can toss all the old writing rules out the virtual window. Don't do it! True, some aspects generate change: the delivery speed and reach of online messages shifts basic concepts of how people communicate. The traditional top-down method, whereby authoritative figures issue 'the word' is eroding quickly. Now everyone can be a journalist, commentator, or contributor. Nevertheless the need to write well holds steady.

Huge numbers of websites, blogs, and tweets are tossed into extremely competitive arenas. Only the well thought out and written ones succeed. Abbreviate all you want with texting and instant messaging (provided you know your audience can follow you) but don't introduce it into other media. Write blogs and posts with bad grammar and spelling, and you lose credibility. Fail to plan your website from the audience's perspective and you don't draw an audience at all.

Chapters 11 and 12 give you the writing know-how you need to communicate in today's digital world.

The online world is the great leveler. Never before has there been so much opportunity for individuals, or small enterprises, to make an impact. Equip yourself to do it effectively and the world may be yours.

Unlike print media and even email, a blog or website isn't personally delivered to someone who then chooses whether or not to read it. You must craft online media to pull in the readers you want. So defining your audience and goals first is at least as important as for any other writing project.

Guidelines for online writing are not radically different from those for print, but they are more intense. Sentences may be as short as a single word, and, generally, no longer than 14. Information must be more concise, crystallizing central ideas into pithy statements with zing. Plus, digital media introduce new demands that center on interactivity. You want people to respond and spread the word, and these goals require targeted techniques.

As you read this, new technologies are no doubt emerging to dazzle and intrigue us. Digital media seems to evolve almost as fast as computer speed. But the newest technology is basically one more delivery system for your messages. I guarantee you still need good writing to succeed and that the techniques presented in this book apply more than ever.

## Globalizing business English

The world may be happy to communicate with you in English. After all, it is now entrenched as the essential language of international business.

But that doesn't mean everyone is on the same wavelength. Every country and culture has distinct values and perspectives. In many parts of the world, for example, work takes second place to family and leisure interests, a viewpoint that some work-obsessed cultures find hard to understand. A number of cultures value courtesy more than efficiency, and do not transact business unless you establish a solid relationship first.

In many cultures you can't open a conversation unless you're able to cite a personal connection. And in some places, directness is not appreciated. Many cultures never voice an outright 'no', so you must interpret polite comments to figure out whether you're being rejected. You also benefit from developing the ability to be similarly indirect with others.

Writing may be the best way to initiate contact with people you don't know. However, you must remember that many people speak and write English only as a second – or third or fourth – language

Fortunately, the basic guidelines in Chapters 13 go a long way toward helping you write messages in a way most non-native speakers anywhere can easily understand. In Chapter 14, I present specific suggestions for writing to business people in eight different countries. I collected the insights directly from people who live or work in each country.

I recommend reading through Part IV even if you have no immediate plan to expand your business overseas. The differences among seemingly similar countries and English speakers are fascinating. Moreover, it's a rare organization today that doesn't need to communicate with non-native English speakers who may be employees, customers or partners.

We all see the world through our own filters, unconsciously constructed of personal experience, cultural values and everything else we grow up with. Glimpsing life through other filters helps you know yourself better.

# Chapter 2

# Planning Your Message: Your Secret Weapon

. . . . . . . . . . . . . . . . . . . . . . . . . . . . . . . . . . . . . . . . . . . . . . .

## In This Chapter

▶ Strategizing for success before you write

▶ Knowing your goal and audience

▶ Making people care about your message

▶ Finding opportunities to build relationships

. . . . . . . . . . . . . . . . . . . . . . . . . . . . . . . . . . . . . . . . . . . . . . .

*T*hink for a minute about how you approached a recent writing task. If it was an email, how much time did you spend considering what to write? A few minutes? Seconds? Or did you just start typing?

Now bring a more complex document to mind: a challenging letter, proposal, report, marketing piece, or anything else. Did you put some time into shaping your message before you began writing – or did you just plunge in?

This chapter demonstrates the power of taking time before you write to consider *who* you're writing to, *what* you truly hope to achieve, and *how* you can deploy your words to maximize success.

## Adopting the Plan-Draft-Edit Principle

Prepare yourself for one of the most important pieces of advice in this book: invest time in planning your messages.

That means *every* message, because even an everyday communication like an email can have a profound impact on your success. Everything you write shows people who you are.

I can't count the times I've received an email asking for a referral, or informational interview, that was badly written and full of errors. Or a long, expensively produced document with an email cover note that's abrupt and sloppy. A poorly done email doesn't help the cause – whatever the cause is.

I'm not suggesting that prior to writing every email you lean back in your chair and let your mind wander into blue-sky mode to see what emerges. The planning I recommend is a step-by-step process that leads to good decisions about what to say and how to say it. It's a process that will never fail you, no matter how big (or seeming small) the writing challenge. And it's quite simple to adopt – in fact, you may experience surprising immediate results. You may also find that you enjoy writing much more.

This strategic approach has no relation to how you learned to write in school, unless you had an atypical teacher who was attuned to writing for results, so start by tossing any preconceived ideas about your inability to write over the side.

When you have a message or document to write, expect to spend your time this way:

- ✔ Planning – one third
- ✔ Drafting – one third
- ✔ Editing – one third

In other words, give equal time, roughly speaking, to the job of deciding what to say – the content; another equal portion to preparing your first draft and finally, a third to fixing what you wrote.

See Chapter 3 for no-fail writing strategies and Chapter 4 for editing tips and tricks.

# *Fine-Tuning Your Plan: Your Goals and Audience*

A well-crafted message is based on two key aspects: your goal and your audience. The following section shows you how to get to know both intimately.

## *Defining your goal: Know what you want*

Your first priority is to know exactly what you want to happen when the person you're writing to reads what you've written. Determining this is far less obvious than it sounds.

Consider a cover letter for your résumé. Seen as a formal but unimportant necessity toward your ultimate goal, to get a job, a cover letter can, just say:

> *Dear Mr Blank, here is my résumé – Jack Slade*

Intuitively you know that isn't sufficient. But analyze what you want to accomplish and you can see clearly why it falls short. Your cover letter must yield the following results:

- ✔ Connect you with the recipient so that you're a person instead of one more set of documents
- ✔ Make you stand out – in a good way
- ✔ Persuade the recipient that your résumé is worth reading
- ✔ Show that you understand the job and the company
- ✔ Set up the person to review your qualifications with a favorable mindset

You also need the cover letter to demonstrate your personal qualifications, especially the ability to communicate well.

If you see that your big goal depends on this set of more specific goals it's obvious why a one-line perfunctory message can't succeed.

A cover letter for a formal business proposal has its own big goal – to help convince an individual or an institution to finance your new product. In order to do this, the letter's role is to connect with the prospective buyer, entice him to actually read at least part of the document, predispose him to like what he sees, present your company as better than the competition and show off good communication skills.

How about the proposal itself? If you break down this goal into a more specific subset then you realize the proposal must demonstrate:

- ✔ The financial viability of what you plan to produce
- ✔ A minimal investment risk and high profit potential
- ✔ Your own excellent qualifications and track record
- ✔ Outstanding backup by an experienced team
- ✔ Special expertise in the field
- ✔ In-depth knowledge of the marketplace, competition, business environment, and so on.

Spelling out your goals is extremely useful because the process keeps you aligned with the big picture while giving you instant guidelines for content that succeeds. Because of good planning on the front end, you're already moving toward *how* to accomplish what you want.

To reap the benefit of goal definition, you must take time to look past the surface. Write every message – no exceptions – with a clear set of goals. If you don't know your goals, don't write at all.

Invariably one of your goals is to present yourself in writing as professional, competent, knowledgeable, empathetic and so on – but don't let me tell you who you are or want to be! Create a list of the personal and professional qualities you want other people to perceive in you. Then remember, every time you write, to be that person. Ask yourself how that individual handles the tough stuff. Your answers may amaze you. This technique isn't mystical, just a way of accessing your own knowledge base and intuition. You may be able to channel this winning persona into your in-person experiences too.

## *Defining your audience: Know your reader*

You've no doubt noticed that people are genuinely different in countless ways – what they value, their motivations, how they like to spend their time, their attitude toward work and success, how they communicate and much more. One ramification of these variables is that they read and react to your messages in different and sometimes unexpected ways.

As part of your planning you need to anticipate people's responses – to both your content and writing style. The key to successfully predicting your reader's response is to address everything you write to someone specific, rather than an anonymous, faceless 'anyone'.

When you meet someone in person and want to persuade her to your viewpoint, you automatically adapt to her reactions as you go along. You respond to a host of clues. Beyond interruptions, comments and questions, you also perceive facial expression, body language, tone of voice, nervous mannerisms and many other indicators. (Check out *Body Language For Dummies* by Elizabeth Kuhnke to sharpen your ability to read people.)

Obviously a written message lacks all in-person clues. So for yours to succeed, you must play both roles – the reader's and your own. Doing this isn't as hard as it may sound.

Unless you're sending a truly trivial message, begin by creating a profile of the person you're writing to. If you know the person, begin with the usual suspects, the demographics. Start by determining:

- ✔ How old? (Generational differences can be huge! See the sidebar 'Generation gaps: Understanding and leveraging them')
- ✔ Male or female?
- ✔ Engaged in what occupation?
- ✔ Married, family or some other arrangement?
- ✔ Member of an ethnic or religious group?
- ✔ Educated to what degree?
- ✔ Social and economic position?

# Generation gaps: Understanding and leveraging them

In business today, understanding young people is important to older ones, and vice versa. If you're a member of Generation X or Generation Y, understanding Baby Boomers is especially useful because they still constitute more than 70 per cent of business owners and probably a similar percentage of all top jobs.

You may quibble about the following descriptions – especially of your own cohort – but the generalizations are still illuminating. Supplement these ideas with your own observations and you discover ways to make higher-ups happy without necessarily compromising your own values.

✔ **Baby Boomers** (born 1946 to 1964) are highly competitive and define themselves by achievement. Many are workaholics. They respect authority, loyalty, position and patience with the hierarchy and slow upward progress. They would like today's young people to advance the same way they did: earning rewards gradually over time. They are good with confrontation and prefer a lot of face-to-face time, so hold meetings often. They resent younger people's perceived lack of respect, low commitment level, expectations of fast progress, and arrogance about their own superior technology skills. And careless writing! Well-planned and proofed messages score high points with Boomers and they are more likely to prefer long detailed accounts. They like phone calls but resent telephone run-arounds and response delays.

✔ **Generation X** (born 1965 to 1980) are literally caught in the middle. They are often middle managers and may constantly translate between those they report to and those who report to them. They are hard-working, individualistic, committed to change, technologically capable but lack the full enthusiasm toward technological solutions of Gen Y. They value independence and resourcefulness (having been the first latchkey children) and like opportunities to develop new skills and receive feedback. Their preferred communication mode is generally email, the short efficient kind. They'd rather skip the meetings.

✔ **Generation Y** (born after 1980) expect their technical skills and input to be recognized and rewarded quickly. They are highly social and collaborative, preferring to work in teams, and like staying in touch with what everyone is doing. They want to be given responsibility but also like structure and mentoring.

They don't see the point of long-term commitment and expect to spend their careers job-hopping. Generation Y'ers prefer to interact through texting, instant messaging and social media, and will use email as necessary, rather than in-person or telephone contact. A subgroup, the Millennials (born 1991 on) are even more techno-centric in their communication preferences.

After demographics, you have *psychographic* considerations, the kind of factors marketing specialists spend a lot of time studying. Marketers are interested in creating customer profiles to understand and manipulate consumer buying. For your purposes, some psychographic factors that can matter are:

✔ Lifestyle

✔ Values and beliefs

✔ Opinions and attitudes

✔ Interests

✔ Leisure and volunteer activities

You also need to consider factors that reflect someone's positioning, personality and, in truth, entire life history and outlook on the world. Some factors that may directly affect how a person perceives your message include the following:

✔ Professional background and experience

✔ Position in the organization: What level? Moving up or down? Respected? How ambitious?

✔ Degree of authority

✔ Leadership style: Team-based? Dictatorial? Collaborative? Indiscernible?

✔ Preferred communication style: In-person? Short or long written messages? Telephone? Texting? PowerPoint?

✔ Approach to decision-making: Collaborative or top-down? Spontaneous or deliberative? Risk-taker or play-it-safer?

✔ Information preferences: Broad vision? Detailed? Statistics and numbers? Charts and graphs?

✔ Work priorities and pressures

✔ Sensitivities and hot buttons

✔ Interaction style and preferences: A people person or a systems and technology person?

✔ Type of thinking: Logical or intuitive? Statistics-based or ideas-based? Big picture or micro oriented? Looking for long-range or immediate results?

✔ Weaknesses, perceived by the person or not: lack of technological savvy? People skills? Education?

✔ Type of people the person likes – and dislikes

Do you know, or can you figure out, what your reader worries about? What keeps him up at night? What is his biggest problem? When you know a person's deepest concerns, you can effectively leverage this information to create messages that he finds highly compelling.

And of course, your precise relationship to the person matters – your relative positioning; the degree of mutual liking, respect and trust; the *simpatico* factor.

No doubt you're wondering how you can possibly take so much into consideration, or why you want to. The good news is, when your message is truly simple, you usually don't. More good news: Even when your goal is complex or important, only some factors matter. I'm giving you a lengthy list to draw on because every situation brings different characteristics into play. Thinking through which ones count in your specific situation is crucial.

For example, say you want authorization to buy a new computer. Perhaps your boss is a technology freak who reacts best to equipment requests when they have detailed productivity data – in writing. Or you may report to someone who values relationships, good office vibes and in-person negotiation. Whatever the specifics, you need to frame the same story differently. I'm not saying to manipulate the facts – both stories must be true and fair.

You succeed when you take the time to look at things through the other person's eyes rather than solely your own. Doing so doesn't compromise your principles. It shows that you're sensible and sensitive to the differences between people and helps your relationships. It shows you how to frame what you're asking for. See the section 'Framing messages with 'you' not 'I'" later in this chapter for more on these techniques.

## *Brainstorming the best content for your purpose*

Perhaps defining your goal and audience so thoroughly sounds like unnecessary busy-work. But doing so helps immeasurably when you're approaching someone with an idea, product or service which you need them to buy into.

Suppose your department is planning to launch a major project that you want to lead. You could write a memo explaining how important the opportunity is to you, how much you can use the extra money, how much you'll appreciate being chosen for the new role. But unless your boss Jane is a totally selfless person without ambition or priorities of her own, why would she care about any of that?

You're much better off highlighting your relevant skills and accomplishments. Your competitors for the leadership position may equal or even better such a rundown, so you must make your best case. Think beyond yourself to what Jane herself most values.

A quick profile (see the preceding section) of Jane reveals a few characteristics to work with:

✔ She likes to see good teamwork in those reporting to her.

✔ She's a workaholic who is usually overcommitted.

✔ She likes to launch projects and then basically forget about them until results are due.

✔ She's ambitious and always angling for her next step up.

Considering what you know about Jane, the content of your message can correspond to these traits by including:

✔ Your good record as both a team player and team leader

✔ Your dedication to the new project and willingness to work over and beyond normal hours to do it right

✔ Your ability to work independently and use good judgment with minimal supervision

✔ Your enthusiasm for this particular project which, if successful, will be highly valued by the department and company

Again, all your claims must be true, and you need to provide evidence that they are: a reminder of another project you successfully directed, for example, and handled independently.

Your reader profile can tell you still more. If you wonder how long your memo needs to be, for example, consider Jane's communication preferences. If she prefers brief memos followed by face-to-face decision-making, keep your memo brief but still cover all the points to ensure that you secure that all-important meeting. However, if she reacts best to written detail, give her more info up front.

Reader profiling offers you the chance to create a blueprint for the content of all your messages and documents. After you've defined what you want and analyzed your audience in relation to the request, brainstorm the points that may help you win your case with that person. Your brainstorming gives you a list of possibilities to review. Winnowing out the most convincing points is easy – and organizing can involve simple prioritizing, as I show you in Chapter 3.

Thinking through how to profile your reader works exactly the same way if you're writing a major proposal, a business plan, a report, a funding request, a client letter, a marketing piece, a PowerPoint presentation, networking message, or website. Know your goal. Figure out what your audience cares about. Then think widely within that perspective. In Parts II and III of this book, I show you how to apply profiling to many communication formats.

## Writing to groups and strangers

Profiling one person is easy enough, but you often write to groups rather than individuals as well as to people you haven't met and know nothing about. The same ideas I discuss in the preceding section apply with groups and strangers, but they demand a little more imagination on your part.

Here's a good tactic for messages addressed to groups: Visualize a single individual – or a few key individuals – who epitomizes that group. The financier Warren Buffet explained that when writing to stockholders he imagines he's writing to his two sisters: intelligent but not knowledgeable about finance. He consciously aims to be understood by them. The results are admirably clear financial messages that are well received and influential.

Like Buffet, you may be able to think of a particular person to represent a larger group. If you've invented a new item of ski equipment, for example, think about a skier you know who'd be interested in your product and profile that person. Or create a composite profile of several such people, drawing on what they have in common plus variations. If you're a business strategy consultant, think of your best clients and use what you know about them to profile your prospects.

## *Imagining your readers*

Even when an audience is entirely new to you, you can still make good generalizations about what these people are like – or, even better, their concerns. Suppose you're a dentist who's taking over a practice and you're writing to introduce yourself to your predecessor's patients. Your basic goal is to maintain that clientele. You needn't know the people to anticipate many of their probable concerns. You can assume for example that your news will be unwelcome because long-standing patients probably liked the old dentist and dislike change and inconvenience, just like you probably would yourself.

You can go further. Anticipate your readers' questions. Just put yourself in their shoes. You may wonder

- ✔ Why should I trust you, an unknown quantity?
- ✔ Will I feel an interruption in my care? Will there be a learning curve?
- ✔ Will I like you and find in you what I value in a medical practitioner – aspects such as kindness, respect for my time, attentiveness, and experience?

Plan your content to answer these intrinsic questions and you can't go wrong. Notice that nearly all the questions are emotional in nature rather than factual. Few patients are likely to ask about a new doctor's training and specific knowledge. They're more concerned with the kind of person he is and how they'll be treated. This somewhat counter-intuitive truth applies to many situations. The questions are essentially the same for an accountant or any other service provider.

When writing, you may need to build a somewhat indirect response to some of the questions you anticipate from readers. Writing something like 'I'm a really nice person' to prospective dental patients is unlikely to convince them, but you can comfortably include any, or all, of the following statements in your letter:

> *I will carefully review all the records so I am personally knowledgeable about your history.*

> *My staff and I pledge to keep your waiting time to a minimum. We use all the latest techniques to make your visits comfortable and pain-free.*

> *I look forward to meeting you in person and getting to know you.*

> *I'm part of your community and participate in its good causes such as . .*

Apply this strategy to job applications, business proposals, online media and other important materials. Ask yourself, whom do I want to reach? Is the person a human resources executive? A CEO? A prospective customer for my product or service? Then jot down a profile covering what that person is probably like and what her concerns and questions are. Everyone has a problem to solve. What's your reader's problem? The HR person must fill open jobs in ways that satisfy other people. The CEO can pretty well be counted on to have one eye on the bottom line and the other on the big picture – that's her role. If you're pitching a product you can base a prospective customer profile on whom you're producing that product for.

If you're an entrepreneur, building a detailed portrait of your ultimate buyers is especially important to your success. The more you know about your prospects, the better you can deliver what they need.

# *Making People Care*

Sending your words out into today's message-dense world is not unlike tossing your message into the sea in a bottle. However, your message is now among a trillion bottles, all of which are trying to reach the same moving and dodging targets. So your competitive edge is in shaping a better bottle. . . or rather, message.

Any message you send must be very well-crafted and very well-aimed, regardless of the medium or format. The challenge is to make people care enough to read your message and act on it in some way. The following sections explore the tools you need to ensure your bottle reaches its target and makes the impact you desire.

## *Connecting instantly with your reader*

Only in rare cases do you have the luxury these days of building up to a grand conclusion, one step at a time. Your audience simply won't stick around.

The opening paragraph of anything you write must instantly hook your readers. The best way to do this is to link directly to their central interests and concerns, within the framework of your purpose.

Say you're informing the staff that the office will be closed on Tuesday to install new air conditioning. You can write:

*Subject: About next Tuesday*

*Dear Staff:*

*As you know, the company is always interested in your comfort and well-being. As part of our company improvement plan this past year, we've installed improved lighting in the hallways, and in response to your request that we . . .*

Stop! No one is reading this! Instead, try this:

*Subject: Office closed Tuesday*

*We're installing new air-conditioning! Tuesday is the day, so we're giving you a holiday.*

*I'm happy the company is able to respond to your number 1 request on the staff survey and hope you are too. . .*

One of the best ways to hook readers is also the simplest: Get to the point. The technique applies even to long documents. Start with the bottom line such as the result you achieved, the strategy you recommend, or the action you want. In a report or proposal the executive summary is often the way to do that, but note that even this micro version of your full message still needs to lead off with your most important point.

Notice in the preceding example that the subject line of the email is part of the lead and planned to hook readers as much as the first paragraph of the actual message. Chapter 6 has more ideas of ways to optimize your emails.

## *Focusing on what's-in-it-for-them*

In marketers' terms, the acronym is WIIFM – what's-in-it-for-me. The air-conditioning email in the preceding section captures readers by telling them first that they have a day off, then follows up by saying that they're getting something they wanted. Figuring out what's going to engage *your* readers often takes a bit of thought.

To make people care, you must first be able to answer the question yourself. Why *should* they care? Then put your answer right in the lead or even the headline.

If you're selling a product or service, for example, zero in on the problem it solves. So rather than your press release headline saying

*New Widget Model to Debut at Expo Magnus on Thursday*

Try

*Widget 175F Day-to-Night Video Recorder Ends Pilfering Instantly*

If you're raising money for a non-profit, you may be tempted to write a letter to previous donors that begins like many you probably receive:

> *For 75 years, Little White Lights has been helping children with learning disabilities improve their capacities, live up to their potential and feel more confident about their educational future.*

But, don't you respond better to letters that open more like this?

> *For his first five years of school, Lenny hated every second. He couldn't follow the lessons, so he stopped trying and stopped even listening. But this September Lenny starts college – because the caring people and non-traditional teaching at Little White Lights showed him how to learn. He's one of 374 children whose lives we transformed since our not-for-profit organization was established, with your help, nine years ago.*

The second version works better not just because it's more concrete, but because it takes account of two factors that all recipients probably share: 1) a concern for children, and 2) a need to be reassured that their donations are well used.

## Highlighting benefits, not features

People care about what a product or service can do for them, not what it is.

- ✔ *Features* describe characteristics – a car having a 200 mph engine; an energy drink containing 500 units of caffeine; a hotel room furnished with priceless antiques.

- ✔ *Benefits* are what features give us – the feeling that you can be the fastest animal on earth (given an open highway without radar traps); the ability to stay up for 56 hours to make up all the work you neglected; the experience of high luxury for the price of a hotel room, at least briefly.

Benefits have more to do with feelings and experiences than actual data. Marketers have known the power of benefits for a long time, but neuroscientists have recently confirmed the principle, noting that most buying decisions are made emotionally rather than logically. You choose a car that speaks to your personality instead of the one with the best technical specs, and then you try to justify your decision on rational grounds.

The lesson for business writing is clear: people care about messages that are based on what really matters to them. Don't get lost in technical detail. Focus on the impact of an event, idea or product. You can cover the specs but keep them contained in a separate section or as backup material. Approach information the way most newspapers have always done (and now do online as well). Put what's most interesting or compelling up front and then include the details in the back (or link to them) for readers who want more.

## *Finding the concrete, limiting the abstract*

The Little White Lights example in the earlier section 'Focusing on what's-in-it-for-them' demonstrates how to effectively focus on a single individual and simultaneously deliver a powerful, far-reaching message. One concrete example is almost always more effective than reams of high-flown prose and empty adjectives.

Make things real for your readers with these techniques:

- ✓ **Tell stories and anecdotes.** They must embody the idea you want to communicate, the nature of your organization or your own value. An early television show about New York City used a slogan along the lines, 'Eight million people, eight million stories.' A good story is always there, lurking, even in what may seem everyday or ordinary. But finding it can take some thinking and active looking. In Chapter 9, I show you how.

- ✓ **Use examples – and make them specific.** Tell customers how your product was used or how your service helped solve a problem. Give them strong case studies of implementations that worked. Inside a company, tell change-resistant staff members how another department saved three hours by using the new ordering process, or how a shift in benefits can cut their out-of-pocket health-care costs by 14 per cent. And if you want people to use a new system, give them clear guidelines, perhaps a step-by-step process to follow.

✔ **Use visuals to explain and break up the words.** Readers who need to be captured and engaged generally shy away from uninterrupted type. Plenty of studies show that people remember visual lessons better, too. Look for ways to graphically present a trend, a change, a plan, a concept or an example. In a way that suits your purpose and medium, incorporate photographs, illustrations, charts, graphs and video. When you must deliver your message primarily in words use graphic techniques like headlines, subheads, bullets, typeface variations and icons – like this book!

✔ **Give readers a vision.** Good leaders know that a vision is essential, whether they're running companies or for public office. You're usually best off framing your message in big-picture terms that make people feel the future will be better in some way. I'm not suggesting you make empty promises; instead, look for the broadest implications of an important communication and use details to back up that central concept and make it more real. Focusing a complicated document this way also makes it more organized and more memorable – both big advantages.

✔ **Eliminate meaningless hyperbole.** What's the point of saying something like, 'This is the most far-reaching, innovative, ground-breaking piece of industrial design ever conceived'? Yet business writing is jam-packed with empty, boring claims.

Today's audiences come to everything you write already jaded, skeptical and impatient. If you're a service provider and describe what you do in words that can belong to anyone, in any profession, you fail. If you depend on a website and it takes viewers 20 seconds to figure out what you're selling or how to make a purchase, you lose. If you're sending out a press release that buries what's interesting or important, you're invisible. The solution: know your point and make it fast!

Go for the evidence! Tell your audience in real terms what your idea, plan or product accomplishes in ways they care about. Show them

✔ How the product improves people's lives

✔ How the non-profit knows its money is helping people

✔ How the service solves problems

✔ How you personally helped your employer make more money or become more efficient.

Proof comes in many forms: statistics, data, images, testimonials, surveys, case histories, biographies, and video and audio clips. Figure out how to track your success and prove it. You end up with first-rate material to use in all your communication.

# Choosing Your Written Voice: Tone

Presentation trainers often state that the meaning of a spoken message is communicated 55 per cent by body language, 38 per cent by tone of voice, and only 7 per cent by the words. Actually this formula has been thoroughly debunked and denied by its creator – the psychologist Albert Mehrabian – but it does imply some important points for writing.

Written messages come without body language or tone of voice. One result is that humor – particularly sarcasm or irony – is very risky. When readers can't see the wink in your eye or hear the playfulness in your voice, they take you literally. So refrain from subtle humor unless you're really secure with your reader's ability to get it. Better yet: be cautious at all times because such assumptions are dangerous.

But even lacking facial expression and gesture, writing does carry its own tone, and this directly affects how readers receive and respond to messages. Written tone results from a combination of word choice, sentence structure and other technical factors.

Also important are less tangible elements that are hard to pin down. You've probably received messages that led you to sense the writer was upset, angry, resistant or amused – even if only a few words were involved. Sometimes even a close reading of the text doesn't explain what's carrying these emotions, but you just sense the writer's strong feelings.

When you're the writer, be very conscious of your message's tone. Consistently control tone so it supports your goals and avoids undermining your message. You've probably found that showing emotion in the workplace rarely gives you an advantage, usually the opposite. Writing is similar. Tone conveys feelings, and if you're not in control of your emotions when you write, tone betrays you.

The following sections explore some ways to find and adopt the right tone.

## Being appropriate to the occasion, relationship and culture

Pause before writing and think about the moment you're writing in. Obviously if you're communicating bad news, you don't want to sound all chipper and cheery.

Always think of your larger audience, too. If the company made more money last month because it eliminated a department, best not to treat the new profits as a triumph. Current staff members probably aren't happy about losing colleagues and are worried about their own jobs. On the other hand if you're communicating about a staff holiday party, sounding gloomy and bored doesn't generate high hopes for a good time. The same is true if you're offering an opportunity or assigning a nuisance job: make it as enticing as possible.

Just as in face-to-face situations, the moods embedded in your writing are contagious. If you want an enthusiastic response, then write with enthusiasm. If you want people to welcome a change you're announcing, sound positive and confident, not fearful or peevish and resentful – even if you don't personally agree with the change.

Make conscious decisions about how formal to sound. After you work in an organization for a while, you typically absorb its culture without really noticing. (In fact most organizations don't realize that they have a culture until they run

into problems when introducing change or a high-level hire.)
If you're new to the place, observe how things work so you
can avoid booby-trapping yourself. Read through files of correspondence, emails, reports, as well as websites and online
material. Analyze what your colleagues feel is appropriate in
content and in writing style. How formal is the communication for the various media used? Adopt the guidelines you see
enacted.

Every passing year seems to decrease the formality of business communication. Just as in choosing what to wear to
work, people are dressing down their writing. This less formal
style can come across as friendlier, simpler and more direct
than in earlier years – and should. But business informal
doesn't mean you should address an executive or board
member casually, use texting or abbreviations your reader
may not understand, or fail to edit and proofread every message. Those are gaffes much like wearing torn jeans to work or
a client meeting.

And you want to be especially careful if you're writing to
someone in another country – even an English-speaking one.
Most countries still prefer a formal form of communication.
(See Part IV of this book for some ideas on effective global
communication.)

## *Writing as your authentic self*

Never try to impress anyone with how educated and literate
you are. Studies show that in reality people believe that those
who write clearly and use simple words are smarter than
those whose writing abounds in fancy phrases and complicated sentences.

*Authentic* means being a straightforward, unpretentious,
honest, trustworthy person – and writer. It doesn't mean
trying for a specific writing style. Clarity is always the goal-
post. This aim absolutely holds true even for materials written
to impress. A proposal, marketing brochure, or request for
funding gains nothing by looking or sounding pompous and
weighty.

# Being relentlessly respectful

Never underestimate or patronize your audience, regardless of educational level, position or apparent accomplishment. People are quite sensitive to such attitudes and react adversely, often without knowing why or telling you. In *all* work and business situations take the trouble to actively demonstrate respect for your reader. Specifically:

- ✔ Address people courteously and use their names

- ✔ Close with courtesy and friendliness

- ✔ Write carefully and proofread thoroughly; many people find poorly written messages insulting

- ✔ Avoid acronyms, jargon, and abbreviations that may be unfamiliar to some readers

- ✔ Never be abrupt or rude or demanding

- ✔ Try to understand and respect cultural differences

Apply these guidelines whether you're writing to a superior, a subordinate or peer. You don't need to be obsequious to an executive higher up the chain than you are (in most cases), though often you should be more formal. Nor should you condescend to those lower down. Consider for example how best to assign a last-minute task to someone who reports to you. You could say:

> *Madge, I need you to read this book tonight and give me a complete rundown of the content first thing tomorrow. Thanks.*

Or:

> *Madge, I need your help – please read this book tonight. The author is coming in tomorrow to talk about engaging us. I'm reading another of his books myself and if we can compare notes first thing tomorrow, I'll feel much more prepped. Thanks!*

Either way Madge may not be thrilled at how her evening looks, but treating her respectfully and explaining *why* you're giving her this intrusive assignment accomplishes a lot: she'll be more motivated, more enthusiastic, more interested in doing a good job, and happier to feel part of your team. At the cost of writing a few more sentences, you improve her attitude and perhaps even her long-range performance.

## Smiling when you say it

People whose job is answering the phone are told by customer service trainers to smile before picking up the call. Smiling physically affects your throat and vocal chords, and your tone of voice. You sound friendly and cheerful and may help the person on the other end of the phone feel that way.

The idea applies to writing as well. You need not smile before you write (though it's an interesting technique to try), but be aware of your own mood and how easily it transfers to your messages and documents.

I'm not saying your feelings of anger, impatience or resentment aren't well-grounded but displaying them rarely helps your cause. Nobody likes to get negative, whiny, nasty messages that put them on the defensive or make them feel under attack.

Suppose you've asked the purchasing department to buy a table for your office and were denied without explanation. You could write to both your boss and the head of purchasing a note such as the following:

> *Hal, Jeanne: I just can't believe how indifferent purchasing is to my work and what I need to do it. This ignorance is really offensive. I'm now an Associate Manager responsible for a three-person team and regular meetings are essential to my . . .*

Put yourself in the recipients' heads to see how bad the impact of such a message can be – for you. At the least, you're creating unnecessary problems and at worst, perhaps permanent bad feelings. Why not write (and just to the purchasing officer) this, instead:

> *Hi Hal, do you have a minute to talk about my request for a small conference table? I was surprised to find that it was denied and want to share why it's important to my work.*

The best way to control your tone is to let emotion-laden matters rest for whatever time you can manage. Even a 10-minute wait can make a difference. Overnight is better if possible in important situations. You're far more likely to accomplish what you want when you come across as logical, reasonable and objective. Positive and cheerful is even better.

Sometimes the challenge isn't to control bad feelings, but to overcome a blah mood that leads your writing to sound dull and uninspired when you need it to sound persuasive and engaging. Knowing your own biological clock is helpful, so you can focus on the task that requires the most energy when you're most naturally up.

If you don't have the luxury of waiting for a good mood to hit before writing, try a method I often use. I churn out the basic document regardless of my spirits, and later when I'm feeling bouncier, graft on the energy and enthusiasm I know the original message is missing. Typical changes involve switching out dull passive verbs and substituting live active ones, picking up the tempo, editing out the dead wood and adding plusses I overlooked when I felt gray. Chapter 3 is chock-full of ideas to enliven your language.

People naturally prefer being around positive, dynamic, enthusiastic people, and they prefer receiving messages with the same qualities. Resolve not to complain, quibble or criticize in writing. People are much more inclined to give you what you want when you're positive – and they see you as a problem-solver rather than a problem-generator.

# Using Relationship-Building Techniques

Just about everything you write is a chance to build relationships with those you report to and even those above them in the chain, as well as peers, colleagues, customers, prospects, suppliers and members of your industry. More and more, people succeed through good networking. In a world characterized by less face-to-face contact and more global possibilities, writing is a major tool for making connections and maintaining them.

As with tone, awareness that building relationships is always one of your goals puts you a giant step ahead. Ask yourself every time you write how you can improve the relationships with that individual. A range of techniques is available to help.

## *Personalizing what you write*

In many countries, business emails and letters that get right down to business seem cold, abrupt and unfeeling. Japanese writers and readers, for example, prefer to begin with the kind of polite comments you tend to make when meeting someone in person: 'How have you been?' 'Is your family well?' 'Isn't it cold for October?' Such comments or questions may carry no real substance, but they serve an important purpose. They personalize the interaction to better set the stage for a business conversation.

 Creating a sense of caring or at least interest in the other person gives you a much better context within which to transact business. If you've thought about your audience when planning what to write (see the preceding section, 'Defining your audience: Know your reader'), you can easily come up with simple but effective personalizing phrases to frame your message. You can always fall back on the old reliables – weather and general health inquiries. If communication continues, you can move the good feelings along by asking whether the vacation mentioned earlier worked out well, or if the weekend was good – whatever clues you can follow up on without becoming inappropriate or intrusive. The idea works with groups, too: You can, for example, begin, 'I hope you all weathered the tornado O.K.'

Some techniques you can use to make your writing feel warm are useful, but they may not translate between different cultures. For example, salutations like *Hi John* set a less formal tone than *Dear John*. Starting with just the name – *John,* – is informal to the point of assuming a relationship already exists. But both ways may not be appropriate if you're writing to someone in a more formal country than your own. A formal address – Mr Charles, Ms Brown, Dr Jones, General Frank – may be called for. In many cultures, if you overlook this formality and other signs of respect, you can lose points before you even begin.

Similarly, it feels friendlier and less formal to use contractions: *isn't* instead of *is not, won't* instead of *will not.* But if your message is addressed to a non-native English speaker or will be translated, contractions may be confusing. Part IV explores other techniques for communicating effectively between cultures.

## *Framing messages with 'you' not 'I'*

Just accept it: people care more about themselves and what they want than they do about you. This simple-sounding concept has important implications for business writing.

Suppose you're a software developer and your company has come up with a dramatically better way for people to manage their online reputations. You may be tempted to announce on your website:

> *We've created a great new product for online reputation management that no one ever imagined possible.*

Or you could say:

> *Our great new Product X helps people manage their online reputation better than ever before.*

The second example is better because it's less abstract and it makes the product's purpose clear. But see if you find this version more powerful:

> *You want a better way to solve your online reputation management challenges? We have what you need.*

When you look for ways to use the word *you* more, and correspondingly decrease the use of *I* and *we,* you put yourself on the reader's wavelength. In the case of the new software, your readers care about how the product can help them, not that you're proud of achieving it.

The principle works for everyday email, letters and online communication too. For example, when you receive a customer complaint, instead of saying

> *We have received your complaint about . . .*

You're better off writing:

> *Your letter explaining your complaint has been received . . .*

Or:

> *Thank you for writing to us about your recent problem with . . .*

Coming up with a 'you frame' is often challenging. Doing so may draw you into convoluted or passive-sounding language – for example, 'Your unusual experience with our tree-pruning service has come to our attention.' Ordinarily I recommend a direct statement (like, 'We hear you've had an unusual experience with. . .') but in customer service situations and others where you want to relate to your reader instantly, figuring out a way to start with 'you' can be worth the effort and a brief dip into the passive. (See Chapters 3, 4 and 5 for ways to expand your resource of techniques for fine-tuning your tone through word choice, sentence structure and customized content.)

In every situation, genuinely consider your reader's viewpoint, sensitivities and needs. Think about how the message you're communicating affects that person or group. Anticipate questions and build in the answers. Write within this framework and you will guide yourself to create successful messages and documents. When you care, it shows. And you succeed.

# Chapter 3

# Making Your Writing Work: The Basics

*In This Chapter*

▶ Tailoring your writing for today's readers

▶ Injecting energy into your language

▶ Implementing elements of good design

*Y*our writing style probably took shape in school where literary traditions and formal essays dominate. This experience may have led you to believe that subtle thoughts require complex sentences, sophisticated vocabulary and dense presentation. Perhaps you learned to write that way – or maybe you didn't. Either way: get over it. The rules of academic writing don't apply to the business world.

Real-world business writing is more natural, reader-friendly and easier to do than academic writing – especially after you know the basics I cover in this chapter.

## Stepping into 21st Century Writing Style

In business you succeed when you achieve your goals. You need to judge business writing the same way – by whether it accomplishes what you want. What works is:

✔ **Clear and simple.** Except for technical material directed at specialists, no subject matter or idea is so complex that you cannot express it in clear, simple language. You automatically move forward a step by accepting this basic premise and practicing it.

✔ **Conversational.** Business writing is reader-friendly and accessible, far closer to spoken language than the more formal and traditional style. It may even come across as casual or spontaneous. This quality, however, doesn't give you a free pass on grammar, punctuation, and the other technicalities.

✔ **Correct.** Noticeable mistakes interfere with your reader's ability to understand you. Further, in today's competitive world, careless writing deducts points you can't afford to lose. People judge you by every piece of writing you create, and you need to live up to your best self. However, good contemporary writing allows substantial leeway in observing grammatical niceties.

✔ **Persuasive.** When you dig beneath the surface, most messages and documents ask something of the reader. This request may be minor ('Meet me at Restaurant X at 4'to major ('Please fund this proposal; a million will do'). Even when you're just asking for or providing information, frame your message to suit your reader's viewpoint. I cover writing for your audience in depth in Chapter 2 and the elements of persuasive writing as they apply to various media in Part II.

All of these indicators of successful business communication come into play in everything you write. The following sections break down the various components of style into separate bits you can examine and adjust in your own writing.

## Aiming for a clear, simple style

Clarity and simplicity go hand in hand. It means your messages communicate what you intend with no room for misunderstanding or misinterpretation. This requires:

✔ Words your reader already knows and whose meaning is agreed-upon – no forcing readers to look up words, no trying to impress

✔ Sentence structure that readers can easily follow the first time through

✔ Well-organized, logical, on-point content without anything unnecessary or distracting

✔ Clear connections between sentences, paragraphs, and ultimately ideas, in order to make a cohesive statement

✔ Correct spelling and basically correct grammar

Writing with the preceding characteristics is transparent: nothing stands in the way of the reader absorbing your information, ideas and recommendations. Good business writing for most purposes doesn't call attention to itself. It's like a good makeup job. A woman doesn't want to hear, 'Great cosmetology!' She hopes for 'You look beautiful.' Similarly you want your audience to admire your thinking, not the way you phrased it.

One result of following these criteria is that people can move through your material very fast. This is good! A fast read is your best shot at pulling people into your message and keeping them from straying off due to boredom. These days people are so overwhelmed and impatient that they don't bother to invest time in deciphering a message's meaning. They just stop reading.

Creating an easy reading experience is hard on the writer. When you write well, you do all the reader's work for them. They don't need to figure out anything because you've already done every bit of it for them. Make the effort because that's how you win what you want.

## Applying readability guidelines

Guidelines for business writing are not theoretical. They're practical, and moreover, supported by research studies on how people respond to the written word. Fortunately, you don't have to read the research. Most word-processing software, including Microsoft Word, and several websites have already digested all the data and offer easy-to-use tools to help you quickly gauge the readability of your writing.

Several readability indexes exist (see the sidebar ': Readability research:What it tells us' in this chapter). In this section, I focus on the Flesch Readability Index because it's the index that Microsoft Word uses. The Flesch Readability Index predicts the percentage of people likely to understand a piece of writing and assigns it a grade level of reading comprehension. The grade level scores are based on average reading ability of students in the US public school system. The algorithm for the Flesch Readability Index is primarily based on the length of words, sentences and paragraphs.

Word's version of the Index also shows you the percentage of passive sentences in a selection, which is a very good indicator of flabby verbs, indirect sentence structure and cut-worthy phrases. See the section 'Finding action verbs' later in this chapter for more on activating sentences that contain passive verbs.

### Matching reading level to audience

Whatever readability index you use, your target numbers depend on the audience you're writing to (one more reason to know your readers).

Highly educated readers can obviously comprehend difficult material, which may lead you to strive for text written at a high educational level for scientists or MBAs. But generally this isn't necessarily a good idea. For most business communication – email, letters, proposals, websites – most readers (yourself included) are lazy and prefer 'easy' material.

At the same time, usually you don't want to gear your use of language to the least literate members of your audience. So take any calculations with many grains of salt and adapt them to your audience and purpose. (And just so you know, the 'average reader' in the US is pegged at a 7th to 9th grade reading level, depending on which study you look at.)

When you want to reach a very diverse group with a message, you can segment your audience, just like marketers, and craft different versions for each. If a company needs to inform employees of a benefits change, for example, it may need different communications for top managers, middle managers, clerical staff, factory workers, and so on. Beyond assuming varying reading comprehension levels, you may need to rethink the content for each as well.

## Assessing readability level

If you're writing in Microsoft Word 2010, to find the Readability Index choose File⇨Options⇨Proofing. In the section 'When correcting spelling and grammar in Word', check the boxes 'Check grammar with spelling' and 'Show readability statistics'. Thereafter, whenever you complete a spelling and grammar check, you see a box with readability scores.

Several readability tests are available free online, including www.readability-score.com. On most sites, you simply paste a chunk of your text into a box and have the site gauge readability.

My personal *print media* targets for general audiences are as follows:

- ✔ Flesch reading ease: 50 to 70 per cent
- ✔ Grade level: 10th to 12th grade
- ✔ Percentage of passive sentences: 0 to 10 per cent
- ✔ Words per sentence: 14 to 18, average (some can consist of one word, while others a great many more)
- ✔ Sentences per paragraph: Average three to five

For online media, my targets are even tighter. Reading from a screen – even a big one – is physically harder for people so they are even less patient than with printed material. Sentences work best when they average eight to 12 words. Paragraphs should contain one to three sentences. I talk about adaptions for digital copy in more depth in Part III.

Select a section or a whole document of something you wrote recently in Word or for a website. Review the Readability Statistics to find out if you need to simplify your writing. If the statistics say that at least a 12th grade reading level is required (on many Word programs, the index doesn't show levels above 12), and less than 50 per cent of readers will understand your document, consider rewriting. Or do the same if you used more than 10 per cent passive sentences.

# Readability research: What it tells us

Serious studies to figure out what produces easy reading began in the early 20th century and continue to be done in many languages in addition to English. The most influential researchers have been Rudolph Flesch – for which the Flesch Readability Index is named – and Robert Gunning, who more picturesquely called his measurement system the Fog Index. Both worked with American journalists and newspaper publishers in the late 1940s to lower the reading grade level of newspapers, and sure enough, newspaper readership went up 45 per cent.

Recent grade-level ratings of what we read are illuminating. Overall, the simpler and clearer the language, the higher the readership. A few examples of necessary grade levels:

✔ Most romance novels: 7

✔ Popular authors including Stephen King, Tom Clancy and John Grisham: 7

✔ The UK's *Sun* and *Daily Mirror:* 9

✔ *Wall Street Journal:* 11

✔ *Sydney Sun-Herald:* 12

✔ *London Times:* 12

✔ *Guardian:* 14

✔ *Times of India:* 15

✔ Academic papers: 15 to 20

✔ Typical Government documents: Over 20

A recent British university study applied readability criteria to online newspapers and the results mirror print studies: *The Sun* was easiest to read, *The Guardian,* most difficult.

I offer lots of suggestions for rewriting in the next section, but consider any or all of the following:

✔ Substitute short, one or two syllable words for any long ones.

✔ Shorten long sentences by breaking them up or tightening your wording.

✔ Break paragraphs into smaller chunks so that you have fewer sentences in each.

✔ Look for words that are a form of the verbs 'have' or 'to
be' ('is,' 'are,' 'will be', and so on). These verbs are weak
and often result in passive verb construction.

✔ Review the rewrite to make sure that your message
still means what you intended and hasn't become even
harder to understand

Then re-check the statistics. If the figures are still high, repeat
the process. See if you can get the grade level down to 10,
then eight. Try for less than 10 per cent passive. Compare the
different versions.

## Finding the right rhythm

You may wonder whether basing your writing on short simple
sentences produces choppy and boring material reminiscent
of a grade school textbook. Aiming for clear and simple definitely should not mean dull reading.

Becoming aware of rhythm in what you read, and what you
write, can improve your writing dramatically. Like all language
English was used to communicate orally long before writing
was invented, so the sound and rhythm patterns are critical
to how written forms as well as spoken ones are received.

Think of the worst public speakers you know. They probably
speak in a series of long, complex sentences in an even tone
that quickly numbs the ear. Good speakers, by contrast, vary
the length of sentences and their intonation. As a writer, you
want to do the same.

In everything you write, aim to build in a natural cadence.
Rhythm is one of the main tools for cajoling people to stay
with you and find what you write more interesting. Just begin
each sentence differently from the previous one and try alter-
nating short plain sentences with longer ones that have two
or three clauses.

Good public speakers vary the lengths of their sentences to
keep reader's ears engaged. They avoid long, complex sentences, and they know that short punchy words and phrases
need to be doled out carefully for maximum impact. As a
writer, you want readers to have a similar experience.

### Fixing the short and choppy

Even a short message benefits from attention to sentence rhythm. Consider this paragraph:

> *John: Our screw supply is low. It takes three weeks for orders to be filled. We should place the order now. Then we won't have an emergency situation later. Please sign this form to authorize this purchase. Thank you. – Ted*

And an alternate version:

> *John: Our screw supply is low. It takes three weeks for orders to be filled, so we should place the order now to avoid an emergency later. Please sign the attached form to authorize the purchase. Thanks – Ted*

For long documents, varying your sentence length and structure is critical. Few people will stay with multiple pages of stilted, mind-numbing prose.

Notice too that when you combine some short sentences to alternate the rhythm, easy ways emerge to improve the wording and edit out unneeded repetition. You may choose to go a step further and write a third version of the same message:

> *John: I notice that our screw supply is getting low. Since an order will take three weeks to reach us, let's take care of it now to avoid an emergency down the line. Just sign the attached authorization and we're all set. – Ted*

Leaving aside how this was edited, which I talk about in the next chapter, notice how much more connected the thoughts seem, and how much more authoritative the overall message feels. With very little rewriting, the writer comes across as a more take charge, efficient professional – someone reliable, someone who cares about the whole operation, rather than just a cog going through the motions.

### Fixing the long and complicated

Many people have a problem opposite to creating short, disconnected sentences. Maybe you tend to write lengthy complicated ones that end up with the same result: dead writing.

The solution to never-ending strings of words is the same – alternate sentence structures. But in this case, break up the long ones. Doing this produces punchier, more enticing copy.

A number of basically good writers don't succeed as well as they might because they fall into a pattern that repeats the same rhythm, over and over again. An example taken from an opinion piece written for a workshop:

> *I strongly support efforts to improve the global economy, and naturally may be biased toward the author's position. While this bias may be the reason I responded well to the piece in the first place, it is not the reason why I consider it an exceptional piece of writing. Not only is this article extremely well researched, its use of cost-benefit analysis is an effective way to think about the challenges.*

The monotonous pattern and unending sentences serve the ideas poorly. One way to rewrite the material:

> *I strongly support efforts to improve the global economy and this probably inclined me to a positive response. But it's not why I see it as an exceptional piece of writing. The article is extremely well researched. Further, its cost-benefit analysis is an effective way to think about the challenge. For an aspiring advocate of globalism, the article is a great example of using history and data to communicate a message in a non-partisan way.*

Again, simply varying the sentence length and structure quickly improves the overall wording and flow. Notice that you can take liberties with the recommended short-long-short sentence pattern and use two short sentences, then two more complex ones, for example.

Spend 10 minutes with a recent piece of your writing that's at least half a page long. Scan it for rhythmic patterns. You may find a balanced flow with varying types of sentences. Or, you may see whole sets of short choppy sentences. Experiment with recombining some of them into longer ones. If you find too many long convoluted sentences, break some of them up so short terse ones are interspersed. Read the reworked text in its entirety and see whether it reads better.

Everyone has particular ways of writing that leave room for improvement. Strive to recognize your own weaknesses and you're a giant step closer to better writing because you can apply fix-it techniques as part of your regular self-editing process. I give you a whole bunch of methods to draw on in Chapter 4.

## Achieving a conversational tone

New business writers are often told to adopt a 'conversational' tone, but what does that actually mean?

Business correspondence written during the 19th century and even most of the 20th, seems slow, formal and ponderous when you read it now. Today's faster pace of life results in a desire for faster communication, both in terms of how you deliver messages and how quickly you're able to read and deal with them.

Conversational tone is something of an illusion. You don't really write the way you talk, and you shouldn't. But you can echo natural speech in various ways to more effectively engage your audience.

Rhythm, which I discuss in the preceding section, is a basic technique that gives your copy forward momentum and promotes a conversational feeling. Sentence variety engages readers while unrelieved choppy sentences or complicated ones kill interest.

Additional techniques for achieving conversational tone include:

- ✔ **Infusing messages with warmth.** Think of the person as an individual before you write and content that's appropriate to the relationship and subject will come to you, and the tone will be right.

- ✔ **Choosing short simple words.** Rely on the versions you use to *talk* to someone, rather than the sophisticated ones you use to try and impress. See the later section 'Choosing reader-friendly words' for examples.

- ✔ **Using contractions as you do in speech.** Go with 'can't' rather than 'cannot,' 'I'm' rather than 'I am'.

- ✔ **Minimizing the use of inactive and passive forms.** Carefully evaluate every use of the 'to be' verbs – *is, was, will be, are,* and so on – to determine if you can use active, interesting verbs instead.

- ✔ **Taking selective liberties with grammatical correctness.** Starting a sentence with 'and' or 'but' is OK, for example, but avoid mismatching your nouns and pronouns.

- ✔ **Adopting an interactive spirit.** As online media teaches, one-way, top-down communication is 'so yesterday'. Find ways in all your writing to invite active interest and input from your reader. Part IV covers a range of ways to make online copy interactive and many of the techniques can be adapted to traditional media.

If you ignore the preceding guidelines – and want to look hopelessly outdated – you can write a long-winded and lifeless message like the following:

> *Dear Elaine:*
>
> *I regret to communicate that the meeting for which we are scheduled on Tuesday at 2 p.m. must be canceled. Unfortunately the accounting information anticipated for receipt on Friday will not be able to meet the delivery deadline.*
>
> *I am contemplating an appropriate rescheduling. Please inform my office of your potential availability at 3 p.m. on the 2nd. – Carrie*

Yawn – and also a bit confusing. Or you can write a clear, quick, crisp version like this:

> *Elaine, I'm sorry to say we're postponing the Tuesday meeting. The accounting info we need won't be ready till Wednesday. Bummer, I know.*
>
> *Is Thursday at 3:00 OK for you? – Carrie*

Although the second example feels casual and conversational, these aren't the actual words Carrie would say to Elaine in a real phone conversation. This exchange is more likely:

> *Hi. How are you? Listen, we got a problem. The project numbers are running way late. I won't have them till Wednesday. Yeah. So no point meeting Tuesday. How's Thursday look?*

Online copy often works best when it carries the conversational illusion to an extreme. Pay attention to the jazzy, spontaneous-style copy on websites you love. The words may read like they sprang ready-made out of some genie's lamp but more than likely they were produced by a team of copywriters agonizing over every line for weeks. Spontaneous-reading copy doesn't come easy: it's hard work. Some people – frequent bloggers, for example – are better at writing conversationally because they practice this skill consciously.

The next time you encounter bloggers or online writers whose voices you like, copy some text and paste it into a blank word-processing document (in order to separate the words from all the online bells and whistles). Read through the words carefully and analyze what you like in terms of words, phrases, and sentences. See if you can identify how the writers pull off their appealing breezy style.

# Enlivening Your Language

Written communication starts with words, so choose them well. But the most important guideline for selecting the best words for business writing may seem counter-intuitive: Avoid long or subtle words that express nuance. These may serve as the staple for many fiction writers and academics, but you're not striving to sound evocative, ambiguous, impressive or super-educated. In fact, you want just the opposite.

## Relying on everyday words and phrasing

The short everyday words you use in ordinary speech are almost always best for business writing. They're clear, practical and direct. They're also powerful enough to express your deepest and widest thoughts. They're the words that reach people emotionally, too, because they stand for the most basic and concrete things people care about and need to communicate about. 'Home' is a whole different story than 'residence,' 'quit' carries a lot more overtones than 'resign.'

Make a list of basic one- and two-syllable words and almost certainly, they come from the oldest part of the English language,

Anglo-Saxon. Most words with three or more syllables were grafted onto this basic stock by historical invaders: the French-speaking Normans and the Latin-speaking Romans for the most part, both of whom aspired to higher levels of cultural refinement than the Britons.

If you were raised in an English-speaking home, you learned Anglo-Saxon words during earliest childhood and acquired the ones with Latin, French and other influences later in your education. Scan these last two paragraphs and you know immediately which words came from which culture set.

For this reason and others, readers are programed to respond best to simple, short, low-profile English words. They trigger feelings of trust (an Anglo-Saxon word) and credibility (from the French). Obviously I don't choose to write entirely with one-syllable words. Variety is the key – just as with sentences. English's history gives you a remarkable array of words when you want to be precise or produce certain feelings. Even in business English, a sprinkling of longer words contributes to a good pace and can make what you say more specific and interesting. But don't forget your base word stock.

If you're writing to a non-native English speaking audience, you have even more reason to write with one- and two-syllable words. People master the same basic words first when learning a new language, no matter what their original tongue, so all new English-speakers understand them. This applies to less educated readers too. Given the diverse and multi-cultural audiences many of your messages must reach, simplicity of language should rule.

This principle holds for long documents like reports and proposals as much as for emails. And it's very important for online writing such as websites and blogs. When you read on-screen, you have even less patience with multi-syllable sophisticated words. Reading (and writing) on smart phones and other small devices makes short words the *only* choice.

## Choosing reader-friendly words

The typical business English you see all the time may lure you toward long, educated words. Resist!

Consciously develop your awareness of short-word options. Clearer writing gives you better results. Opt for the first and friendlier word in the following pairs.

| Use. . . | Rather than. . . |
|---|---|
| help | assistance |
| often | frequently |
| try | endeavor |
| need | requirement |
| basic | fundamental |
| built | constructed |
| confirm | validate |
| rule | regulation |
| create | originate |
| use | utilize |
| prove | substantiate |
| show | demonstrate |
| study | analyze |
| fake | artificial |
| limits | parameters |
| skill | proficiency |
| need | necessitate |

I don't mean that the longer words are bad – in fact, they may often be the better choice. But generally, make sure that you have a reason for going long.

## *Focusing on the real and concrete*

*Concrete nouns* are words that denote something tangible: a person or any number of actual things: cat, apple, dirt, child, boat, balloon, computer, egg, tree, table, Joseph, and so on.

*Abstract nouns* on the other hand typically represent ideas and concepts. They may denote a situation, condition, quality or experience. For example: catastrophe, freedom, efficiency, knowledge, mystery, observation, analysis, research, love, democracy, and many more.

Concrete nouns are objects that exist in real space. You can touch, see, hear, smell or taste them. When you use concrete nouns in your writing, readers bring these physical associations to your words, and this lends reality to your thoughts. Moreover, you can expect most people to take the same meaning from them. This isn't true of abstract words. Two people are unlikely to argue about what an apricot is, but they may well disagree on what exactly 'independence' means.

When your writing is built on a lot of abstract nouns, you are generalizing. Even when you're writing an opinion or philosophical piece, too much abstraction doesn't fire the imagination. A lot of business writing strikes readers as dull and uninspiring for this reason.

Suppose at a pivotal point of World War II Winston Churchill had written in the manner of many modern business executives:

> *We're operationalizing this initiative to proceed as effectively, efficiently and proactively as possible in alignment with our responsibilities to existing population centers and our intention to develop a transformative future for mankind. We'll employ cost-effective, cutting-edge technologies and exercise the highest level of commitment, whatever the obstacles that materialize in various geographic situations.*

Instead he wrote, and said:

> *We shall not flag or fail. We shall go on to the end. We shall fight in France, we shall fight on the seas and the oceans, we shall fight with growing confidence and growing strength in the air, we shall defend our island, whatever the cost may be. We shall fight on the beaches, we shall fight on the landing grounds, we shall fight in the fields and in the streets, we shall fight in the hills; we shall never surrender.*

Which statement engages the senses and therefore the heart, even three-quarters of a century after this particular cause was won? Which carries more conviction? Granted, Churchill was writing a speech, but the statement also works amazingly when read.

While you probably won't be called on to rouse your country-men as Churchill was, writing in a concrete way pays off for you too. It brings your writing alive. Aim to get down to earth in what you say and how you say it.

Using short words goes a long way toward this goal. Notice how many words of the mock business-writing piece contain three or more syllables. Churchill's piece uses only three. And running both passages through readability checks (see the preceding section 'Applying readability guidelines') predicts at least a 12th grade reading level to understand the business-speak with only 2 per cent of readers understanding it. By contrast, Churchill's lines require only a fourth grade reading level and 91 per cent of readers understand them.

You may often find yourself tempted to write convoluted, indirect, abstract prose – because it's common to your cor-porate culture, or your technical field, or the Request for Proposal you're responding to. Don't do it. Remind yourself that nobody likes to read that kind of writing, even though they may write that way themselves. Take the lead in deliver-ing lean lively messages and watch the positive response this brings.

## Finding action verbs

Good strong verbs invigorate. Passive verbs, which involve a form of the verb 'to be,' deaden language and thinking, too. Consider some dull sentences and their better alternatives:

> *All of the department heads were invited to the celebration by the CEO.*

> *The CEO invited all department heads to the celebration.*

> *A decision to extend working hours was reached by the talent management office.*

> *The talent management office decided to extend working hours.*
> Or: *The talent management office is extending work hours.*

> *The idea is an improvement on the original design.*

> *The idea improves the original design.*

*The annual report numbers were contradicted by the auditors.*

*The auditors contradict the annual report numbers.*

Try also to avoid sentences that rely on the phrases 'there is' and 'there are,' which often bury the meaning of a sentence. Compare the following pairs:

*There is a company rule to consider in deciding which route to follow.*

*A company rule determines which route to follow.*

*There are guidelines you should use if you want to improve your writing.*

*Use the guidelines to improve your writing.*

For most dull passive verbs the solution is the same: ***Find the action.*** Be clear about *who* did *what* and then rework the sentence to say that.

You may need to go beyond changing the verb and rethink the entire sentence so it's simple, clear and direct. In the process, take responsibility. Passive sentences often evade it. A classic example:

*Mistakes were made, people were hurt and opportunities were lost.*

Who made the mistakes, hurt the people, and lost the opportunities? The writer? An unidentified CEO? Mystery government officials? This kind of structure is sometimes called 'the divine passive': some unknown or unnameable force made it happen.

To help you remember why you generally need to avoid the passive, here's my favorite mistake. I asked a group to write about their personal writing problems and how they planned to work on them. One person contributed:

*Many passive verbs are used by me.*

Take the time to identify the passive verbs and indirect constructions in all your writing. Doing so doesn't mean that you must always eliminate them. You may want to use the passive because no clearly definable active subject exists – or doesn't matter:

*The award was created to recognize outstanding sales achievement.*

Or you may have a surprise to disclose which leads you to use the passive for emphasis:

*This year's award was won by the newest member of the department: Joe Mann.*

Using the passive unconsciously and often undermines your writing success. Substitute active verbs. They can be short and punchy, such as *drive, end, gain, fail, win, probe, treat, taint, speed.* Or they can be longer words that offer more precise meaning, such as *underline, trigger, suspend, pioneer, model, fracture, crystallize, compress, accelerate.* Both word groups suggest action and movement, adding zing and urgency to your messages.

## Crafting comparisons to help readers

Comparisons help your readers understand your message on deeper levels. You can use similes and metaphors which are both analogies, to make abstract ideas more tangible and generally promote comprehension. These devices don't need to be elaborate, long or pretentiously literary. Here are some simple comparisons:

*Poets use metaphors like painters use brushes – to paint pictures that help people see under the surface.*

*Winning this award is my Oscar.*

*Life is like a box of chocolates.*

*The new polymer strand is 10 nanometers in width – while the average human hair is 90,000 nanometers wide.*

*From 15,000 feet up the world looks like a peaceful quilt of harmonious colors where no conflict could exist.*

# Making up fresh comparisons

Playing with comparisons is a classic schoolroom game and you can experiment today as a means of finding new ways to express your ideas. Simply think about bringing together two different things so one is seen differently.

Take 15 minutes and assemble a short list of things, activities or experiences on the left-hand side of a page of blank paper or screen. For example, you can list your new project, writing your résumé, making your boss happy, the new product you're selling, playing a computer game, and so on.

Think about what that item is like – how you can describe it visually or through the other senses. Think about how it makes you feel. Brainstorm about other things that have similar characteristics. Try to avoid clichés and come up with something you find interesting.

Write your idea for each item on your list on the right side of the paper. Come up with an idea for every item just to give yourself the practice, even if some of your comparisons aren't brilliant. Use your new skill when you're writing an important document, trying to explain something difficult or make your best persuasive argument.

For example, you might brainstorm for a comparison by 'finishing' statements such as:

Winning this contract is as good as...

This new service will change your thinking about life insurance just like __X_ changed _Y___

Saving a few dollars by investing in Solution A instead of Solution B is like....

For an entirely different way to explore comparisons, visit GistOut. com (gistout.com). Type in whatever you like in the searchbox, and using Google search data, GistOut assembles comparisons that others have used elsewhere online. The results may stimulate your own imagination or suggest an idea you can adapt.

When I entered 'writing,' I got 192 results complete with attributions. Here are a few that caught my eye:

- ✔ *I love cooking, and writing is like that. You think, 'Ah, I'll put a bit of that in, now that's right.' You have a feeling that somehow it will make a good meal.*

- ✔ *Writing a novel is like creeping along on your belly with shells exploding around you. It's only occasionally that there's a ceasefire and you can get up and run.*

- ✔ *If writing a first draft is like jumping off a building, revising is like suddenly sprouting wings and taking flight.*

Whatever device you use, effective comparisons

- ✔ **Create mental images.** You can give readers a different way to access – and *remember* – your ideas and information.

- ✔ **Align things from different arenas.** Using the familiar to explain the unfamiliar can be especially helpful when you introduce new information or change.

- ✔ **Heighten the impact of everyday practical writing.** Just as in well-written fiction, a great comparison in a business document engages the reader's imagination and boosts your message's memorability.

- ✔ **Make intriguing headlines that grab attention.** I saw a blog post recently titled, 'How Learning to Ride a Bike is Like Working at Home'. I read it just to find out what the two things have in common.

# Using Reader-Friendly Graphic Techniques

Good written messages and documents are well thought out, as I cover in Chapter 2, and presented clearly and vividly, as I show you in the preceding sections of this chapter. But I have one more aspect to highlight. Your writing must not only meet audience needs and read well; it must look good.

Whether your material appears in print or online, every message and document you create is a visual experience. More than readability is at stake; others judge your message's value and credibility by how it looks. Whether you want to write an effective résumé, proposal, report – or just an email – design can make or break your writing.

The following sections show you how to use various graphic techniques to maximize your message's appeal. And rest assured, you don't need to purchase special software or other tools to easily implement these good design principles.

# Building in white space

To coin a comparison (see the sidebar 'Making up fresh comparisons'):

> *Add white space to your writing for the same reason bakers add yeast to their bread – to leaven the denseness by letting in the light and air.*

Help your writing breathe by providing plenty of empty space. The eye demands rest when scanning or reading. Don't cram your words into a small tight space by decreasing the point size or squeezing the space between characters, words, or lines. Densely packed text is inaccessible. If you have too many words for the available space, cut them down. I show you many ways to do that while also improving your impact in Chapter 4.

Always look for opportunities to add that valuable emptiness to your message. Check for white space in everything you deliver. Factors that affect white space include the size of the typeface, line spacing, margin size, column width, and graphic devices such as subheads, sidebars, and integrated images.

# Toying with type

Type has numerous graphic aspects and effects. Following are some of the most powerful, as well as easiest to adjust.

### Fonts

Using an easy-to-read simple typeface (or font) is critical. For printed text, *serif fonts* – fonts with feet or squiggles at the end of each letter – are more reader-friendly because they smoothly guide the eye from letter to letter, word to word. However, *sans-serif fonts* (ones without the little feet) are favored by art directors because they look more modern and classy. The sans-serif face Verdana was specifically designed for screen work and often used for it.

You need to choose your font according to your purpose. For long print documents serif remains the better choice for the same reason that books still use it – ease of reading. But you can to some extent mix your faces. Using sans-serif headlines and subheads can make a welcome contrast. (For example, Times New Roman and Helvetica work nicely together.) But generally, resist the temptation to combine more than two different typefaces.

Avoid fancy or cute typefaces for any purpose. They're not only distracting but may not transfer well to someone else's computer system. They can end up garbled or altogether missing in action. Recruitment officers sometimes find a candidate's name entirely missing from a résumé because their systems lack a corresponding typeface and end up omitting these very important words.

And never type a whole message in capitals or bold face, which give the impression that you're shouting. Avoid using italics on more than a word or two because such treatments are hard to read.

### Point-size

Like font choice, the best point size for text depends on the result that you're trying to achieve. Generally, somewhere between 10 and 12 points works best, but you need to adjust according to your audience and the experience you want to create. Small type may look great, but if you want readers 55 and up to read your annual report, 8-point type will kill it.

Online text suggests a similar 10 to 12 point range for body copy, but calculating the actual onscreen experience for a wide range of monitors and devices is complicated. Online text often looks different on different platforms. Err on the side of a generous point size.

Never resort to reducing the size of your typeface to fit more in. I once had to persuade the top boss to cut back his 'Message from the CEO' because it was longer than the allocated space. He resisted sacrificing more than a few words. Then I showed him what his message would look like in the 6-point type we needed to run the whole thing. He quickly slashed half his copy to create a better presentation.

### Margins and columns

For both online and print media, avoid making columns of type so wide that the eye becomes discouraged in reading across. If breaking the copy into two columns isn't suitable, consider making one or both margins wider. Also avoid columns that are only three or four words wide, because they're very hard to read and annoying visually.

Be selective in how you justify text. The text in this paragraph is justified on the left, which is almost always your best choice for body copy. Right-justified text is difficult to read because each new line starts in a different spot. Fully justified copy (on both left and right) often visibly distorts words and spacing to make your words fit consistently within a block of text. Worse yet, full justification eliminates a good way to add white space through uneven lines.

## *Keeping colors simple*

Using color to accent your document can work well, but stay simple. One color, in addition to the black used for the text, is probably plenty. See whether an accent color sparks your message by using it consistently on headlines and/or subheads.

Using a lot of different colors – even on a website – strikes people as messy and amateur these days. Designers prefer simple, clean palettes that combine a few colors at most. So should you. And do not place any type against a color background that makes it hard to read. This means that backgrounds should be no more than a light tint. *Dropped or reversed-out type* – for instance, white type on a black or dark background – can look terrific but only in small doses, such as a caption or short sidebar. A whole page of reversed-out type, whether in print or onscreen, makes a daunting read.

If you're producing a substantial document or website in tandem with a graphic designer, never allow graphic impact to trump readability and editorial clarity. To most designers, words are just part of a visual pattern. If a designer tells you the document has too many words, certainly listen; it's probably true and you do want the piece to look good. But 'just say no' if playing second fiddle to the visual undermines your copy. Graphics should strengthen, not weaken, your message's impact and absorbability.

## Adding effective graphics

On the whole, if you've got good images and they're appropriate, flaunt them. This doesn't really apply to an email or letter, but certainly, graphics help long documents and anything read online.

Appropriateness of graphics depends on your purpose. A proposal can benefit from charts and graphs to make financials and other variables clear and more easily grasped. A report may include photographs of a project under way. A blog with a fun image related to the subject is more enticing. Additional possibilities for various media include images of successful projects to support credibility, illustrations of something yet to be built, change documentation and visualizations of abstract ideas.

Of course, your own resources and time may be limited. But when visual effect matters – to attract readers or when you're competing for a big contract, for example – take time to brainstorm possibilities. Wonderful online resources proliferate, and many are free. Your computer can help you produce a good chart or graph. It may take some imagination and research.

Images must feel appropriate to your readers. If not, you create a negative reaction. Even with websites, research shows that people value the words most and are put off by images unrelated to the subject. And generally stay away from clip art that's packaged with your word-processing software or other design tools. Clip art must be totally appropriate to your medium and message or cleverly adapted to look original or else it instantly cheapens your message in the viewer's eye.

## Breaking space up with sidebars, boxes and lists

Print media in the past decade have increasingly used graphic techniques to draw readers in with as many ways as they can come up with. Today's readers are scanners first. Think of your own behavior when opening up a newspaper or magazine. You most likely scout for what interests you and then read the material, in whole or at least in part, if it appeals to you. When you get bored, you quickly stop reading and start scanning again.

Good headlines and subheads are critical to capture readers' attention and guide them through a document. I show you how to write these bits in Chapter 9. But you must also pay major attention to writing:

✔ Captions accompanying photos and other images

✔ Sidebars and boxes offering additional background, sidelights or information

✔ Interesting quotes or tidbits used as 'pullouts' in the margins or inside the text

✔ Small tight summaries of the article, or introductions, at the beginning

✔ Bulleted or numbered lists of examples or steps

✔ Icons (such as the Tip and Remember icons in this book) that denote something of special interest

All these devices serve three important purposes.

✔ **Along with images, they break up unrelieved blocks of type that discourage the eye.** In fact, on a printed page, some print editors use the 'ten-dollar note test': if you can lay down a note on a page and it doesn't touch a single graphic device, then add one in.

✔ **They offer different ways to capture a reader's attention.** You may be drawn by a summary, a caption, or a box to read the whole piece, or at least some of it.

✔ **Using graphic devices helps to convey ideas and information more clearly and effectively.** People absorb information in different ways. Taking lessons from the online world, today's editors offer readers choices of what they want to read, and where they want to start.

All these graphic techniques should be part of your writing repertoire. Do you need them for every email you write? Of course not. But strategies like subheads and bullets can still help get your message across. For long documents and materials intended to be persuasive, draw on all the techniques that suit your goals and audience.

# Chapter 4

# Self-Editing: Professional Ways to Improve Your Own Work

. . . . . . . . . . . . . . . . . . . . . . . . . . . . . . . . . . . . . . . . . . . .

## In This Chapter

▶ Switching to the editor's role

▶ Reviewing the big picture

▶ Assessing your writing's readability

▶ Avoiding pitfalls that undermine clarity and impact

. . . . . . . . . . . . . . . . . . . . . . . . . . . . . . . . . . . . . . . . . . . .

*I*f you expect to create a successful email, letter or business document in just one shot, think again. Don't ask so much of yourself. Very, very few professional writers can accomplish a finished piece – whether they write novels, plays, articles, websites or press releases – with their first draft. This especially includes writers known for their simplicity and easy reading.

Editing is how writers write. For them, the writing and editing processes are inseparable because they wouldn't dream of submitting work to anyone that is less than their very best. Unfortunately, many people are intimidated by the notion of editing their own work. But equipped with effective methods and techniques, you can edit with confidence.

Mastering hundreds of grammar rules is not necessary to becoming a good editor. Know the clues that reveal where your writing needs work, and you can sharpen what you write so it accomplishes exactly what you want. This chapter gives you the groundwork.

# Changing Hats: Going from Writer to Editor

The writer and editor roles reinforce each other.

- ✔ In writing, you plan your message or document based on what you want to accomplish and your analysis of the reader (which I cover in Chapter 2), brainstorm content possibilities, organize logically, and create a full draft. Always think of this piece as the *first draft* because every message, whatever its nature and length, deserves editing and will hugely benefit from it.

- ✔ In editing, you review your first draft and find ways to liven word choice, simplify sentences, and ensure that ideas hang together. You also evaluate the 'macro' side: whether the content and tone deliver the strongest message to your audience and help build relationships. (I cover all this in Chapter 2.) Furthermore, as you make a habit of regularly editing your writing, your first-draft writing improves as well.

- ✔ In proofreading, you review your writing in nitty-gritty detail to find and correct errors – mistakes in spelling, grammar, punctuation, facts, references, citations, calculations and more as relevant to the material.

Don't expect to discard the editing process down the line as you further refine your writing abilities. Professional writers never stop relying on their editing skills, no matter how good they get at their craft.

Improving your editing abilities goes a long way toward improving the impact of everything you write. The following tools and tricks make you a more capable and confident self-editor.

## Choosing a way to edit

You have three main ways to edit writing. Try each of the following and see which you prefer – but realize you can always switch your editing method to best suit a current writing task or timeline.

### Option 1: Marking up print-outs

Before computers, both writers and editors worked with 'hard copy' because it was the only choice. For about a century before computers, people wrote on typewriters, revised the results by hand, and then retyped the entire document. If you were reviewing *printer's proofs* –preliminary versions of material to be printed – you used a shorthand set of symbols to tell the typesetter what to change.

These symbols offered uniformity; every editor and printer knew what they meant. Typing and printing processes have changed radically, but the marks are still used today and remain a helpful way for communicating text changes between people.

Many professional writers still edit their work on hard copy print-outs because onscreen editing strains the eyes and makes you more error-prone. You may find physically editing your copy with universal marks to be more satisfying; you have something to show for your editing efforts when you're done. Editing on paper can help you switch over to the editor's side of the table. Of course, you must then transfer the changes to your computer.

Proof marks vary between the US and UK, and some organizations have special marks or special meanings.

### Option 2: Editing onscreen

After you draft a document, you can simply read through it and make changes. Younger writers may never have considered any other system. You can substitute words, reorganize the material by cutting and pasting with a few mouse clicks or keystrokes. The down side to this method of editing is that you're left with no record of the change process. (See the next section for a useful alternative.)

When maintaining a copy of your original text matters, save your new version as a separate document. Amend its name to avoid hassle later, in case a series of revised versions develops.

Keep your renaming simple yet specific. If the document is titled 'Gidget article,' title the edited version 'Gidget 2,' for example, or date it –'Gidget 11.13.' When you edit someone else's document, tack on your initials: 'Gidget.nc' for example.

Be sure your titling allows for easy identification of the various versions to avoid time-wasting confusion later.

### Option 3: Tracking your changes

Most word-processing software offers a handy feature to record every change you make to the text in a document. In Word 2010, select Review, then Track Changes.

When you choose to track changes, all changes show up on the copy in a color other than black or in small text boxes off to the side (depending on your choice of screen view). Deletions appear as strikethrough text or off to the side.

The system takes some personal trial and error but provides a useful tool for your editing experiments.

When you're tracking changes on an extensive edited document, you can end up with something quite complicated. You can spare yourself the nitty-gritty of every deletion and insertion by selecting to view as 'Final' with all your proposed changes included. You don't lose your edits, they're just hidden from immediate view.

When you finish editing, save a version that shows the revisions, then go back to the Review tab and choose 'Accept or Reject Changes.' Accept all changes, or go through your document section by section or even sentence by sentence. You emerge with a clean copy; save this version separately from the original. Proof the new version carefully because new errors creep in when you edit.

The Track Changes tool can help you improve your writing process and offers a way to share refinement stages with others when needed. (Numerous online tools, such as GoogleDocs, help you share document development.) But when you ultimately send the message to your audience, be sure your final saved version does not reveal the change process: Turn Track Changes off.

## *Distancing yourself from what you write*

The first step for a self-editor is to consciously assume that role. Forget how hard some of the material was to draft, or how attached you are to some of the ideas or language. Aim to judge as objectively as you can whether your message succeeds and how to improve it.

Your best tool to achieve this distance is the one that cures all ills: time. I suggest in Chapter 2 that for everything you write, allocate roughly one-third the available time to planning, one-third to drafting, and one-third to editing. But ideally, that last third isn't in the same continuous timeframe as the first two stages.

---

# Practicing the stripper's art: In writing, less is usually more

Your goal for every message and business document is 'just enough.' This applies both to overall content and specific word choices:

✔ **Content:** Aim to makes your point and achieve your goal without overkill that loses your reader or damages your argument

✔ **Words:** A windy presentation dilutes impact and may slow reading to the point of no return. Aim to state your case, make or respond to a request, present an argument or accomplish any given purpose in the most concise way.

Build every message with complete words, sentences and commonly accepted grammar. (Abbreviated messages do have their place, however. See 'Texting and instant messaging' for more.)

Many documents suggest their own lengths. If you're answering an RFP (Request for Proposal) that's 10 pages long, a one-page response doesn't suffice. You must supply detail and backup. If you're applying for a job, even a well-done paragraph can't take the place of a résumé. Always take a document's purpose into account to judge appropriate length and depth.

Try to build in a pause between drafting and editing. Pausing overnight (or longer) is highly recommended for major business documents. If your document is really long or important, try to edit and re-edit in a series of stages over days or even weeks. Some copy, such as a website home page or marketing piece, may never be 'finished.' It evolves over time.

For short and/or less consequential messages, an hour or two between drafting and editing helps. A top-of-your-head email or text message that doesn't seem important can still land you in a lot of trouble if you send it out without vetting. If an hour isn't possible, just a quick trip to the coffee maker to stretch your legs can clear your mind and refresh your eyes.

So put the message away and then revisit it after a planned delay.When you return, you see your words with fresh eyes – an editor's rather than the writer's.

# Reviewing the Big and Small Pictures

Your job when self-editing is to review what you wrote on two levels:

- **The macro level:** The thinking that underlies the message and the content decisions you made.

- **The micro level:** How well you use language to express your viewpoint and ask for what you want. (I talk about this in Chapter 5)

## Assessing content success

Start your edit with a big-picture review, using the fresh eyes and mind you gain by putting the piece aside for a while.

Read through the entire document and ask yourself:

- Is what I want very clear from reading the message?

- Does the content support that goal?

✔ Is anything missing from my argument, my sequence of thoughts or my explanations? Do I include all necessary backup?

✔ Do I give the reader a reason to care?

✔ Do I include any unnecessary ideas or statements that don't contribute to my central goal or that detract from it?

✔ Does the tone feel right for the person or group I'm communicating with?

✔ Does the whole message present 'me' in the best possible light?

✔ How would I react if I were the recipient rather than the sender?

✔ Are there any ways my reader can possibly misunderstand or misinterpret my words?

The initial editing challenge is to drill to the core of your message. If you followed the step-by-step process to create the document that I present in Chapter 2, check now that you met your own criteria and that every element works to accomplish your goal.

Your objective answers to these nine questions may lead you to partially or substantially revamp your content. That's fine – there's no point working to improve presentation until you have the right substance.

You may choose to do the big-picture revise right away, or plan for it and proceed to the second stage, the micro-level of editing: crafting the words. It's much easier to make the language more effective when you know exactly what message you want to deliver.

## *Assessing the effectiveness of your language*

You have two ways to get instant, objective feedback on how well you used language.

✔ **Use a readability index.** Most word-processing software can give you a good overview of the difficulty of any written piece. As Chapter 3 details, Word's Readability Statistics box provides helpful information on word, sentence and paragraph length; the number of passive constructions; and the degree of ease with which people can read and understand your message. Use these statistics to pinpoint your word-choice problems.

✔ **Read it aloud.** Reading what you write aloud is a favored method for many writers. As you speak your writing quietly – even under your breath – you identify problems in flow, clarity, and word choice. Asking someone else to read your words aloud to you can put you even more fully in the listener role.

In addition to telling you whether you achieved a conversational tone (see Chapter 3), the read-aloud test alerts you to eight specific problems common to poor writing. I recommend solutions to four of these problems in Chapter 3.

✔ **Problem 1:** A sentence is so long it takes you more than one breath to get through it.
**Solution:** Break it up or shorten it.

✔ **Problem 2:** You hear a monotonous pattern with each sentence starting the same way.
**Solution:** Change some of the sentence structures so you alternate between long and short, simple and complex.

✔ **Problem 3**: All or most sentences sound short and choppy, which creates an abrupt tone and dulls the content.
**Solution:** Combine some sentences to make the read smoother.

✔ **Problem 4:** You stumble over words.
**Solution:** Replace those words with simpler ones, preferably words that are one or two syllables long.

The read-aloud method can reveal four additional challenges. I deal with each problem in greater detail in following sections, but here's a quick overview.

✔ **Problem 5:** You hear yourself using an up-and-down inflection to get through a sentence.
**Solution:** Make the sentence less complicated.

✔ **Problem 6:** You hear repeat sounds produced by words ending in *-ize, -ion, -ing, -ous* or another suffix. **Solution:** Restructure the sentence.

✔ **Problem 7:** You notice numerous prepositional phrases strung together.
**Solution:** Change your wording to make fewer prepositions necessary.

✔ **Problem 8:** You hear words repeated in the same paragraph.
**Solution**: Find substitutes.

If you read your copy aloud and practice the fix-it techniques I prescribe in Chapter 3 and the following sections, you give yourself a gift: the ability to bypass grammar lessons. After you know how to spot a problem, you can use shortcut tools to correct it. Even better, track your own patterns and prevent the problems from happening.

Everyone writes with his or her own personal patterns. The better handle you gain on your own patterns, the better your writing, and the faster you achieve results.

Now for some detail on handling problems 5, 6, 7 and 8.

## *Avoiding telltale up-down-up inflection*

'Fancy' words, excess phrases and awkward constructions force sentences into an unnatural pattern when read aloud. The effect is rather like the typical up-down-up-down inflection of the tattletale: **I** know who **DID** it.

Read the following sentence aloud and see what pattern you force on your voice:

> *All of the writing that is published is a representation of our company, so spelling and grammatical errors can make us look unprofessional and interfere with the public perception of us as competent businesspeople.*

Simply scanning the sentences tips you off to its wordiness. This single sentence contains two phrases using 'of,' two statements with the passive verb 'is,' and three words ending in '-ion.' They produce an awkward, wordy construction. Plus the sentence contains 34 words – far more than the average 18 I recommend – and more than five words have three or more syllables (see Chapter 3).

You don't need to be a linguistic rocket scientist to write a better sentence. Just go for simple and clear. Break up the long sentence. Get rid of the unnecessary words and phrases. Substitute shorter friendlier words. One way:

> *All our company's writing represents us. Spelling and grammar errors make us look unprofessional and incompetent.*

After you simplify, you can often find a third, even better way to write the sentence. A third pass may read:

> *When we make spelling and grammar mistakes, we look unprofessional and incompetent.*

## Looking for repeat word endings

Big clues to wordy, ineffective sentences come with over-used suffixes – words ending in *-ing, -ive, -ion, -ent, -ous* and *-y*. Almost always, these words are three or more syllables and French or Latinate in origin. Several in a sentence make you sound pompous and stiff. They often force you into convoluted, passive constructions that weaken your writing and discourage readers. (See 'Moving from Passive to Active' later for more on activating passive construction.)

Sprinkle these words throughout your written vocabulary but never let them dominate. Try for one per sentence, two at most. Avoid using a string of these words in a single sentence. Find these stuffy words either visually, by scanning what you write, or orally – -read the material out loud and you'll definitely notice when they clutter up your sentences.

In the following sections I show you examples of overly-suffixed wording and how to fix it. If you are unenthusiastic about grammar lessons, proceed happily: my goal is to help you develop a *feel* for well put-together sentences and how to build them. Once you notice problems you can correct them without thinking about rules.

### The -ing words

Consider this sentence:

> *An inspiring new idea is emerging from marshaling the evolving body of evidence.*

One short sentence with four words ending in *-ing!* Read it aloud and you find yourself fall into that up-down inflection. You can fix it by trimming down to one *-ing* word:

> *An inspiring new idea emerges from the evidence.*

Here's a sentence I wrote for this chapter:

> *Besides, there's something more satisfying about physically editing your copy and using the universal markings.*

I didn't spot the five words that ended in *-ing* until my third round of editing! Once you see a problem like this, play with the words to eliminate it. Then check that it matches your original intent. I rewrote the sentence this way:

> *Besides, you may find it more satisfying to physically edit your copy with the universal marks.*

When you're both the writer and editor, you're doubly responsible for knowing what you want to say. Fuzzy, verbose writing often results from your own lack of clarity. So when you spot a technical problem, think first about whether a simple word fix will work. But realize that you may need to rethink your content more thoroughly. After you're clear, a better way to write the sentence emerges, like magic.

If you edit someone else's work, knowing the writer's intent is harder. You may not understand what the author is going for, and then it's all too easy to shift her meaning when you try to clarify. You may wish to ask the author how to interpret what she wrote. Or make the changes and as appropriate, check that they are OK with the writer. Don't be surprised if he or she objects. The writer/editor relationship is often a tense and complicated one.

### The -ion words

The following is cluttered with *-ion* words and incredibly dull:

> *To attract the attention of the local population, with the intention of promoting new construction, we should mention recent inventions that reduce noise pollution.*

Reading aloud makes this sentence's unfriendliness instantly clear. Also note that piling up lots of *-ion* words leads to a very awkward passive sentence structure.

The problem with too many *-ion* words can be way more subtle, as in this sentence from an otherwise careful writer:

> *Whether they are organizing large demonstrations, talking with pedestrians in the street, or gathering signatures for a petition, their involvement was motivated by the realization that as individuals within a larger group, they had the potential to influence and bring about change.*

In addition to four words with the *-ion* suffix, the sentence also contains three ending in-*ing*. The result is a rambling, hard to follow, overly long sentence that feels abstract and distant. This sentence is challenging to fix. One way:

> *They organized large demonstrations, talked with pedestrians and gathered signatures. Their motivation: knowing that as individuals, they could influence and bring about change.*

Does it say exactly the same thing as the original? Perhaps not, but it's close. And more likely to be read.

Notice that after I cut down the *-ion* and *-ing* words, some of the cluttery phrases become more obvious.

> ✔ Of course, pedestrians are 'in the street' – so why say it?

> ✔ 'for a petition' and 'had the potential' are both overkill.

Always look for phrases that add nothing or offer unnecessary elaboration – and cut them. Your writing will improve noticeably.

### The -ize words

Similarly to *-ion* and *-ing* words, more than one *-ize* per sentence works against you.

> *He intended to utilize the equipment to maximize the profit and minimize the workforce.*

In fact, you rarely need these kind of Latinate words at all. In line with the principle of using short simple words as much as possible, shift *utilize* to *use* and *maximize* to *raise*. And you can more honestly state *minimize* as *cut*.

Modern business language keeps inventing *-ize* words, essentially creating new verbs from nouns. 'Incentivize' is a good example. Consider this quote from a government official that appeared in a newspaper article:

> *It would be a true homage to her memory if we are able to channelize these emotions into a constructive course of action.*

Aside from the fact that 'channel' is better than 'channelize' for the purpose, note how made-up, long words are typically embedded in abstract, verbose thinking.

### The -ent, -ly and -ous words

Words with these suffixes are usually complicated versions of words available in simpler forms.

A silly example that combines all these forms shows how using long words forces you into that unnatural rhythm, passive structure and wordy phrases full of unnecessary prepositional phrases.

> *Continuous investment in the pretentiously conceived strategic plan recently proved to be an impediment to the actualization and inadvertently triggered the anomaly.*

Unfortunately, much modern business writing is filled with convoluted language, clichés, and hyperbole at the expense of substance. When you try to edit some of it – -such as the preceding silly example – -you're left with nothing at all. The fact that no one is impressed with empty writing, or likes to read it, doesn't stop people from producing it. This is a mystery I can't solve.

But I'm hopeful: Research is under way to correlate good writing and communication with the bottom line. Towers Watson, a global management consulting firm, conducts high-profile surveys on the financial impact of effective communication and the American Management Association is interested in the ROI-writing connection. Meanwhile the lesson is clear: Don't write in empty business-speak – it won't reward you.

## *Pruning prepositions*

Another good way to reduce wordiness is to look for unnecessary prepositional phrases – that is, expressions that depend on words like *of, to* and *in.* Here are a few examples along with better alternatives.

> **Original:** *Our mission is to bring awareness of the importance of receiving annual checkups to the people of the community.*
> **Revised:** *Our mission is to build the community's awareness of how important annual checkups are.*

> **Original:** *But it is important not to forget that you have to still use the rules of traditional writing.*
> **Revised:** *But remember, you must still use traditional writing rules.*

> **Original:** *He invested 10 years in the development of a system to improve the performance of his organization.*
> **Revised:** *He spent 10 years developing a system to improve his organization's performance.*

Try any and all of the following to cut down wordy phrases

- ✔ **Use an apostrophe.** Why say the *trick of the magician,* when you can say *the magician's trick?* Why write *the favorite product of our customers,* when you can write *our customers' favorite product?*

- ✔ **Use a hyphen.** Rework *the CEO's fixation on the bottom line* to *the CEO's bottom-line fixation.*

- ✔ **Combine two words and remove an apostrophe:** The phrase *build the community's awareness* can also read well as *build community awareness.*

## *Cutting all non-contributing words*

Extra words that don't support your meaning dilute writing strength. Aim for concise. Use the set of clues I describe in the preceding sections and zero in on individual sentence for ways to tighten. Here's a case in point:

> *With the use of this new and unique idea, it will increase the profits for the magazine in that particular month.*

Extra words hurt the sentence's readability and grammar. Even though the sentence is fairly short already, it manages to jam in two prepositions (*of* and *for*), an altogether useless phrase (*with the use of*), and an unnecessary word repetition – *new* and *unique*. Of course, the sentence construction is confusing as a result. A better version:

> *This new idea will increase the magazine's profits in that particular month.*

An objective look at your sentences may reveal words and phrases that obviously repeat the same idea. Here's a sentence I wrote for this chapter, which talks about editing hard copy from a computer print-out.

> *Of course, you must then transfer your changes to the original on your computer.*

In context, the original document was clearly on the computer, so I cut the unnecessary phrase:

> *Of course, you must then transfer the changes to your computer.*

Consider this explanation of how Track Changes works:

> *Now when you make a change, the alteration is indicated in a color and any deletion is shown on the right.*

The rewrite:

> *Your changes then show up in color, and deletions appear outside the text on the far right.*

The revision works better because it eliminates unnecessary words and with them, the passive construction of *alteration is indicated* and *deletion is shown.*

# Texting and instant messaging: When and where to use the style

The terse style of texting and instant messaging follows time-honored traditions.

Probably since the first humans drew on cave walls, people have looked for faster and easier ways to communicate big ideas with written symbols. The Romans chipped their messages into stone tablets and monuments. This was such hard going that they jammed in whole strings of abbreviations and acronyms that still challenge historians. The ancient Egyptians also depended on word shortcuts to make their point on stone surfaces. They liked abbreviations and often skipped words that were obvious (to them, at least). In the 19th century, news was sent by telegraph and people found tapping out every letter of every word too slow. Again, words were abbreviated to their minimal intelligible form or omitted altogether.

There's nothing inherently wrong with finding faster ways to type on tiny keyboards. In fact, many language gurus believe that texting improves writing because it teaches conciseness. But when you assume everyone understands those abbreviations and symbols, you may have a problem.

Generally speaking, many older people may not readily read text-style messages (see the information on generation gaps in Chapter 2), and even younger readers may not like it as a common language. Writing in a manner your readers are unlikely to understand simply doesn't make sense.

Further, many readers who are comfortable with texting shortcuts still expect a more formal style in other media, including email. So don't risk your credibility by transferring informal texting strategies to other business writing. Limit texting style to appropriate media and audiences that you're sure will respond in kind.

Take aim at common phrases that slow down reading. Substitute simple words. The words on the left are almost always non-contributors; choose those on the right.

| Wordy | Better |
|---|---|
| at this time | now |
| for the purpose of | for, or to |
| in accordance with | under |
| in an effort to | to |
| in order to | to |
| in regard to | about |
| in the amount of | for |
| in the event of | if |
| in the near future | soon |
| is indicative of | indicates |
| is representative of | represents |
| on a daily basis | daily |

# Moving from Passive to Active

Most people write much too passively. They use far too many verbs that are forms of *to be*, which force sentences into convoluted shapes that are hard for readers to untangle. Worse, all those *to be* verbs make writing so dull that many readers don't even want to try. I talk about passive verbs in context of writing in Chapter 3, but now I cover the topic from the editing angle.

 Active verbs say everything more directly, clearly, concisely and colorfully. If you want to transform everything you write – quickly – pay attention to verbs and build your sentences around active ones.

## *Thinking 'action'*

Active voice and action verbs are not the same thing grammatically, but this isn't a grammar guide. For practical purposes don't worry about the distinction. Just remember to cut back on the following word choices:

- ✔ **Is + an -ed ending:** as in, *Your attention is requested.*

- ✔ **Are + an -ed ending:** as in, *The best toys are created by scientists.*

- ✔ **Were + an -ed ending:** as in, *The company executives were worried about poor writers who were failing to build good customer relations.*

- ✔ **Was + an -ed ending:** as in, *The ice cream was delivered by Jenny.*

- ✔ **Will be + have + an -ed ending:** as in, *We will be happy to have finished studying grammar.*

- ✔ **Would be + an -ed ending:** as in, *The CEO said a new marketing plan would be launched next year.*

The solution in every case is the same: Figure out *who* does *what,* and rephrase the idea accordingly:

- ✔ *We request your attention.*

- ✔ *Scientists create the best toys.*

- ✔ *Company executives worry that bad writers fail to build good relationships.*

- ✔ *Jenny delivered the ice cream.*

- ✔ *We're happy to finish studying grammar.*

- ✔ *The CEO plans to launch a new marketing plan next year.*

Verbs endings with *-en* raise the same red flag as those ending in *-ed.* For example, *I will be taken to Washington by an India Airways plane* is better expressed as *An India Airways plane will fly me to Washington.*

When you rid a sentence of *to be* verbs, you win a chance to substitute active **present tense verbs** for boring, passive past tense ones. Many professionals work this tactic out on their own through years of trial and error (trust me on this).

Writing in the present tense takes a bit more thought at first but quickly becomes a habit. Use present tense everywhere you can and see your writing leap forward in one giant step.

 Look closely at all your sentences that contain *is, are* and the other *to be* verbs. See whether an action verb can bring your sentences to life. Often you can use the present tense of the same verb:

> *He is still a pest to the whole office about correct grammar.*

is better stated as,

> *He still pesters the whole office about correct grammar.*

At other times, think of a more interesting verb entirely:

> *She is intending to develop a surprise party for the boss.*

is more engaging as,

> *She is hatching a surprise party for the boss.*

## Trimming 'there is' and 'there are'

 Big-time culprits in the passive sweepstakes are the combinations *there is* and *there are*. This problem is easy to fix – just commit never to start a sentence with either. Keep away from *there will be, there have been,* and all the variations. Don't bury them inside your sentences, either.

Check out the following examples and improvements:

> **Original:** *There were 23 references to public relations in the report.*
> **Revised:** *The report cited public relations 23 times.*

> **Original:** *There is a helpful section called "new entries" at the top of the page.*
> **Revised:** *A helpful section called "new entries" appears at the top of the page.*

> **Original:** *It's expected that in the future, there will be easier ways to communicate.*
> **Revised:** *We expect easier ways to communicate in the future.*

In every case, using an active verb does the trick, and almost all reworked sentences are in the present tense.

## Cutting the haves and have nots

Like the *to be* verbs, using the various forms of the verb *to have* signals lazy writing. Find substitute words as often as possible. A few examples and possible rewrites:

> **Original:** *He said he had intentions to utilize the equipment he had been given by the company.*
> **Revised:** *He said that he plans to use the equipment the company gave him.*

> **Original:** *We have to make use of the talents we have.*
> **Revised:** *We must use our own talents.*

## Using the passive deliberately

Despite all the reasons for minimizing passive sentences, passive verbs are not 'bad.' You need them on occasions when the 'actor' is obvious, is unknown or unimportant, or is the punchline. For example:

> *The computer was developed in its modern form over a number of years.*

> *After long trial and error, the culprit was finally identified as the Green Haybarn.*

You can also make a case for using the passive voice when you need to frame a message in terms of *you* rather than *we* or *I*. When writing to a customer, for example, you may be more effective to begin,

> *Your satisfaction with the product is what we care about most.*

Rather than,

> *We care most about your satisfaction with the product.*

The second statement gives the impression that 'it's all about us.' Of course, don't write an *entire* letter like the first opening – just the first sentence.

The passive is also useful when you don't want to sound accusatory. *The bill has not been paid* is more neutral than *You failed to pay the bill.*

# Sidestepping Jargon, Clichés and Extra Modifiers

Relying on words that have little meaning wastes valuable message space and slows down reading. Over-used expressions also dilute impact, and 'insider' language can confuse 'outside' readers. Jargon, clichés and unhelpful adjectives are hallmarks of unsuccessful business writing.

## Reining in jargon

Almost every specialized profession has its *jargon:* terminology and symbols that shortcut communication and in some cases, make group members feel more professional and 'inside.' If a physicist is writing to other physicists, she doesn't need to spell out the formulas, symbols and technical language. Her audience shares a common knowledge base.

Similarly a lawyer can write to colleagues in the peculiar language he and his peers mastered through education and practice. A musician can exchange performance notes with other musicians in a way that means little to non-musicians.

The risk arises when people talk or write to anyone other than fellow-specialists and use inside jargon. You forget that the general public does not share your professional language. If, for example, you're a scientist who needs to explain your work to a journalist, report on progress to company executives, order supplies, negotiate employment or chat at a party, you're best avoiding scientific jargon entirely.

Outside of specialized fields, we are all generalists. We want to be addressed in clear simple language we can immediately understand. Judging by their messages to clients, many attorneys and accountants are among those who forget this basic principle – or perhaps no longer remember how to communicate in plain English.

But business writers face an additional challenge. A specialized, jargon-laden language flourishes full of buzzwords that means little – even to those who use it. For example, a technology company states in a publication:

> *These visible IT capabilities along with IT participation in the project identification process can drive the infusion of IT leverage on revenue improvement in much the same way as IT has leveraged cost cutting and efficiency.*

What does it mean? Who knows? All too often, corporate writers string together a set of buzzwords and clichés that communicate little beyond a reluctance to think.

Of course, sometimes a writer or organization deliberately chooses to bury a fact or a truth behind carefully selected words and phrases. Then you might argue that a message built on empty business jargon works well. But I don't recommend deliberately distorting the truth, writing without substance, or masking either situation with bad writing. Doing so just doesn't work, and it may boomerang. This widely-circulated Citigroup press release made the bank look ridiculous:

> *Citigroup today announced a series of repositioning actions that will further reduce expenses and improve efficiency across the company while maintaining Citi's unique capabilities to serve clients, especially in the emerging markets. These actions will result in increased business efficiency, streamlined operations and an optimized consumer footprint across geographies.*

Translation: We're firing a lot of people to improve our numbers.

To avoid producing empty business-speak steer clear of words and phrases such as:

| | |
|---|---|
| best practice | from the helicopter view |
| blue-sky thinking | full service |
| boil the ocean | optimization |
| boots to the ground | over the wall |
| core competency | peel the onion |
| drinking the Kool-Aid | robust |

| | |
|---|---|
| scalable | 360-degree view |
| shift a paradigm | value proposition |
| take it to the next level | vertical |
| think outside the box | world class |

If you're writing a press release, website or other promotional copy, check it for buzz-wordiness by asking yourself: Could this copy be used by any company, in any industry, to describe any product or service? If I substitute down-to-earth words for the clichés, does the message have meaning? Will my 17-year-old nephew laugh when he reads it?

## Cooling the clichés

Jargon can be seen as business-world clichés. English, like all languages, has an enormous trove of 'general' clichés, expressions that are so over-used they may lose their impact. A few random examples that can turn up in business communication: *All's well that ends well, barking up the wrong tree, beat around the bush, nice guys finish last, a stitch in time, read between the lines.*

Clichés are so numerous they often seem hard to avoid. Often they're idioms, a way of shorthanding ideas, found in every language. They're popular for a reason – they communicate a meaning in shorthand. And they can be used well in context. But I do suggest being on the lookout for any that don't carry your meaning or trivialize it. Instead, say what you want more simply, or perhaps develop an original comparison, which I talk about in Chapter 3. And never forget that idioms and clichés are rarely understood by non-native English speakers, so try to avoid them altogether when writing to these audiences. I talk about this in Part IV.

## Minimizing modifiers

The best advice on using descriptive words – adjectives and adverbs – came from the great 19th century American novelist Mark Twain.

*I notice that you use plain, simple language, short words and brief sentences. That is the way to write English – it is the modern way and the best way. Stick to it; don't let fluff and flowers and verbosity creep in.*

*When you catch an adjective, kill it. No, I don't mean utterly, but kill most of them – then the rest will be valuable. They weaken when they are close together. They give strength when they are wide apart. An adjective habit, or a wordy, diffuse, flowery habit, once fastened upon a person, is as hard to get rid of as any other vice.*

Twain wrote this advice in 1880 to a 12-year-old boy who sent him a school essay, but he's right on target for today's business communicators.

If depending on buzzwords and clichés is Sin #1 of empty business-speak, over-use of adjectives is Sin #2. Consider for example

*The newest, most innovative, cutting-edge solution to the ultimate 21st century challenges...*

What, another solution?

Adopt whenever possible the fiction writer's mantra: Show, don't tell. Adjectives generally communicate little. In fiction, and especially scriptwriting, writers must find ways to bring the audience into the experience so they draw their own conclusions about whether a character makes bad decisions, is unethical, feels ugly or pretty, is suffering pain, and so on.

In business writing, 'show, don't tell' means giving your audience substance and detail: facts, ideas, statistics, examples – whatever it takes to prove they need your product or idea. Stating that something is innovative proves nothing. Adding an adverb, such as 'very' innovative, just multiplies the emptiness.

Take a piece of marketing or website copy, either your own or someone else's, and highlightall the adjectives and adverbs. Then eliminate most or all of the words you identified. Examine what's left. Does it say anything meaningful? If not, can you replace the copy with something real?

Welcome opportunities to replace empty rhetoric with substance! There's no substitute for good content. Use good writing techniques (as presented throughout this book) to make that content clear, straightforward and lively.

In Chapter 5, I show you how to move from sentence building to create solid paragraphs, solve organization problems, use strong transitions, and fix the technical problems that typically handicap many business writers.

# Unclear writing is against the law!

By long tradition the worst examples of opaque, confusing, and hard to understand writing come from none other than government. 'Plain language' movements have gathered steam in a number of countries, including the U.S. and Britain, since the 1970s. Advocates point out that clear writing is essential for people to access services, follow regulations and understand the law.

In the U.S. sustained work by several non-profit groups led to passage of the Plain Writing Act of 2010, which requires federal agencies to write all new publications, forms, and publicly distributed documents in a 'clear, concise, well-organized' manner that follows the best practices of plain language writing. Extending the law to government regulations is the next effort.

In England the campaign against small-print, bureaucratic language is similarly vigoros but a corresponding law has not been passed.

In both countries, efforts to clarify legal writing are underway as well. And an organization called PLAIN – the Plain Language Association International (www.plainlanguagenetwork.org) – serves as a central resource for the plain language movement globally.

A special point of interest: Some studies demonstrate that the guidelines for better writing are basically the same across different languages: short words, short simple sentences, fewer descriptive words and good graphic techniques (see Chapter 3) work well for Swedish writing, just as for English.

Other interesting U.S. sites include The Plain Language Association (www.plain-writing-association.org) and the Center for Plain Language (www.centerforplainlanguage.org).

These and related websites offer a wealth of useful information and good 'before' and 'after' writing examples from both the public and private sectors. Movement leaders hope that promoting clear language in government will have a much-needed impact on corporate writing.

# Chapter 5

# Troubleshooting Your Writing: Fixing Common Problems

● ● ● ● ● ● ● ● ● ● ● ● ● ● ● ● ● ● ● ● ● ● ● ● ● ● ● ● ● ● ● ● ● ● ● ● ● ● ● ● ● ● ●

## In This Chapter

▶ Solving organization challenges

▶ Honing sentences and fine-tuning phrases

▶ Catching common language mistakes and correcting them

▶ Proofing what you write

● ● ● ● ● ● ● ● ● ● ● ● ● ● ● ● ● ● ● ● ● ● ● ● ● ● ● ● ● ● ● ● ● ● ● ● ● ● ● ● ● ● ●

*A*s I explore in Chapter 4, good self-editing requires you to look at your writing on two levels – macro and micro. Chapter 4 focuses on how you assess your content and present your material effectively. This chapter drills down to even more specific editing issues: techniques for organizing material and improving sentences and words.

Each of us has our own writing demons, persistent problems that show up in everything you write. Happily, most of these issues fall into common categories that you can correct with common-sense approaches. Even better, you don't need to master hundreds of grammar rules. This chapter gives you a repertoire of practical fix-it techniques. After you absorb them and begin putting them into practice, they enable you to head off problems *before* they pull you off-message or undermine your success.

# Organizing Your Document

Many people, including a number of experienced writers, say that organization is their biggest challenge. If you follow the process I outline in Chapter 2, which shows you how to plan each message within the framework of your goal and audience, you may be able to sidestep the organization challenge substantially.

But this may not altogether solve your problems, especially when documents are lengthy or complicated, written by more than one person, or simply strike you as confusing or illogical once drafted. You may need to review organization at that point and reshuffle or recast material. The following techniques help. You can implement them at the writing stage – or the editing stage.

## Paragraphing for logic

You may remember being told in school to establish a 'thesis sentence' and develop each paragraph from that. If you found this advice a little dumfounding, you're not alone.

Here's a much easier way to look at paragraphs. Just accept the idea that each chunk should contain no more than three to five sentences. If you write your document that way, you easily achieve an inner logic and produce a series of self-contained units, or paragraphs.

If you routinely produce uninterrupted strings of sentences, don't despair: make the fixes later, during the editing stage. Read over what you've written and look for logical places to make breaks.

Can't decide where to insert breaks? Use the following technique:

1. **Scan your text to find places where you introduce a new idea or fact – or where you change direction.**

   Break the flow into paragraphs at these points.

2. **If your paragraphs are still more than three to five sentences, go through the whole piece again and**

**make decisions on an experimental basis. You'll check later to see if they work.**

**The three- to five-sentence guideline is a general one that applies to print material. But an occasional one-sentence paragraph is fine and adds variety. When you write for online reading paragraphs should be sorter, as I cover in Part III.**

3. **Look carefully at the first sentence of each newly created paragraph.**

   See whether the new first sentence makes sense in connecting with what follows – or whether it connects better with the preceding paragraph. If the latter, then move the sentence up a paragraph and break to a new paragraph where it now ends.

   If a sentence seems not to belong with either paragraph, it may need to stand as its own paragraph – or be rephrased.

4. **Look at your paragraphs again in order and check whether any wording needs adjustment.**

   Pay particular attention to the first and last sentences of each paragraph. You want each paragraph to link to the next. Using transitions helps with this – read more about these in the later section 'Working with transitions'.

   If when you scan the whole message you don't like the sequence of paragraphs, fool around with shuffling them. Adjust the language as necessary so that your paragraphs still clearly relate to each other.

You often find repeat words or whole ideas during this step, so make the necessary cuts and smooth everything out.

The point of paragraphing is clarity. You want to deliver information in absorbable or usable chunks that lead from one to the next, rather than a single, long, confusing word dump.

Sometimes the reason you have trouble organizing your material is because you don't yet understand it well enough to effectively present it to others. Ask yourself: What *is* my point? What are the components of my argument? Number or list them if you haven't yet done so. (Omit the numbers later if that's better for your purpose.) Also ask, am I missing critical pieces and need to research for them?

## Building with subheads

Another strategy for organizing, useful on its own or to supplement the paragraphing strategy I discuss in the preceding section, is to add a few simple subheads. I mention subheads as an excellent graphic technique in Chapter 3. They are also very useful guideposts for planning what you write, and during the editing process, can be added to help clarify your message.

Suppose you're composing an email telling your staff that new technology will be installed department-wide. The new system is quite technical so you anticipate plenty of questions and some resistance. You want your memo to head off many of the possible challenges.

To organize your own thoughts and avoid writer's block, turn your brainstorming of content (see Chapter 2) into a series of subheads. Perhaps:

✔ System X24A: Rollout starts March 6

✔ Who is affected?

✔ Advantages of the new system

✔ Changes in how we'll work

✔ Tech training plans

✔ March 6: Department Q&A meeting

Arrange your subheads in a logical order and then just fill in the information under each subhead. As you write under each heading additional topics may emerge that you didn't think of initially – for example, how the new system affects your team's interface with payroll. Find a logical place in your sequence of subheads and add the new one.

In your final message, discard the subheads if you wish – or leave them in. Subheads usually work well to pull your readers through a message and keep them organized as well. The overall impact on readers, even those who only scan the message, is that they see you've got the situation well in hand and have thoroughly thought everything out. This feeling alone inspires greater confidence in both you and the new system, making people more receptive to the change.

Long, complex documents benefit from the subhead strategy too. For a report or proposal, for example, identify the necessary sections and, rather than subheads, write a headline for each. Then write a set of subheads for each section.

Drafting headings and subheads is a great way to be sure that you cover all the right bases, identify missing pieces early on, and build in good organization from project start. You also break up the writing process into do-able bits so it's far less formidable. I talk more about using this approach with long-form documents in Chapter 8.

Use a consistent style for all your headings. Your Word program offers built-in styles, so it just takes a click to apply one.

## *Working with transitions*

Transitions, those low-key words and phrases, are like the connective tissue that holds your skeleton together and empowers you to move where you want. Transitions tell readers how all the ideas, facts and information in a piece of writing connect to each other. They smooth your writing and pull people along in the direction you want to take them.

Good transitions signal good writing and good thinking. They help you organize your own ideas as a writer. And for the reader, they promote the feeling that your argument is sensible and even unassailable. Transitions are important tools for all writing – and for persuasive copy, they're essential.

Transitions can consist of single words, phrases, or sentences. They can be put to work within a sentence, to link sentences, and to connect paragraphs. Think of them in several categories:

To continue a line of thought – or to shift a line of thought:

| | |
|---|---|
| additionally | on the other hand |
| also | but |
| and | however |
| consequently | alternatively |
| for example | originally |
| furthermore | nevertheless |

| | |
|---|---|
| mainly | despite |
| so | in other words |
| sometimes | conversely |

To establish a sequence or time frame:

| | |
|---|---|
| as soon as | ultimately |
| at the moment | finally |
| first . . . second . . . third | later |
| to begin with | next |
| to conclude | for now |

To reinforce a desired focus or tone:

| | |
|---|---|
| disappointingly | it sounds good, but. . . |
| invariably | counter-intuitively |
| luckily | of particular interest |
| unfortunately | at the same time |

Transitions give you a good way to begin paragraphs or sections, while putting that information in context of the full message. The following are examples of whole sentences that serve as transitions:

*Based on this data, we've made the following decisions.*

*Here's why the problem arose.*

*We should pay special attention to the sales figures.*

*We now have four choices.*

*A number of questions were raised at the meeting. The most significant:*

Notice how these introductory statements set up a super-simple way to organize subsequent material, including within long complicated documents.

As with all writing principles, there can be too much of a good thing. When you give your writing the read-aloud test and it sounds stilted and clumsy, review your transitions – you may need to remove some. Do so and you still have a well-organized, convincing message.

# Working in lists: Numbers and bulleting

Lists offer an excellent way to present information in a compact, to-the-point manner. They suit readers' Internet-trained text-skimming habits, and most people like them. They also automatically promote graphic variation, another plus for your document (see Chapter 3).

## Numbered lists

Use numbered lists to present sequences – of events, procedures and processes. For example, a numbered list can guide readers on how to do something:

> *Follow these steps to activate the new software.*
> *1. Turn on your computer*
> *2. Choose **Preferences** in your graphics program*
> *3. Select **Formatting,** then. . .*

Scout actively for opportunities to organize a sequence by dates or milestones:

> *1. Jan. 7, Deadline 1: Submit preliminary budget estimates*
> *2. Feb. 10, Deadline 2: Submit adjusted numbers*
> *3. March 4, Deadline 3: Finalize department budget*

These techniques may sound simple-minded, but they bestow a clarity that is so unambiguous, few people can misinterpret your meaning – no matter how hard they try.

You can also use numbered lists in more sophisticated ways. Bloggers use them, for example, to present blog posts in a very popular and reader-friendly style: A number-centered headline followed by each numbered point, spelled out. For example:

> *The 7 Tricks for Warp-Speed Writing that Professionals Don't Want You to Know*

As I discuss in Chapter 9, many experienced bloggers think up a headline like that first, marshal their ideas around it and then write the copy. The Parts of Ten at the end of this book follow the same pattern. In addition to its reader appeal, this format channels your knowledge in a different way and helps you uncover ideas you didn't know you knew.

When I wrote 'Ten Ways to Advance Your Career with Writing' (Chapter 15) for example, I committed to the topic because it seemed well worth covering. Then I brainstormed a list of possibilities, angling in on my knowledge base from a new perspective. I ended up with almost 20 ideas and chose the best.

Numbering is also a staple for speechwriters:

> *I'm going to give you five ways to boost your power to close the sale.*

The technique works every time because audiences like knowing how much is ahead of them, and they love ticking off the speaker's progress (and their own). It helps people retain information a bit better, too.

You need to know when to stop, though. In a speech, going above more than five numbered items is usually more than listeners can handle. In print, as with bullets, I would say limit yourself to seven. However, there's something magnetic about '10.'

Also as with bullets, make items on your lists parallel in structure – begin them with the same part of speech. And they should work visually by being of approximately the same length.

### Bulleted lists

Between onscreen writing habits and PowerPoint everywhere, writing has become a bullet-heavy experience.

Like numbering, bullet lists convey information tightly and neatly. They're appropriate for summarizing, offering checklists, and providing information-at-a-glance. What's more, readers like them – but only up to a point. Used incorrectly, bullets can kill. Audience interest, that is.

To successfully use bulleting, take account of these guidelines.

✔ **Don't use too many.** Research shows that people can't absorb more than about seven bullets at one go. They tune out after that because each bullet typically makes a separate point and gives little logical connection to hold onto.

If you must present more than seven bullets, break them into more than one list and intersperse some narrative material.

✔ **Use the same sentence structure for every bullet.** Start each item similarly. Sentence structure must be parallel so as not to confuse readers.

You can begin bullet points with action verbs, for example, like when you present accomplishments in a résumé:

- *Authorized...*
- *Generated...*
- *Streamlined...*
- *Overhauled...*
- *Mentored...*

Or you can compose a bullet list that starts with nouns, such as:

*When you weekend in Timbuktu, be sure to pack:*
- *Tropical microfibre clothing*
- *Sunglasses with a good UV coating*
- *Sunhat with extra-long visor*

Don't be lazy and create bulleted lists of unrelated mix-and-match thoughts, like this:

*Here are goals to aim for in business writing:*
- *You want a conversational but professional tone*
- *When you quote numbers, check that your readers use those systems*
- *Don't be emotional or make things up*
- *Jane is trying to standardize a similar look on charts and graphs. Once she does so, use that standard.*

You can refine this list by rearranging points two through four to start like the first one:

- *You want to check that all numbers quoted are in line with systems your readers use*
- *You want to avoid emotion or making things up*

But that approach produces an annoying repetition of *you want*. The solution: Find an intro sentence that covers the points you want to make. For example:

*In business writing, try to use:*
- *conversational but professional style*
- *non-emotional tone*
- *number systems familiar to your readers*
- *real facts and anecdotes*

✔ **Punctuate and format bullets consistently.** In this book, the first phrase or sentence is often bold, and we don't use periods at the ends of bullet points. In some bulleted lists, each item begins with a capital letter, in others they're all lowercase. That's *For Dummies* style.

No one way of punctuating and formatting is right for every organization and every situation. Figure out your style, or your organization's, and apply it consistently to all your lists.

✔ **Give bullet points meaning.** Don't depend on bullet points to convince people of something or expect readers to fill in the gaps between them. Bullets are only formatting. If you've seen as many poor PowerPoint presentations as I have, you know that when bullets are not given meaning, they possess very little.

Tell readers what your bullets mean with good narrative writing or a quick introduction that puts the bullets in context. In a bio or résumé, for example, using all bullets to describe your assets defies readability. Begin with a well-written overall description of your current job followed by a list of your accomplishments – but put the information in context. For example, a job description can end – 'Consistent performance beyond company goals for three years', followed by your bullet evidence. But no more than five to seven, and stated in parallel sentences.

Don't make formatting decisions, such as using bullets and numbered lists, lightly. They may be easy to write but if they don't present your message as clearly as possible, you undermine your success. When you use such formatting devices take a hard look during the editing stage to see if your material might present better (and be more persuasive) in narrative form.

# Catching Common Mistakes

Unlike the common cold, common writing problems can be treated and even prevented. The prescription is simple: Be aware of your own mistakes, which are nearly always consistent.

Improving your grammar is somehow a personal thing, so if you want solid grounding, I recommend that you scout what's out there in books and on the Internet. Choose a resource compatible with your learning style and dig in. Consider starting out with *English Grammar For Dummies* or *English Grammar Workbook For Dummies,* both by Geraldine Woods.

My grammar-related goal in this book, more modestly, is to:

✔ Raise your consciousness so that you can recognize some of your own problems

✔ Give you practical tips for fixing those problems that require little grammar know-how

✔ Relieve you of some of your worries. What you're doing may be perfectly OK for today's less formal communication.

Infinitely more can – and has – been written about writing it right. See the sidebar 'The Journalist's Grammar Guidelines' later in this chapter for what may be the most succinct run-down ever created.

In the following sections, I tip you off to the problems I most often find in even solid writers – all are easily fixed to make your writing a whole lot more effective right away. One general guideline to help you relax: When your own writing faces you with a grammar problem that's hard to resolve, or you just can't figure out, write the sentence differently to sidestep the challenge altogether.

## *Using comma sense*

Stop stressing about commas! If visual cues don't work for you, use oral ones. The reading-aloud trick I recommend in Chapter 4 works sure-fire to tell you when you need a comma. Note the difference:

*Eat Grandpa!*

*Eat, Grandpa!*

If you read the words aloud to say what you presumably intend – that Grandpa should eat – the first option sounds this way:

*Eat* (pause and downward inflection) *Grandpa*

A pause signals the comma is needed. And most assuredly, this sentence needs the comma.

Too many commas can also be a problem:

> *The use of the Internet, is part of a new culture, that more and more of the younger generations are entering into.*

Read this sentence and you hear that it works better without pauses where the two commas are placed. They interfere with smooth reading and should be cut.

Badly placed commas in cases like this often signal a wording problem. A better version, once the too-obvious parts are cut:

> *Using the Internet is part of a new younger-generation culture.*

Reading aloud can also cure runaway or run-on sentences that typically depend on misused commas. Here's one that emerged from a writing seminar:

> *Grammar is something that everyone can always touch up on, the writers should use simple punctuation, properly place the punctuation marks, things like too many commas and semicolons can confuse the reader.*

The read-aloud test shows that a sustained pause calls for a new sentence after *touch up on.* The comma between the two middle thoughts doesn't work either because an *and* should connect them. Insert that conjunction and it's then clear that you need a period after *marks,* because to read meaningfully demands another sustained pause. The result:

> *Grammar is something that everyone can always touch up on. Writers should use simple punctuation and properly place the punctuation marks. Things like too many commas and semicolons can confuse the reader.*

Another way of fixing this paragraph is to connect the whole second part with a transition, and cut some redundancy, as in:

> *Writers should use simple punctuation and properly place the punctuation marks, because too many commas and semicolons can confuse the reader.*

Train your ear and with a little practice, you improve your punctuation quickly. I once argued with the best grammarian I know about the reading-aloud method, running through a whole list of examples. Finally she said, 'The problem is it only works 97 per cent of the time!' I figure I'll take my chances with the 3 per cent and you may also prefer to.

## Using 'however' correctly

As with commas, reading aloud gives you the clue about how to include *however* in your writing.

Many perfectly decent writers undercut themselves with sentences like these:

> *I'd like to go to the office, however, my car won't start.*

> *Expense reports are due on Jan 15, however, exceptions can be made.*

Reading these sentences aloud shows that long pauses are necessary before each *however*. You can break up both statements into two sentences with periods after *office* and *Jan. 15*. The second sentence in each case starts with *However*.

Alternatively, you can sidestep the 'however' problem and also refine your wording by:

✔ Replacing the *however* with *but*. If this substitution works, go with the *but*. It's correct and less stuffy as well.

✔ Using *however* only to begin sentences.

✔ Moving a *however* that falls in the middle of the sentence to the beginning and see whether the meaning holds. For example:

> *He agreed with Jane, however, she was wrong.*

> *He wants to know, however, so he can plan his vacation.*

Moving *however* to the front makes nonsense of the first sentence. With the second sentence, however, moving it retains the basic sense.

## *Matching nouns and pronouns*

Using the wrong pronoun is incredibly common, even in the work of professionals. For most communication jobs today, candidates must take a writing test. All those I've seen include a disproportionate number of questions geared to reveal this failing.

*Pronouns* have a simple function – to stand in for nouns so you don't have to keep repeating them. One cause of confusion is when to use *me* as opposed to *I, he* rather than *him,* and so on. For example:

> *Just between you and I, Jean was correct.*
>
> *Mark, Harold and me will go to the conference.*

Both sentences are wrong. One way to figure that out: Switch some of the wording so the correct pronoun becomes obvious. In the first sentence, if you substituted *us* for *you and I,* it works fine. But if you substitute *we,* the sentence sounds absurd and you're clearly wrong.

In the second sentence, you can choose to say *We will go to the conference,* and the singular for *we* is *I,* so that pronoun is correct. Or, you can eliminate Mark and Harold from the scene altogether, in which case you obviously must say *I* not *me.*

 As a general rule, go with what seems natural; but check yourself out. Try adding or subtracting words, as in the preceding examples.

Another cause of confusion is when to use a plural pronoun (like *their*) as opposed to singular (*his, its*). In these situations, stay alert to the original noun.

> *A journalist must always be attuned to their readers' interests.*
>
> *Everyone should use their discount when ordering online.*

Both are wrong because both nouns (*journalist* and *everyone*) are singular, not plural. But the first sentence raises other issues. If I correct the first sentence to:

> A journalist must always be attuned to his readers' interests.

Will I be accused of sexism? Perhaps, but the jury is still out on how to avoid this. You can

- ✔ Say *his or her readers,* but that repetition gets tiresome.
- ✔ Switch back and forth between the masculine and feminine. This approach works in longer documents, and that's what I do often in this book.
- ✔ Change the original noun to plural:

    *Journalists must always be attuned to their readers' interests.*

- ✔ Rework the sentence to avoid the problem entirely:

    *Journalists must always be attuned to reader interest.*

    You can alter the second sentence to:

    *Use your discount when ordering online.*

Some pronoun issues reflect cultural differences. In the US, an organization is considered singular, so you say:

> *The company is widely criticized for its actions.*

But in the UK the plural is used:

> *The company is widely criticized for their actions.*

## Weighing 'which' vs. 'that'

Almost always, choose *that* rather than *which.* The latter word refers to something very specific. When you're not sure which to use, try using *that* and see whether the sentence has the same meaning. If it does, keep the *that.* For example:

> *The report that I wrote at home is on John's desk now.*

But if you find that *that* doesn't reflect your meaning, you may mean *which.*

Note that you can write the sentence this way:

> *The report, which I wrote at home, is on John's desk now.*

The second version calls attention to *where* you wrote it. And observe that you need two commas to set the clause off. *Which* always requires two commas unless the phrase appears at the end of the sentence. Another instance:

> *We provide afternoon breaks which, we know, help reduce stress.*

You're using *which* correctly if you can eliminate the phrase inside the commas (*we know*) without changing the sentence's basic meaning. If you remove the non-essential phrase, the sentence becomes:

> *We provide afternoon breaks that help reduce stress.*

Does this sentence carry exactly the same meaning as the original? Basically yes, but if the 'we know' is important, it doesn't. In order for a sentence to carry your meaning you must know what you want to communicate.

## Pondering 'who' vs. 'that'

For reasons I can't understand or explain, contemporary writing is chock-full of *thats* and very few *whos*. People have become depersonalized into objects. The following sentences are all incorrect:

> *The new office manager that started on Monday already called in sick.*
>
> *My friend, that I've known for 20 years, is planning to visit.*
>
> *The first person that said he was ready changed his mind.*

Always use *who* when referring to people. Inanimate objects and ideas are *that*. You may choose to refer to animals as *who*, but some prefer *that*.

## Choosing 'who' vs. 'whom'

This is foggier territory. Grammar enthusiasts insist that you differentiate between the word used as a subject (*who*) and as an object (*whom,* as in *to whom*). But adhering to the rule can land you in some stuffy places.

> *To whom should I address the package?*
>
> *With whom should I speak?*
>
> *To whom it may concern. . .*

In the first two sentences, the less correct version works better for general business writing:

> *Who should I address this package to?*
>
> *Who should I speak to?*

In the case of the last example, don't use such an archaic phrase at all. Always find a specific person who may be concerned, and use her name. If that's impossible use a title (*Dear Recruitment Chief*) or a generic address (*Dear Readers*).

# Beginning with 'and' or 'but'

Like other wording choices I address in this section, grammatical standards have relaxed, and only the rare individual complains about sentences that begin with *and* or *but*. *The Wall Street Journal* does it, the *New York Times* does it. And so can you.

But don't do it so often that it loses its effect. Starting sentences with these conjunctions adds to your rhythmic variety and gives you a way to add a little verve, especially to online writing. It works best with short sentences.

*Because* can be used the same way, although I still hear people repeating the schoolroom mantra against starting sentences with that word. And so can *or* and *yet* start a sentence.

# Ending with prepositions

An often-quoted piece of wit attributed to Winston Churchill underscores the silliness of strictly obeying some rules:

> *This is the sort of bloody nonsense up with which I will not put.*

Obviously it's more natural to say,

> *This is the sort of bloody nonsense I won't put up with.*

Similarly, sentences such as these that end with prepositions are fine:

> *Leave on the horse you rode in on.*
>
> *See if the answers add up.*
>
> *He's a man I can't get along with.*
>
> *We didn't know where he came from.*
>
> *Don't make fun of grammarians, just because some of their ideas don't go where you want to.*

Many stock phrases end with prepositions and there's no reason not to use them wherever they fall in a sentence. This especially applies if writing 'correctly' requires an unnatural-sounding manipulation of language. The general guideline for business writing is: Use what feels comfortable in conversation.

## The Journalist's Grammar Guidelines

Business writers can learn a lot from journalists, whose full-time work is figuring out how to present ideas and information in the clearest, most succinct and interesting way possible. Unfortunately, as the newspaper industry shrinks, it provides an ever-smaller training ground for writers.

This classic list of rules was originally taken from a bulletin board at Denver's *Rocky Mountain News* and has appeared, with different add-ons, in a number of journalism books. *The Rocky Mountain News* stopped publishing in 2009, but many a writer keeps this demonstration of grammar pitfalls on hand.

1. Don't use no double negatives.

2. Make each pronoun agree with their antecedent.

3. Join clauses good, like a conjunction should.

4. About them sentence fragments.

5. When dangling, watch your participles.

6. Verbs has to agree with their subjects.

7. Just between you and I, case is important too.

8. Don't write run-on sentences they are hard to read.

9. Don't use commas, which aren't necessary.

10. Try to not ever split infinitives.

11. It's important to use your apostrophe's correctly.

12. Proofread your writing to see if you any words out.

13. Correct speling is essential(!)

14. Avoid unnecessary redundancy.

15. Be more or less specific.

16. Avoid clichés like the plague.

# Reviewing and Proofreading: The Final Check

Before sending out your message or document into the world or to its target audience of one, review it at both the big-picture macro level (see Chapter 4), and the close-in micro level (everything I cover in this chapter).

Editing is essential but almost always, the process can unintentionally shift meaning and introduce new mistakes. So plan to review any passages you reworked at least one extra time.

## Checking the big picture

Once you've edited your message or document and are satisfied with the writing, it's time to return to the big picture and assess your overall message in terms of content, impact and tone. It's not sufficient to send a technically perfect message that isn't geared to accomplishing what you want!

Forgetting all the work and the decisions that went into what you've written and edited, look at your text as a self-contained piece and consider:

  ✔ Is my *purpose* – what I want to accomplish – absolutely clear?

  ✔ Does the piece support my sub-agenda? For example, does it promote the relationships I want to build, represent me in the best professional light and contribute toward my larger goals?

✔ Do I get to the point quickly and stay on message? Does every element of the message support the result I want?

✔ Does the message move well and smoothly from section to section, paragraph to paragraph?

✔ Is the level of detail right? Not too much, not too little, just enough to make my case?

Step even further back and read your document from your recipient's viewpoint.

✔ Will the reader know what I want and exactly how to respond?

✔ Is the message a good match in terms of tone, communication style, and audience characteristics? Does it focus on what's important to the reader?

✔ If I were the recipient, would I care about this message enough to read it – and respond?

✔ Did I provide appropriate evidence to support the case I'm making? What unanswered questions could the reader possibly have?

✔ If I were the reader, would I give the writer what he wants?

✔ Can anything in the message possibly be misinterpreted or misunderstood? Could it embarrass anyone?

✔ How does it look: Accessible? Easy to read? Plenty of white space? Good graphic devices? Visuals as called for?

And finally,

✔ Will I feel perfectly fine if this document is forwarded to the CEO, tweeted to thousands of strangers, mailed to my grandmother, or printed in a daily newspaper?

Correct any problems using ideas and tips in this book, plus your own common sense. Chapter 2 tells you how to understand your goals and your audience and build messages that draw the response you want. Choosing appropriate graphic options is covered in Chapter 3, and the preceding sections of this chapter.

## *Proofreading your work*

In professional communication circles, proofreading is seen as separate from writing and editing. But in these economically tight times, copywriters, journalists and even book authors often wear all three hats. Many publications now outsource their proofing services, or eliminate them altogether. If you've noticed a growing number of mistakes in what you read, that's the reason.

On a daily basis obviously proofreading is all up to you. But you can still reach out for help. Many writers use a buddy system to back them up on important material, and you can too. A colleague, friend or partner may be happy to supply editing advice with you in exchange for the same help. As the saying goes, two sets of eyes are better than one.

## Surefire proofreading tips

Here are some ways to do the best job proofing your own work, or someone else's. They're based on my own hard-won experience and I share them, like everything in this book, to save you all that trial and error.

1. Use one of the systems I explain at the beginning of Chapter 4 so your proofreading is systematic and clear.

2. Make sure in the case of a major document to keep an original unedited version.

3. Try to proofread when your eyes and mind are fresh and take frequent breaks.

4. Proofread more than once – ideally three times – allowing some time between sessions.

5. Carefully check sentences before and after every change you make because editing often generates new errors.

6. Pay special attention to the places where you find an error because errors often clump together (perhaps you were tired when you wrote that part).

7. Look for words that are often misspelled (every grammar book has these lists or you can easily find one online; keep a copy on your desk).

8. Examine all the 'little words,' including on, in, at, the, for, to. They may repeat or go missing without your noticing if you don't pay attention.

*(continued)*

*(continued)*

9. Look up all words you aren't sure about. Choose an online dictionary you like, or just Google the word.

10. Triple-check names, titles, numbers, subheads, and headlines.

11. Rest your eyes regularly, especially if you're proofreading onscreen. Looking out a window into the distance helps. So does setting your computer screen to a comfortable brightness.

12. Try enlarging the onscreen type for easier viewing – but not so much that you don't see the whole sentence, paragraph or section.

13. Read challenging portions of text backwards: this approach is often useful with material that is highly technical or contains numbers.

14. Re-check all the places where a mistake would prove most embarrassing: Headlines, lead sentences, quotes

## *Creating your very own writing improvement guide*

Most writers are highly consistent in the errors they make, so creating a list of your writing shortfalls helps you sharpen up – and ultimately speed up – your writing.

Treat yourself to an in-depth session to review either a major document or a batch of smaller messages. Or gather information and insights over time. Better yet, do both.

Start by thoroughly editing your selected work using the various criteria I explain in this book. Look for patterns of errors and less-than-wonderful writing. Addressing these particular problems will really benefit you.

Record the challenges – and the solutions – systematically. For example, in editing the chapter you're reading now, I made notes about what I found to need improvement. That list appears on the left. Then I wrote down the solutions on the right.

| *My Problems* | *Solutions* |
|---|---|
| Too many words ending in *ing* | Find substitutes for most and rewrite as necessary |
| Too many sentences longer than 17 words | Break them up or tighten by cutting |
| Need to fix sentence rhythm often | Read them aloud and add or cut words so they move better |
| Too many sentences per paragraph | Break them up |
| Too many long words | Replace with short ones, mostly |
| Too much passive tense | Keep an eye on Word's Readability Index; find more interesting verbs that promote an action feel |
| General wordiness | Cut, tighten, and/or rewrite |
| Too many qualifiers (*you might, you can, you should*) and extra phrases | Cut the hedge words and WRITE IN PRESENT TENSE! |

This analysis produces a roadmap I can use to review everything I write, from an email to a home page to a proposal.

Get even more specific and add categories, like words you often misspell or incorrect use of possessives. Scout for solutions in this book and other sources, and equip yourself with tools to lick the problem. Identifying your personal roadblocks goes 64 per cent toward fixing them. (I made that figure up but believe it's true.)

## Doesn't my computer catch grammar goofs?

Microsoft Word and other word-processing software have grammar-checking features that identify possible mistakes and indicate potential fixes. While these tools can help, accepting the corrections unquestioningly is like trusting a smart phone's word-guessing function.

Pay attention to the corrections and changes your word processing software wants to make, in both spelling and grammar, and evaluate them thoroughly.

# How do I know I'm done editing?

Painters have the same question about knowing when they've finished a painting. With writing, stop editing before you begin to change the meaning of your message. And stop before you compress all the life out of it. Overly general, bland writing doesn't work well. Don't cut the examples, anecdotes or details that engage readers and help them understand.

You're better off saying less but saying it fully. For example, plan a series of emails on a subject rather than jamming the information into one overly long one. Or focus an article on one aspect of a subject and keep the color.

To care about what you write is a different way of thinking. Do you really need to plan, draft, edit, cut, rewrite, add, subtract, edit, and proofread everything you write? You be the judge. But before you decide most of the process isn't necessary, consider whether or not your reputation and effectiveness is on the line nearly every time you write. I bet it is.

Try out the plan/draft/edit process in small ways, like for everyday messages, and see if you start getting what you want more often. I believe you will. The good – no, great news – is that when you practice the plan/draft/edit process on the small stuff, you're ready to use it for the big stuff: proposals, reports, articles, websites, blogs, marketing materials.

# Part II
# Putting Your Skills to Work for Everyday Business Writing

## *Top Five Ways to Boost Your Business Communication*

- ✔ Craft every email to accomplish your company and personal goals.
- ✔ Create strong leads that engage and inform your reader.
- ✔ Ask clearly for what you want.
- ✔ Treat every message as a chance to build relationships.
- ✔ Use letters to gain an edge when you're competing.

For more tips on how to keep your business writing clear and professional, check out this free article at `http://eu.dummies.com/how-to/content/how-to-keep-your-business-writing-clear-and-profes.html`.

Part II

Brushing Up Your Skills to Communicate Effectively Through Business Writing

## In this part . . .

- ✔ Utilize email in your business and benefit from the advantages it can bring.

- ✔ Become an expert in letter writing and use this skill to network, build working relationships and pitch your product or service.

# Chapter 6

# Writing Emails That Get Results

*In This Chapter*

▶ Understanding why email still matters and where it can take you

▶ Writing emails that achieve immediate and long-range goals

▶ Using strategies and techniques that work – and avoiding pitfalls

*L*ove it or hate it, you can't leave it – email is the nervous system of business life all over the world. Companies may declare e-free Fridays or add newer media like instant messaging or social networks for basic communication but you probably still find that your work life centers on managing your in and out boxes.

The volume and omnipresence of email in your life gives you the opportunity to accomplish your immediate and long-range goals, or screw up both. This chapter shows you how to make the most of this powerful medium and sidestep the traps.

Of course another communication channel may replace email soon, but it hasn't happened yet. In any case, the guidelines in this chapter apply to whatever comes next, maybe with minor adaptations to formatting and style. The essentials of good communication hold steady.

## Email's ever-widening reach

By the end of 2016, according to research by the Radicati Group, Inc., a technology market research firm, 4.2 billion email accounts will exist worldwide – up a billion from 2012. Radicati also projects that the number of business emails will steadily increase during that timeframe by 13 per cent yearly, reaching 143 billion *per day.* Although the study notes the explosive growth of social networking and growing popularity of instant messaging, it also tracks steady growth of corporate email. Furthermore, nearly half of all email users worldwide are in the Asia Pacific region, home to China and India. North America accounts for about 14 per cent, and Europe, 22 per cent. So you can safely anticipate that email will remain your first choice for connecting with audiences across the globe.

# *Fast-Forwarding Your Agenda In-House and Out-of-House*

If you're wishing for a way to show off your skills, judgment, competence, and resourcefulness and have decision-makers pay attention, *shazam* – email is *the* opportunity.

Yes, everyone is overwhelmed with too much email and wants most of it to go away. The reasons are two-fold: most email is unrelated to your interests and needs, and most of it is badly thought out and poorly written. Take a look through your own inbox. You're likely to find that most of it falls into one of those two categories – or both.

Then take a look at your outbox. Ask yourself (and why not be honest) how many messages you carelessly tossed off without planning or editing. You may feel that this is the nature of the medium – here one minute, gone the next, so not worth investing time and energy. But email is the tool you depend on to get things done, day in and day out.

Moreover, email has become the delivery system for many forms of communication. In earlier times you'd write a cover letter to accompany a résumé, for example, and today you deliver it electronically. But a cover letter for a job application is still a cover letter – no matter how it's delivered. A short business proposal may also be sent by email, but like a cover letter, needs to be very well written. Resist the temptation to write such material in an off-the-top-of-your-head fashion. If you're writing what is essentially a letter, check out Chapter 7. If it's a proposal, or a marketing pitch, see Chapters 8 and 9, respectively.

Good emails bring you the results you want. Even more, writing good emails every time – no exceptions – brings you amazing opportunities to reach the people you want to reach with a message *about you:* how intelligent, resourceful and reliable you are, for example, and how well you communicate. Even those humdrum in-house emails contribute incrementally to your positive image as an efficient professional, and give you a long-range advantage way past accomplishing your immediate goal.

Send direct, well-written emails that have a clear purpose and respect people's time, and you get respect back. People notice and respond to well-written messages, though admittedly, most do so unconsciously.

The higher you go in an organization's hierarchy, the more people tend to recognize good writing and value it because they see so little of it these days. Executives are acutely aware of how badly written emails, even on mundane matters, can create:

- ✔ Misunderstandings that generate mistakes
- ✔ Needless dissent among employees and departments
- ✔ Inefficiency, because countering unclear messages demands much more communication
- ✔ A staggering waste of collective time and productivity.

Smart leaders are even more aware of how poor email messaging can affect an organization's interface with the world at large, resulting in

- ✔ Weakened company image and reputation
- ✔ Disaffected customers
- ✔ Missed opportunities to connect with new customers
- ✔ Long-term damage to relationships with the public, investors, suppliers, lenders, partners, media, regulators, and donors – all of which directly affect the company's bottom line.

Take email seriously and it will give you many happy returns. Decision-makers in your workplace who value clear communication will value you all the more. In addition:

✔ **Email offers huge opportunities to develop relationships in the course of doing business.** To build and sustain a network of trusted colleagues and contacts in-house and out can only benefit you over the long term.

✔ **Email gives you access to the loftiest heights.** Fifteen years ago the idea that you could directly write to your CEO, or the hiring manager of your dream employer, was unthinkable. Now you can, and she may read it and even respond – if you make your message good.

✔ **Email is your entrée to reaching people all over the world.** Without it, international trade would depend on mail systems and faxes for making initial contact. Surely email is the unsung hero of globalization.

If you're an independent entrepreneur, consultant, freelancer or outside contractor, recognize that emails can make or break your enterprise. Written well, emails can help generate what you need: in-person meetings, opportunities to compete for business, new agreements, relationships of trust, and ways to promote what you do.

# Getting Off to a Great Start

Your first imperative in drafting an email: draw your reader to open it – and read it. Sound easy? Not at all, given the sheer volume of messages that motivates most people to press the Delete key for any excuse they can come up with. That's another reason why every email you send must be good: you don't want a reputation for sending pointless, hard-to-decipher messages that lead people to ignore the important ones that you craft carefully.

With email, the lead has two parts – the subject line and the opening sentence or paragraph. I explore each in detail in the following sections.

## *Writing subject lines that get your message read*

Take another look at your inbox and scan the subject lines. Note which ones you opened and why. Most of them probably fall into one of these categories:

- ✔ Must-read because of essential information

    *Subject: New location, May 3rd meeting*

- ✔ Must-read because of urgency

    *Decision on Plan A needed today*

- ✔ Must-read because of who the writer is (in which case the 'From' matters, too)

    *From: President White*

    *Subject: Department reorganization planned*

- ✔ Want-to-read because you need the information or it may be valuable

    *Subject: Free tools to recover deleted files*

- ✔ Want-to-read because it looks like a good deal

    *Subject: Lowest iPhone price ever*

- ✔ Want-to-read because it's from a trusted source

    *From: Kickstarter*

    *Subject: Projects we love: mobile murals*

- ✔ Want-to-read because it sounds interesting or fun:

    *From: Bronx Zoo*

    *Subject: Come see our tiger cubs!*

Few messages are required reading. Your challenge in writing email subject lines is to zero in on what's most likely to concern or interest your reader. But you must always be fair. Don't promise something in the package that isn't actually there after your reader opens it.

To create a good subject line that keeps fingers off that Delete key:

1. **Figure out what's most relevant to your reader in the message – why the person should care.**

2. **Think of the absolutely most concise way of saying it.**

3. **Put the key words as far to the left as possible so your recipient understands the meat of your message quickly and easily.**

Subject lines work best when they're as specific as possible. Here are two examples of emails I didn't open because the subject lines were too vague and general to capture my interest. I also suggest ways the message could work better.

Poor: Important question

Better: *Where is tomorrow's workshop?*

Poor: *June newsletter*

Better: *New Twitter techniques in June issue*

Ensuring that the most important words appear in your recipient's inbox window and aren't cut off for lack of space – or because they're reading on smartphones and other hand-held devices – is worth the thought every time. Very few people pay attention to this simple principle so build this habit to reap a big advantage.

Following are a few examples of truncated subject lines from my own computer that I didn't open.

*The Coach's Corner: 9 ways to. . .*

*Did you ever wish that y. . .*

*Express yourself with a perso. . .*

As an experiment, I opened the last one to see what it was about and found that the full subject line was: 'Express yourself with a personalized dish'. Had the line begun: 'Your personalized dish', or 'Your name on stoneware', I'd have opened the email.

Investing in good, accurate subject lines always rewards you. You may not be able to deliver the whole of your subject in the limited amount of characters your recipient's inbox allows, but try to get the gist across. Ordinarily you needn't aim to be clever; but if the message is important, spend some time to make the first few words intriguing.

If you can't come up with a tight subject line that communicates the core of your message, consider the possibility that your message may not have a core – or any meaning at all to your reader. Review both the subject line and the entire message to see whether you're perfectly clear on why you're writing and what outcome you want.

Be sure to review your subject line after you write the whole message. You may shift tack in the course of writing. In fact, the writing process can lead you to think through your reason for creating the message and how to best make your case. Drafting the message first and then distilling the subject line is often easier.

Don't be lazy about changing the subject lines of long message threads. If you don't, people may overlook your new input. Later on, both you and the recipient may be frustrated when looking for a specific message. Try for some continuity, however, so it doesn't look like a whole different topic. If the first email of a series is identified as 'Ideas for Farber proposal', for example, a new subject line might say 'Farber proposal 3rd November update'. Keep the subject lines obviously relevant to everyone concerned.

Most people use email as their personal database to draw on as needed, so always label messages in ways that make them findable.

## Using salutations that suit

The greeting you use is also part of the lead. Draw on a limited repertoire developed for letters:

> *Dear. . .*
>
> *Hi. . .*
>
> *Hello. . .*

You can use 'Greetings' or something else but be sure it doesn't feel pretentious.

Follow with first name or last as appropriate, using the necessary title (Miss, Ms, Mrs, Mr). For the plural, Mesdames and Messieurs definitely feel over the top for English speakers. For groups you can sometimes come up with an aggregate title, such as 'Dear Software X Users', 'Dear Subscribers', 'Hi Team', and so on. Don't be homey or quirky. Using 'folks', for example, can grate on people sooner or later. Avoid generalizations like 'Dear Customer' if you're writing to an individual. These days, people expect to be addressed by name.

Often people who know each other well or are transacting business in a series of emails dispense with the title, and simply start the message with the person's name, for example, 'John'. That's fine if doing so feels comfortable. Generally speaking, don't omit a name altogether and plunge right into your message. You miss an important chance to personalize. You can, however, build a name into the opening line, as in: 'I haven't heard from you in a while, Jerry, so thought I'd check where things stand.'

## Drafting a strong email lead

The first sentence or two of your message should accomplish the same goal as the lead of a newspaper article: attract your readers' attention, present the heart of what you want to say, and give them a reason to care. Plus, you need to tell readers what you want.

Because email leads usually include the same information that appears in the subject line, try not to repeat the same wording or the same information. Email copy occupies valuable real estate. Your best chance of enticing people to read the whole message is to make the lead and everything that follows read fast and tight.

Your email lead can consist of one sentence, two sentences or a paragraph as needed. When the subject line clearly suggests your focus, you can pick up the thread. For example:

> *Subject: Preparing for the August meeting*
>
> *Hi Jenn,*
>
> *Since we need the materials for the Willow conference in less than a week, I'd like to review their status with you ASAP.*

Often you need a context or clarifying sentence before you get to your request.

*Subject: Timing on design hire*

*Hilary, you mentioned that you'd like to bring in a graphic designer to work on the stockholder report ASAP. However, I won't be able to supply finished copy until April 3rd.*

Note how quickly both of the preceding messages get to the point. Your everyday in-house messages should nearly always do so, whether addressed to peers, subordinates or immediate supervisors. But never sacrifice courtesy. The right tone is essential to make your message work. I talk about that later in the sidebar 'Finding the right tone for email'.

In the case of messages to people who are outside your own department or company, you often need to include more framing. Suppose you're responsible for fielding customer complaints and must write to an irate woman who claims your company sold her a defective appliance.

*Dear Ms Black,*

*Your letter about your disappointment with the new Magnaline blender has been brought to my attention. I am happy to help resolve the problem.*

## Best time to send email?

Probably 6 a.m. according to research by Dan Zarrella of the web marketing firm Hub Spot. As reported in the *Wall Street Journal,* Zarrella's study of billions of emails showed that the early bird messages are most likely to be read because people tend to check their inboxes at the beginning of the day, like a newspaper. A 6 a.m. message tends to appear high in the inbox, too.

Your email program may have a 'delay delivery' feature so you can write your messages at a convenient time and sent them out at 6 or so, without having to be there yourself to push the button.

A good subject line and lead rarely just happen: you achieve them by thoughtful planning. That doesn't mean you can't draft the complete email and then go back and strengthen or change the lead. In fact, you may prefer to figure out the main point through the writing process itself. Just be sure you leave time to edit when you proceed that way. See Chapters 4 and 5 for more on editing and revising.

# Building Messages That Achieve Your Goals

You build a successful email at the intersection of goal and audience. Intuition can take you far, but analyzing both factors in a methodical way improves all your results. Knowing your goal and your audience is especially critical when you're handling a difficult situation, trying to solve a problem or writing a message that's really important to you.

## Clarifying your own goals

Email often seems like a practical tool for getting things done. You write to arrange a meeting, receive or deliver information, change an appointment, request help, ask or answer a question, and so on. But even simple messages call for some delving into what you really want.

Consider Amy, a new junior member of the department, who hears that an important staff meeting was held and she wasn't invited. She could write the following:

> *Tom, I am so distressed to know I was excluded from the staff meeting last Thursday. Was it just an oversight, or should I take it as a sign that you think my contribution has no value?*

Bad move! Presenting herself as an easily offended childish whiner undermines what she really wants – to improve her positioning in the department. Instead of using the opportunity to vent, Amy can take a dispassionate look at the situation and build a message that serves her true goal:

> *Tom, I respectfully request that I be included in future depart-ment meetings. I am eager to learn everything I can about how we operate so I can do my work more efficiently and contribute more. I'll very much appreciate the opportunity to better understand department thinking and initiatives.*

With external communication, knowing your goal is just as important. For example, if you're responsible for answering cus-tomer complaints about defective appliances and believe your goal is to make an unhappy customer go away, you can write:

> *We regret your dissatisfaction, but yours is the only com-plaint we have ever received. We suggest you review the operating manual.*

If you assume your job is to mollify the customer on a just-enough level you may say:

> *We're sorry it doesn't work. Use the enclosed label to ship it back to us, and we'll repair it within six months.*

But if your acknowledged goal is to retain this customer as a future buyer of company products, while generating good word of mouth and maybe even positive rather than negative tweets, you're best off writing:

> *We're so sorry to hear the product didn't work as you hoped. We're shipping you a brand new one today. I'm sure you'll be happy with it, but if not, please call me right away at my personal phone number. . .*

For both Amy's and the customer service scenarios, keeping your true, higher goals in mind often leads you to create entirely different messages. The thinking is big picture and future-ori-ented: In Amy's case, the higher purpose is to build a relation-ship of trust and value with a supervisor and gain opportunities. In the unhappy customer case, you want to reverse a negative situation and cultivate a loyal long-term customer.

Be the best person you can in every message you send. Every email is a building block for your reputation and future. And email is never private: electronic magic means your message can go anywhere anyone wants to send it – and you can't erase it, ever.

## *Assessing what matters about your audience*

After you're clear on what you want to accomplish with your email, think about your audience – the person or group you're writing to. One message, one style does not fit all occasions and individuals. As I point out in Chapter 2, when you ask someone to do something for you in person, you instinctively choose the best arguments to make your case. You adapt your arguments as you go along according to the other person's reactions – his words, body language, expression, tone of voice, inflection, and all the other tiny clues that tell you how the other person is receiving your message in the moment you're delivering it.

An email message, of course, provides no visual or oral feedback. Your words are on their own. So your job is to think through, in advance, how your reader is most likely to respond and base what you write on that.

Anticipating a reader's reaction can take a little imagination. You may find you're good at it. Try holding a two-way conversation with the person in your head. Observe what she says and how she says it. Note any areas of resistance and other clues.

You also have another sure-fire way to predict your reader's reaction: systematically consider the most relevant factors about that person or group. Chapter 2 gives you a comprehensive list of factors that may relate to what you want to accomplish.

Do you need to consider so many aspects when you're drafting every email? No, if your goal is really simple, like a request to meet. But even then, you're better off knowing whether this particular recipient needs a clear reason to spend time with you, how much notice she prefers, if she already has set feelings about the subject you want to discuss, and so on. You can tilt the result in your favor – even for a seemingly minor request – by taking account of such things.

The more major your message is, the more factors you may need to consider. Or perhaps just one facet of the person's situation or personality may be overwhelmingly important. To shape the right message check out the section 'Defining your audience: Know your reader' in Chapter 2 for what's relevant to the person and the case at hand. Think about the factors that are most relevant in the context of what you're asking for.

Audience analysis becomes instinctive with practice. And your better results soon reinforce its value.

Certain characteristics are always important. Considering your reader's age, for example, may seem rude or politically incorrect, but business writer beware – especially with emails. Different generations have genuinely different attitudes toward work, communications, rewards, authority, career development and much more. If you're a Gen Y (born after 1980) or Gen X (born 1965 to 1980), you need to understand the Boomer's (born 1946 to 1964) need for respect, hierarchical thinking, correct grammar, courtesy, in-person communication, and more. I talk about this fully in Chapter 2.

I often ask participants in writing workshops to create detailed profiles of their immediate supervisors. Pretend that you're an undercover secret agent and you're asked to file a report on the person you report to. Take 20 minutes and see what you can put together. First scan the demographic, psychographic, positioning, and personality traits I outline in Chapter 2 and list those you think seem relevant to defining that person (for example, age; position; information preferences; hot buttons; decision-making style). Then fill in what you know or intuit about the person under each category. You probably find that you understand far more about your boss than you think.

Read through the completed profile and you see major clues on how to communicate with that important person on a routine basis, as well as how to work with him successfully overall and make yourself more highly valued. You may uncover ways to strengthen your relationship or even turn it around.

Suppose you're inviting your immediate supervisor, Jane, to a staff meeting where you plan to present an idea for a new project. You hope to persuade her that your project is worth the resources to make it happen. First clarify your goal, or set of goals. Perhaps, in no particular order, you aim to:

- ✔ Obtain Jane's buy-in and endorsement

- ✔ Get input on project tweaks sooner rather than later

- ✔ Gain the resources you need for the project

- ✔ Demonstrate what a terrific asset you are (always, always a constant)

You know Jane is heavily scheduled and the invite must convince her to reserve the time. What factors about her should you consider? Your analysis may suggest the following:

- ✔ **Demographics:** Jane is young for her position, and the first woman to hold that job. Observation supports the idea that she feels pressured to prove herself. She drives herself hard and works 60-hour weeks.

- ✔ **Psychographics:** She is famously pro-technology, a true believer and early adaptor.

- ✔ **Positioning:** She has the authority to approve a pilot program but probably not more. She's probably being groomed for higher positions and is closely monitored.

- ✔ **Personality/communication style:** She likes statistics. She likes evidence. She's an impatient listener who makes decisions when she feels she has just enough information. Her hottest button is being able to show her own manager that she's boosted her department's numbers. How to do that probably keeps her up at night, along with how generally to impress her boss toward her next promotion. She takes risks if she feels reasonably sheltered from bad consequences.

Presto! With these four points, you have a reader profile to help you write Jane a must-come email – and even more important, a guide that enables you to structure an actual meeting that accomplishes exactly what you want.

## Determining the best content for emails

After you know your goal and audience, you have the groundwork in place for good content decisions. You know how to judge what information is likely to lead the person or group to respond the way you want. (See Chapter 2 for guidance on how to address groups and construct a reader that epitomizes that group.)

To figure out what you need to say, play a matching game: what information, facts, ideas, statistics, and so on will engage the person and dispose him to say 'yes'?

Think about audience *benefits*. This important marketing concept applies to all persuasive pitches. Benefits speak to the underlying reasons you want something. A dress, for example, possesses features like color, style, and craftsmanship, but the benefit is that it makes the wearer feel beautiful. When you're planning a message and want it to succeed, think about the audience and goal, and write down your first ideas about matching points and benefits.

For example, to draw Jane from the preceding section to that meeting, based on your analysis, the list may include:

- ✓ Evidence that the idea works well somewhere else

- ✓ Information on how cutting-edge technology will be used

- ✓ Potential for the idea to solve a major problem for the department

- ✓ Suggestion that other parts of the company will also be interested and impressed

## Finding the right tone for email

In everyday emails, your tone contributes hugely to coming across as empathetic, so never overlook it. I talk about tone as it applies to all writing in Chapter 2 but here I address tone in electronic communications.

Often you can identify the appropriate tone by thinking about the person you're writing to briefly. Imagine yourself in conversation with him and determine where, along the spectrum of formal and professionally reserved to casual and friendly, the atmosphere falls. Your email tone can correspond.

If you're writing to someone you don't know, or to a group, edge toward the more formal but avoid sounding stilted or indifferent. Conveying a degree of warmth and caring is nearly always appropriate because people respond well to that.

Strive for positive energy in all your emails unless for some reason it feels inappropriate. Granted, you have limited ways to express enthusiasm and must balance word choice and content to achieve a positive tone. Punctuation offers the option of exclamation points. Many people use them more freely nowadays because electronic communication offers so few ways to sound excited. But don't scatter them everywhere and make yourself look childish. This recommendation also holds for emoticons, all those cute symbols popularized by texting. Unless you know your reader well, do not use them at all. Older people especially may regard you as lightweight. Remember, too, that some graphic emoticons don't translate between various technologies and may auto-replace them with who knows what!

Many other ideas may be relevant – it's great for the environment, it gives people more free time – but probably not to Jane.

# Structuring Your Middle Ground

Think of your email message like a sandwich: The opening and closing hold your content together and the rest is the filling. Viewed in this way most emails are easy to organize. Complicated messages full of subtle ideas and in-depth instructions or pronouncements are inappropriate to the medium anyway.

Email's typical orientation toward the practical means that how you set up and how you close count heavily – but the middle still matters. Typically the in-between content explains why – why a particular decision should be made, why you deserve an opportunity, or why the reader should respond positively. The middle portion can also explain in greater detail why a request is denied, provide details and technical backup, or a series of steps to accomplish something.

Figure out middle section content by first brainstorming what points will accomplish your goal in terms of your target audience as I outline in the preceding sections. Then do the following:

1. **Write out a neat, simple list of the points to make.**
   One example is the list I created to convince Jane to come to a meeting with a positive mindset in the 'Determining the best content for emails' section.

2. **Scan your list and frame your lead.**

   Your *lead* is the sentence or paragraph that clearly tells readers why you're writing and what you want in a way most likely to engage their interest.

   Starting with the bottom line is almost always your best approach for organizing a message. Remember the reporter's mantra: 'Don't bury the lead.'

Skipping the subject line for now, a get-Jane-to-the-meeting message can begin like this:

> Hi Jane,
>
> *I'm ready to show you how using new social media can help us increase market share for our entire XL line. After checking the online calendar for your availability, I scheduled the demo for March 5 at 2. Can you meet with me and my team then?*

To structure the middle, consider the previously identified points that are most important to Jane:

✔ Evidence that the idea works well somewhere else

✔ Opportunity to use cutting edge technology

✔ Potential to solve a major problem

✔ Potential for wide company interest

You then simply march through these points for the body of the message. For example:

> *My research shows that two companies in related industries have reaped 15 to 20 per cent increases in market share in just a few months. For us, the new media I've identified can potentially move XL out of the sales doldrums of the past two quarters.*
>
> *Further, we'll be positioning our department at the cutting edge of strategic social media marketing. If we succeed as I anticipate, I see the whole company taking notice of our creative leadership.*

The thinking you did before you started to write now pays handsome dividends. With a little reshuffling of the four points, you have a persuasive memo that feels naturally organized and logical. You not only know your content, but how it fits together.

This process may sound easy to do with an invented example, but actually, working with real ideas and facts is even easier.

Your biggest strength in building a successful message in any format is to know your story. Organizing a clear email is rarely a problem after you determine your content. You simply need to know such factors as:

✔ How the person you want to meet with may benefit by seeing you

✔ Why your recipient will find your report or proposal of interest

✔ Why the employment manager should read *your* résumé.

Review the list you assemble, decide which points to include and put them in a logical order. Your list may include more thoughts than you need for a convincing message, and you can be selective. That's fine. 'Just enough' is better than too much.

This basic premise works with longer more formal documents as well, as I show in Chapter 8.

## Closing Strong

After you write your lead and the middle, you need to close (and perhaps circle back to fill in or hone your subject line).

When you use the guidelines in the preceding sections to begin messages and develop the middle, your close needs to only reinforce what you want. An email doesn't need to end dramatically. You just want to circle back to the beginning and add any more relevant information to the 'ask'.

✔ If you requested a decision on something, saying something like, 'I look forward to knowing your decision by October 21st,' is sufficient.

✔ If you're delivering a report, your close may be, 'I appreciate your review. Please let me know if you have any questions or if you'd like additional information.'

✔ In the case of the memo to Jane, the closing might be simply, 'Please let me know if March 5th at 2 p.m. works for you. If not, I'm happy to reschedule.'

Sign of with courtesy and tailor the degree of formality to the occasion and relationship. If you're writing to a very conservative person or a businessman in another culture, a formal closing like 'Sincerely' is often best. The same is true for a résumé cover letter, which is essentially a letter in email form and should look like a letter.

But in most situations, less formal end-signals are better:

'Thanks!' 'I look forward to your response.' 'Best regards,' or a variant. Generally avoid cute signoffs like 'Cheers.' I recommend always ending with your name – first name if you know the person or are comfortable establishing informality. Even if your reader is someone who hears from you all the time, using your name personalizes the message and alerts her that the communication is truly finished.

Actually, your finished message needs one more thing – the subject line. Consider at this point the total thrust of your content. What words and phrases work best to engage your audience's interest.

The 'Jane' subject line, for example, needs to get across that your message is a meeting invitation, suggest what it's about and emphasize that it is worth her time. Perhaps:

*Need you there: 3rd May Demo, Social Media Project*

# Perfecting Your Writing for Email

Email deserves your best writing, editing and proofreading skills. Often the message is *who you are* to your audience. You may be communicating with someone you'll never meet, in which case the virtual interaction determines the relationship and the success of the transaction. At other times, crafting good emails wins you the opportunity to present your case in person or progress to the next stage of doing business.

People look for clues about you and draw conclusions from what you write and how you write it. Even if your ideas are good, incorrect grammar and spelling lose you more points than you may suspect no matter how informal your relationship with the recipient seems.

The following sections run through some of my top tips for crafting text that perfectly suits email.

## Monitoring length and breadth

Keep emails to fewer than 300 words and stick to one idea or question. Three hundred words can go a long way (the memo I wrote to draw Jane to the meeting in the preceding section ended up only 145 words total).

Such limits are hard to consistently observe, but you're wise to remember how short people's attention spans are, especially for online reading. That's why you benefit from knowing your central point or request and opening with it. Don't bury it as a grand conclusion. Nor should you bury any important secondary questions at the end.

Aim to make emails as brief and tight as you can. If your message starts to grow too much, reconsider whether email is the appropriate format. You may choose to use the message as a cover note and attach the full document. Or you may want to break the message up into components to send separately over a reasonable space of time. But realize that you risk losing your audience if you send a series of messages.

## Signalling style

Choose words and phrases that are conversational, friendly, business-like, and unequivocally clear. Email is not the place for fanciful language and invention. Put your energy into the content and structure of your message.

Try to make your presentation transparent, eliminating all barriers to understanding. Your messages may end up less colorful than they could be, and that's OK. Clear, concise language is especially relevant to messages directed at overseas audiences, as I show in Chapter 13.

## Going short: Words, sentences, paragraphs

The business writing guidelines I present in Chapter 3 apply even more intensely to email. You want your message to be readable and completely understood in the smallest possible amount of time.

Draw on the plain old Anglo-Saxon word-stock, mostly one-syllable words. Use two syllable words when they express ideas better; three syllables when they're the best choice, but reserve more lengthy and complex words for when they serve real purpose.

Short sentences work for the same reason. Aim for 10 to 15 words long on average. Paragraphs should be one to three sentences long to support comprehension and build in helpful white space.

## Using graphic techniques to promote clarity

The graphic techniques I discuss here don't require special software or a degree in fine arts. They're simply ways to visually present information and make your writing more organized and accessible.

Do everything you can to incorporate generous *white space* (areas with no text or graphics) into your writing. Don't crowd your messages and leave them (and the reader) gasping for air. White space allows the eye to rest and focuses emphasis where you want it. Short paragraphs with double returns instantly create white space.

### Add subheads

Subheads are great for longer emails. You can make the type bold and add a line of space above it. Subheads for email can be matter of fact:

**Why decide now**

**Step 1 (followed by Step 2 and so on)**

**Final recommendation**

**Pros and cons**

**Background**

This technique neatly guides the reader through the information and also enables you as a writer to organize your thinking and delivery with ease.

Drafting all your subheads *before* you write can be a terrific way to achieve good organization. Pick a message that you already wrote and found challenging. Think the subject through to come up with the major points or steps to cover and write a simple, suitable subhead for each. Put the subheads in logical order and add the relevant content under each. (Each section need not be more than a paragraph long.) Now check if all the necessary information to make your point is there – if not, add it. Your message is sure to become clearer and more cohesive and persuasive.

Providing your own structure in this way may make writing easier, particularly if you feel organizationally challenged. It helps ensure that you don't leave out anything important, too.

Here's an extra trick. If you feel that you have too many subheads after drafting the entire message, just cut some or all of them out. You still have a solid, logically organized email. Just be sure to check that the connections between sections are clear without the subheads.

### Bring in bulleted and numbered lists

Bullets offer another excellent option for presenting your information. They are:

- ✔ Readily absorbed
- ✔ Fast to read
- ✔ Easy to write
- ✔ Useful for equipment lists, examples, considerations, and other groupings

However, observe a few cautions:

- ✔ Don't use more than six or seven bullets in a list. A long stretch of bullets loses all impact; they become mind-numbing and hard to absorb.
- ✔ Don't use them to present ideas that need context or connection.
- ✔ Don't mix and match. The items on your list must be *parallel,* so that they begin with the same kind of word – a verb, a noun, or in the case of my first bullet list, an adverb.

Never use bullet lists as a dumping ground for thoughts that you're too lazy to organize or connect. If you doubt this advice, think of all the bad PowerPoint shows you've seen – screens rife with random-seeming bullets.

Numbered lists are also helpful, particularly if you're presenting a sequence or step-by-step process. Instructions work well in numbered form. Give numbered lists some air so that they don't look intimidating – skip a space between each number.

### Consider bold face

Making your type bold gives you a good option for calling attention to key topics, ideas, or subsections of your message. You can use bold for lead-ins:

> **Holiday party coming up.** *Please see the task list and choose your way of contributing. . .*

You may also use bold to highlight something in the body of the text:

> *Please see the task list and choose your way of contributing* **by December 10.**

Of course, don't overload your message with bold face or it undermines its reason for being. Keep in mind that boldface doesn't always transfer across different email systems and software, so don't depend on it too much for making your point.

Underlining important words or phrases is another option.

### Respect overall graphic impact

Avoid undercutting your content through bad graphic presentation. Plain and simple is the way to go. Use plain text or the simplest HTML – no tricky, cute, or hard to read fonts. Don't write whole messages in capitals or italics, and don't use a rainbow of color – that's distracting rather than fun for readers. Avoid that crammed-in feeling. People simply do not read messages that look dense and difficult. Or they read as little of them as possible. Like everything you write, an email must look inviting and accessible.

## Using the signature block

Contact information these days can be very complex. Typically you want people to find you by email or telephone. Plus there's your tagline. Your company name. Your website. Your blog. The book you wrote. The article you got published. Twitter. Facebook. LinkedIn. Professional affiliations and offices. And potentially much more.

Decide on a few things you most want to call attention to and refrain from adding the rest. Better yet, create several signature blocks for different audiences. Then you can select the most appropriate one for the people you're writing to. Don't include your full signature block every time you respond to a message, especially if you incorporate a logo, which arrives as an attachment. Check your email program's settings so the automatic signature is minimal, or altogether absent.

## Practicing email smarts

Email is a great facilitator in many ways, but definitely has limits. Email's 'easiness' can lead you to inappropriate use. Don't use it to:

✔ **Present complicated issues or subjects.** Of course you can attach a report, proposal or other long document to an email, but don't expect an email in itself to produce an investment, donation, or other high-stakes buy-in.

✔ **Wax philosophical or poetic.** Readers look to email for practical communication and are annoyed by windy meanderings – even (or especially) if you're the boss.

✔ **Spam.** Send email only to people directly concerned with the subject and don't send unnecessary replies. Don't forward cute anec-

dotes or jokes unless you're very sure the particular person welcomes that. And don't forward chain letters: they can really upset recipients. Don't forward anything without reading it. Thoroughly and carefully.

✔ **Amuse.** Generally avoid sarcasm and irony (and most humour) because it can be misinterpreted against your interests.

Never respond to poorly considered and written emails with poor emails of your own. You don't know who else may see them, and even those who write poorly – perhaps through a feeling of executive privilege – may disrespect you for doing the same. Enjoy feeling superior (without expressing it, of course)! Your excellent emails reward you over the long run as almost nothing else can.

# Chapter 7

# Creating High Impact Business Correspondence

● ● ● ● ● ● ● ● ● ● ● ● ● ● ● ● ● ● ● ● ● ● ● ● ● ● ● ● ● ● ● ● ● ● ● ● ● ● ● ● ● ●

*In This Chapter*

▶ Crafting winning cover letters

▶ Networking and building relationships with letters

▶ Complaining well and getting personal

▶ Focusing on facts in letters of record

▶ Pitching your product or service

● ● ● ● ● ● ● ● ● ● ● ● ● ● ● ● ● ● ● ● ● ● ● ● ● ● ● ● ● ● ● ● ● ● ● ● ● ● ● ● ● ●

*Y*ou may be under the impression that you don't write business letters and never need to in today's fast-paced world. Think again. When you write to ask for a meeting or reference, you're writing a letter. So is a pitch for a product or service, a thank you for a courtesy or opportunity, or a cover letter for an application or report.

Yes, you probably send such messages by email. But don't be fooled by the fact that you're using an electronic delivery system and don't need a stamp. Acknowledge that your missive is a letter, and you do a much better job of achieving your goal.

Think of your message as a 'letter' whenever you're writing a short to medium-length document that is relatively formal and introduces you in some way. You usually want to make a good personal impression, as if you're courting the reader. In many instances, a letter often serves as an official record. It's helpful to remember too that while the privacy of electronic communication is a murky area, 'the secrecy of correspondence' concept practiced in many countries protects letters in transit from being opened. So letters are typically more private than digital communication.

You won't find formulas and templates for various types of letters in this chapter. Instead, I build on and refine the planning strategies of Chapter 2. Many of the ideas I present about writing emails in Chapter 6 also apply to letters. The goal is to help you write the best letters possible for an array of situations you're likely to encounter in your professional life.

# Succeeding with Cover Letters

Take time to write a good original targeted cover letter for every application and proposal you submit, whether the goal is to get funding, a job, a grant, a work benefit, a professional honour – whatever. A well-crafted cover letter is essential even if you're responding to specifications that say cover letters aren't necessary. Exception: if the posting says 'absolutely no cover letters,' don't disobey. But review your résumé or the application form and look for ways to work in helpful information you might otherwise include in the cover letter.

Writing effective cover letters is tough but worth the trouble because:

- ✓ **Letters offer golden opportunities to personalize an interaction.** In most letters you're asking for something that's important to you and, if the initial process is conducted through writing, you must humanize your request.
- ✓ **Letters enable you to shine.** A letter supplements what may be dry information if an application or proposal form give you little room to present yourself as an individual.
- ✓ **Letters set up your reader to give your submission the perspective you choose.** You can provide a context for your accomplishments, point at what's most relevant, add depth to a noteworthy qualification, or create your desired tone.

The following sections show you how to organize and execute a cover letter that strengthens your application or proposal.

## *Planning a cover letter*

The basic decision-making system that I introduce in Chapter 2 and apply to emails in Chapter 6, works for cover letters too.

Start by focusing your goal. Often you need to go through a narrowing process. While your ultimate purpose may be to get a job or secure a contract, you rarely achieve this result from paperwork alone. At the first stage of competing for an opportunity, aim more realistically to survive the contest and be picked for further review.

Framing the goal this way helps you make good content choices. Consider the following question in brainstorming what to include in your letter.

- ✔ What personal facets are you unable to include in the application that would strengthen your bid if brought to the reviewer's attention?

- ✔ Do you have any connection with your reader or the organization worth referring to– a common acquaintance or alma mater, for example?

- ✔ What are the key qualifications and qualities the organization is looking for– and what are your best matching points?

- ✔ Should your cover letter reflect the qualities the organization is seeking? For example, should you aim to demonstrate creativity or attention to detail in your letter?

- ✔ Why do you want this opportunity? Can you say something genuine and positive about your motivation or what you plan to do if you're chosen?

- ✔ Can you say something genuine and positive about the person or organization you're applying to? And why you think this is a good match?

Never treat the cover letter as an afterthought. Most of your competitors invest all their energy into their proposals and tack on careless, perfunctory notes rather than letters. In more than a few cases, a bad cover note eliminates someone from the running altogether because tired reviewers welcome the chance to 'just say no' to an applicant. Don't let this be your situation. The planning process gives you insights on how to stand out.

Ideally, you can use your planning to shape the content of two pieces of writing that supplement and reinforce each other – the cover letter and the résumé, application or proposal itself. Consider your letter's purpose and possibilities separately from the documents it accompanies. When practical, write the application or proposal first, and for the cover letter then draw on the thinking you worked out. You might deliberately bank an idea or two for the cover letter – see the section called 'Saving something special for cover letters' for more on this technique.

## Opening with pizazz

Like email, the subject of Chapter 6, letters should get to the point as quickly as possible and focus on what most matters to readers so they are enticed to keep reading. But very often, letters need context. If you're responding to a job ad, or funding opportunity, you're usually impelled to begin along the lines, 'I'm writing in response to your ad for an SEO specialist in the Daily Techie's July 1 issue, page 13.'

There is a way around this boring lead. At the top of the letter, preferably on the right, type 'In application for the SEO specialist job, Daily Techie July 1.' Or, 'Responding to Citizens for Clean Air grant announcement.' Then you can create an engaging lead that zooms right in on your own strength, or the reader's hot button, according to the situation.

If you're delivering your letter via email, another option is using the subject line to identify your reason for writing.

Often it's worthwhile to take some trouble with your letter's opening sentence and paragraph. Most emails address practical matters, so identifying the subject and getting to the point are paramount. Letters usually face a more formidable challenge – you're trying to convince your reader of something. I present more ideas on crafting persuasive copy in Chapters 8 and 9.

## Using cover notes to build your image

Even short notes should in many cases merit careful construction. When you deliver a report or other document to a client or higher-up, for example, you may be tempted to scribble something like, 'Hi Jake— here's the info you wanted.' That's often short-sighted. Everything you write adds to a collective impression of your capabilities and value.

Many members of the Baby Boomer generation (see Chapter 2) and many younger VIPs expect full courtesy and respect, even in short messages. They are unlikely to compliment you on well-done cover notes, but trust me, they may complain to your boss if your messages are terse, confusing, or grammatically questionable. I receive more than a few requests to help team members upgrade their 'courtesy skills' from frustrated company owners and executives who observe their employees alienating clients, board members, and other key people.

## *Targeting a cover letter's multiple audience*

For more clues on what to say and how to say it, after refining your goal, think about all the people who will review your letter and other materials. (See Chapter 2 for audience characteristics relevant to specific situations.) Getting past an initial gatekeeper matters, but letter is likely to travel with your application or proposal.

Explore what you know or are able to intuit about your readers. Account for specific audience characteristics based on the situation. If you're writing to an accountant about funding for an art installation, for example, he's likely to focus on the numbers; an arts administrator is going to be more interested in the project's artistic merit.

While you rarely know who exactly is going to review your materials, you can safely assume that these people:

- ✓ Feel pressured to make a good decision that will satisfy others and be validated over time

- ✓ Want the selection process to run as quickly and efficiently as possible

✔ Have carefully hammered out a set of criteria for making their decision or choice

✔ Want to see proof that a candidate meets the criteria

✔ Need evidence that the candidate understands the organization and aligns with its mission

✔ Desire a candidate who really wants the opportunity

✔ Prefer a sense (in more cases than you may expect) that the selected candidate will be nice to work with

Strategize your cover letter by asking the essential questions for planning any message: 'What's in it for them if they give me what I ask for?' and, 'Why should they give it to me?' Know the answers yourself and use this information to shape your writing.

## Saving something special for cover letters

Content brainstorming (see 'Planning a cover letter') pays off handsomely. Suppose your company periodically funds several employee projects aimed at saving money, and you're submitting an application for one you've identified as worthwhile – reducing warehouse shrinkage. After thinking through goal and audience for clues to the best cover letter content, you realise that you:

✔ Have 10 years' experience as a member of staff, so you really know the company

✔ Can cite an excellent track record with assigned projects

✔ Have written feedback in hand on your cost-effectiveness and attention to detail

✔ Believe your project can potentially save money for the department by reducing warehouse theft 15 per cent

✔ Can estimate reasonable cost projections

✔ Have been shaping the idea for 8 months with input from relevant managers

✔ Are very enthusiastic about undertaking the project

You cover the first five points in the proposal, which follows your company's prescribed format for pitching new projects. But you didn't address the last two points – how long you've been developing the idea and how you feel about it – which are more personal and don't fit well into the company proposal format. You now have the option of using these ideas to setup the reader to see your application in a positive light.

Even if an application form accommodates all the points you want to make, you can choose to save one or more as ammunition for the cover letter. Often the ideas worth using this way are the ones you feel personally passionate about, and those that put the proposal in a positive perspective – or underline what makes you the most qualified person for the job at hand. It can be okay to repeat the most important ideas in both an application and cover letter, but take the time to phrase them differently.

As I explore in Chapter 2, the *tone* of every message works either for or against you. Just as a formal proposal or application in a question-answer type format doesn't allow much scope for passion, it doesn't offer many opportunities to bring (appropriate) emotion into the proceedings. But the cover letter does.

In most cases aim for a formal but fluid tone and style that is grammatically correct but still warm – and conveys enthusiasm. Nothing is more attractive to decision-makers than enthusiasm or even passion for the job, assignment, or contract at their disposal. All things being equal, or nearly so, the gung-ho bird is the one that gets the worm.

You now have the guidelines to craft your cover letter. Here's one version.

> *Dear Mel:*
>
> *Thank you so much for the opportunity to submit a proposal for this year's Personal Project Award.*
>
> *I've outlined my idea for a shrinkage reduction program which, based on research I've undertaken in my own time over the past eight months, can potentially save us 15 per cent in warehousing costs.*
>
> *The experiment requires a minimal outlay for new technology and can be handled by my office as part of our normal workload.*

*During my 10 years with the company, I've been credited with a number of successful projects, including the Morris Initiative, which you may recall. I'm excited by the chance to carry out my new idea and further contribute to Grand Co.'s success.*

*If any information is not included in the proposal that will be helpful, I'm very happy to provide it.*

*Sincerely,*

*Pat*

*Patricia James*

Write your cover letter choosing content and style comfortable for *you.* You can choose more than one way to write a successful message. But check that your approach supports your goals. In the preceding case, your message needs to setup the audience to find the proposal worthwhile and does this through strong matching points with company interests, key qualifications, and that extra ingredient – enthusiasm.

Of course, you can choose to write a cover letter such as: 'Dear Mel, Herewith my application for the Project Award. Let me know any questions. Pat.' But you're wasting a big opportunity.

The same basic thinking structure works when you're crafting cover letters for business proposals, job applications, grant applications, and much more. For more detailed strategies targeted to specific purposes, see *Cover Letters For Dummies* by Joyce Lain Kennedy.

---

## Saying tough things with tact

Take special care to avoid a chastising tone if you're writing to remind a significant person that she forgot to send promised information, is running late, failed to ground you in necessary background or is imposing an unfair demand. Never show impatience. Figure out a tactful way to deliver the message. For example:

*I know how busy you are . . .*

*We'll move to meet the deadline as soon as we have the information about . . .*

*Don't hesitate to tell me if there's any way I can help you prepare the material . . .*

> I'm happy to handle the new project, but need your help to prioritize my other assignments
>
> Which material will be most helpful for me to give you first?

> I welcome this assignment and will appreciate any background information you can point me at
>
> I'll appreciate your attention to this when that becomes possible.

# Networking with Letters

Typically you write networking messages to follow up a meeting, ask for a connection, express appreciation, or something similar. Most of your networking messages are probably sent as emails, but they deserve as much careful crafting as traditional letters.

In every case, your message is *you* to the reader, whether he's met you or not. You're evaluated based on what you say and how you say it. If you send careless sloppy messages, don't expect people to do you many favors.

More and more, the professional world is blending with the personal. Many a friend is in a position to bestow a critical favor, and even professional relationships can be personalized. Everyone prefers doing business with people who they trust and like to work with. Letters are invaluable in establishing this comfort zone.

## Making requests: Informational interviews, references and intros

Be aware that with requests, you ask people of influence to a) give you their valuable time and b) stake their own reputations on you.

If you ask in the right way, most people are extraordinarily willing to help. People may choose to spend half-an-hour telling you about their work in an informational interview, either in person or by telephone, if you:

- ✔ Target the appropriate person
- ✔ Define and limit your expectation

✔ Show respect and appreciation for the prospective conversation

✔ Demonstrate that you will be a credit to the person, and his industry, when you interact with others in his circle

✔ Come across as someone worth knowing in future

Clearly, requests demand your best writing and thinking skills.

Ask the classic 'What's in it for them' question to frame content for any request. If you're asking for an informational interview from a relatively young person, he may be pleased to know you consider him knowledgeable and influential. More established people are often motivated to 'give back' – to their alma mater, their profession, or simply in recognition of their good fortune. They may recall someone who reached out on their behalf at an earlier time in their career. And, many successful people with children of their own take satisfaction in helping young people.

In addition to altruistic motives, smart businesspeople like making connections and bringing worthwhile people together. They value being known for their networking skills. When you craft your messages, you rarely address such 'what's-in-it-for-them' factors directly. But being aware of probable motivation guides you to the right tone and content.

If you share a connection use that entrée early in your message – the lead if possible. For example, 'Our mutual friend Pat Jones suggested I contact you because I'm aiming for a career in your field, biomedical engineering, and would deeply appreciate your advice.'

If you don't have a ready-made connection research the people who you're writing to and see if you can find one. For example, do you have a college, career path, or professional association in common? Did you hear the person speak at a conference or read his article? Do you have a reason for admiring him?

Do your homework and make sure that it shows in your request. You need to have a good reason to write to a particular person and organization. An individualized message has an entirely different impact from a hit-and-miss email that could be addressed to anyone.

To see what I mean, think about your reactions to the following two messages.

**Message 1:**

*Dear Rob Walker:*

*I'm a new grad with a degree in Business Admin and think I might like to work for an international non-profit-.. I see that you do that now. I'm in your area next Thursday available from 2 to 4, OK for me to come in then? Thanx much. – Mark*

**Message 2:**

*Dear Mr Walker:*

*I write at the suggestion of Allison James, who interned with your office this past summer and spoke highly of the experience. I hope very much you might find the time to talk with me about my career path – 10 minutes would mean a lot to me.*

*I've just graduated from Marshall State with a degree in non-profit management. During the past five years I've held internships with four international development agencies and feel confident that this is the work I want to spend my life doing. I've spent several months in Nigeria, Sri Lanka and Peru.*

*In hopes of preparing for work like yours, directing overseas field volunteers, I see several possible career routes and would appreciate your perspective.*

*Would you consider scheduling time for a brief telephone interview? I can be available at your convenience almost anytime next week.*

*Thank you for considering this request.*

*Sincerely, Melanie Black*

If you think the politeness of message 2 is exaggerated, perhaps so. But if you were Rob Walker, would you talk to Mark or Melanie? Which one sounds like a good investment of your time – not only because of how much they may value the opportunity, but because of their relative long-term prospects? Melanie comes across as someone worth helping.

To succeed with network messaging, think through your content options, draft a message tailored to the particular reader, then carefully edit and proof as I explain in Chapters 4 and 5. You may be amazed at what opportunities and people move within reach.

If you're performing a virtual introduction between two people, spell out what's in it for both parties – why you're suggesting the connection.

Don't use the power of virtual networking to replace or avoid in-person networking or human contact in general. You can sit at your computer all day and exchange written messages, but that's no substitute for a conversation or live interaction. No one hires a piece of paper or an email.

If you want the best assignments, job leads and relationships, *show up.* The benefits of networking face-to-face within an industry and through professional associations are huge. Use your writing skills to achieve in-person opportunities. (For tips on introducing yourself with a brief 'elevator pitch,' see Chapter 10.)

## *Saying thank you*

Suppose you achieve the informational interview you want and speak to the person. Should you write a thank you note? Don't even ask: the answer is not 'yes', but 'always'. That applies even if you didn't find the person all that helpful, and it applies every time someone gives you information, advice, an interview, a contact, or an introduction. If you don't write, the discourtesy may be held against you.

A good thank you is notoriously challenging. I often ask graduate students of public relations to thank, in writing, a special guest who participated in a seminar. Most are surprised at how much thought a brief note takes.

To the writing rescue once more – the idea of defining goal and audience!

To thank someone for an informational interview, a job lead, a reference, or other favor, your *goal* is to express appreciation and also to keep the door open for future interaction or help. In considering the *audience,* decide:

- ✔ What did the person do that you appreciate?
- ✔ What feedback would this person value?

Consider Roger whose client, Jen, has referred him to one of her own clients in need of services in his province. Roger sends this note:

> *Jen, followed up the referral to your client Bob Black, went well! Thanks. Roger*

You're probably not impressed because major elements are missing. First, detail. The information is vague and gives no concrete idea of the interaction or outcome between Roger and Bob. Second, the tone is careless. Added to minimal feedback from Roger, Jen (who staked her reputation on Roger) is likely to feel uneasy about making the connection and reluctant to reach out on his behalf again. Here's a version that works better:

> *Dear Jen,*
>
> *Thanks so much for connecting me with Bob Black. I met with him at his office this morning, and we had a good conversation about his technology update program, and how my group is equipped to help.*
>
> *Bob asked me to prepare an informal proposal for review by his team. Of course I'm delighted to have the opportunity.*
>
> *Jen, I really appreciate your opening this door for me and will keep you updated on developments.*
>
> *Sincerely, Roger*

Besides being carefully constructed and written – itself a necessary tribute to Jen's generous spirit – the note reassures her that Roger made a good impression on her client rather than flubbing it. In this instance, what's-in-it-for-Jen is creating a connection that benefits both parties and makes her look and feel good.

Depending on the situation, consider too whether a more definitive thank you is called for: offering your favor-giver a cup of coffee or lunch, for example. Surprisingly few people actively reciprocate a good turn. Returning the favor at some point is the most effective response, of course. Each thank-you situation deserves individual thought.

If your thank you note is written in the wake of a job interview or pitch for a project, it probably becomes part of your application package. Treat the thank you note as a test of your communication skills and a chance to customize what the decision-makers know about you. If you spoke to someone on site or experienced the environment, you have new insights on what qualifications the organization most values. Or perhaps you realize you didn't mention something important in writing or in person. Such additions are first-rate material for thank you notes.

The note is also a good way to reinforce your belief in how good a match you see between the company and what you can do for it.

Don't overlook saying a cordial thank you in situations such as receiving a grant. Organizations and people seldom take the trouble. Here, express a sincere appreciation for the confidence vested in you or your organization, and perhaps say something about how productive the project will be.

Odd as it may sound, take the time to thank someone for the opportunity even when you're not a winner of a job, contract or grant. The same people are likely to make the decision next time, and your positive attitude may pay off. Thanking someone for the opportunity underscores your professionalism and makes you a bit more memorable.

Many people positioned to bestow jobs, projects and other awards find the world discourteous. Act as the exception and see what happens.

## Putting pen to paper

Give short, more personal messages an extra boost by handwriting them on notepaper or a card – and mailing them. This approach is perfect for thank-you notes, giving you a chance to stand out.

Don't dismiss the handwritten idea without trying it. In an impersonal world, many people are grateful for humanizing gestures. You are likely to see your note pinned to your client's bulletin board when you next visit and may well receive an effusive thank you.

Smart consultants and independent contractors keep their ear to the ground for chances to write personal messages whenever a client:

✔ Wins an honor or recognition, either personal or professional

✔ Achieves a promotion or reaches a milestone

✔ Appears in the news (favorably)

✔ Writes an article or good blog post

✔ Gives a well-received speech

✔ Completes an important project

✔ Shares good family news, such as a marriage, birth, graduation, or other event

Of course, judge carefully whether your congratulations are appropriate and will be welcome. Don't use language more intimate than suited to a business relationship. Keep your sentiments brief.

If a sympathy note is in order, make it brief but heartfelt.

Just like a typed message, plan what to say. You may find that handwriting the note suggests different ideas than may typically occur to you, and the results may sound warmer and more sincere. But keep the tone and content in check.

# Writing to Complain

In both your personal and professional lives, you may occasionally find cause to write complaints. When that happens, you get much better results if you do it well. A written complaint offers a great demonstration of how to use the planning process (see Chapter 2).

In any situation, first, thoroughly review the pros and cons of putting a complaint in writing at all. You may not have achieved what you wanted or may feel disappointed, but written complaints last a long time – forever, more or less. People take written complaints and criticism very seriously. So never draft and send such a message in the heat of the moment. Step-by-step planning helps you remove yourself from the emotional context and attendant risks.

Bringing up the problem in a telephone or in-person conversation may be a smart way of dealing with the complaint, depending on the situation and whether you can keep your cool. For example, you might say, 'Hi Jack, how's it going? We noticed there's a long delay 'till our calls for service get handled. What's up?' This is a good, neutral way to start the interaction.

If making a call or having a conversation doesn't seem to help, plan a letter. Suppose a supplier has disappointed you with the quality of goods or services delivered.. Perhaps computer maintenance work has been poorly performed. Articulating your *goal* is critical.

Your goal in a complaint letter is never – no matter how you feel– to let off steam. Writing from anger is a self-indulgent approach that frequently boomerangs. You may not know an important part of the story, so proceed very cautiously before burning bridges. In any case, the world is small, and a person you attack may have friends you may encounter in the future.

Your goal may better be stated as one or more of the following:

- ✔ Resolve a dispute
- ✔ Solve a problem
- ✔ Gain a concession
- ✔ Get a refund
- ✔ Get an apology or acknowledgment

Controlling your *tone* also helps you achieve your purpose. Putting your reader on the defensive is never to your advantage. Stick to the facts, not how you feel. Adopt a tone that conveys an assumption that the problem can be fixed. As the saying says, no point biting off your nose to spite your face.

Is the disappointing supplier the only one who has what you need? Will finding a new source threaten your production deadlines or up the costs? Review the ramifications to help you feel more objective. Resolve to give the other party a chance to perform.

For example, you can complain about a computer maintenance issue:

> *Dear Bob,*
>
> *I looked into several complaints from three of my departments last week, and the records show that service on our network has been slow.*
>
> *During the first quarter of this year, we made 16 calls to your office and in 12 cases, response took two to three days. As you know, the network's critical to all our operations and such delays are expensive for us.*
>
> *Of course, this is not the service level we signed on for or experienced in the prior year.*
>
> *Please look into this and get back to me at your earliest convenience. I'd like to know why the problem is happening and what steps you can take to deliver the service we need.*
>
> *Thank you for your immediate attention. I hope these issues can be quickly resolved.*
>
> *Best, Elaine*

The tone and language are low-key and neutral, and Bob will notice that Elaine sees the problem as fixable. But he'll have no trouble recognizing that the contract is at risk. Note how using specific facts supports the goal and provides the best shot at remedying the situation.

# Crafting Letters of Record

Sometimes you must write a letter as a record: to review your own or someone else's performance, to detail a formal agreement or contract termination, to document an event or problem, or to make a statement of some kind. Many such letters have legal implications and can (and should) involve lawyers. This is beyond my province.

But I can share one strategy I know to be useful in a variety of situations: a chronological accounting of the dispute. Like complaint letters (see the earlier section 'Writing to Complain'), letters of record are all about the facts.

To start, marshal your facts completely and arrange them in a timeline. Then create a letter that simply marches down each item on your list in a dispassionate, matter-of-fact way: no frills, no flowery adjectives, no emotion whatsoever. Start each item with the date.

Suppose you're an independent graphic designer and a client hasn't paid your last bill, due six months earlier. He now hints that the work wasn't done to his satisfaction. You don't want to go to court, but you do want the money you're entitled to.

Your letter can go this way:

> *Dear Mel:*
>
> *On July 6 of this year, you contacted my firm, Dropdead Graphics, to inquire about website services for your firm, Travesty Ltd.*
>
> *On July 8 we met at your office for two hours to discuss Travesty's needs and goals.*
>
> *On July 21 I sent you an agreement specifying that Dropdead would provide a particular set of services at a proposed fee (see attached contract). Payment terms called for 1/3 in advance, 1/3 on delivery of preliminary design, 1/3 on finished approved version.*
>
> *On July 22 we signed the contract. You remitted the 1/3 payment due.*
>
> *On August 10 I presented the preliminary design. You said 'with some revision it would be exactly what you wanted' and that you'd mail the second payment at week's end.*
>
> *On August 19 I presented the revised version based on your input. You said, 'It looks fantastic, let me take a more careful look with my staff, and I'll check about the payment you didn't receive.'*

And so on. Further entries would include the dates the invoices were sent, when the new web design went live, and every additional detail that's relevant. The close would say:

> *Mel, clearly I have met every obligation of our contract in a timely manner and with your enthusiastic approval. The site is online exactly as I designed it but six months later, you have not paid two-thirds of the fee to which you agreed in writing. Kindly remit the balance owed immediately.*

> *Very truly yours, Natasha*

This may be the only place in this book that I recommend a stilted, formal language with archaic wording. To the recipient, this type of letter sounds as if a lawyer is advising you. Or at the least, the reader can recognize that you have a good case and are ready to seek legal redress.

Will you get paid? Not necessarily, but it's a good shot. The recipient may at least offer to negotiate a settlement. Or after you make your case you may in fact see the value in taking the legal route if Mel doesn't come through. Your letter becomes part of that process.

The approach works just as well if you're on the other side of the fence. For example, if you don't want to pay an unfair bill, your chances are even better, because if you clearly state that you have no intention of paying, the other party's recourse is limited.

Underscore your letter's legal undertones by mailing it – or better yet, certify delivery and have the recipient sign for it.

# Introducing Yourself in Letter Form

When you assume a new role in your company, take over a professional practice or join one, or open a new business, take time to introduce yourself by letter. A letter of introduction is like making a first impression in person, but it can last even longer. Obviously, this kind of letter needs to be very well done.

Start by thinking about your *audience*. This usually includes people directly affected by your news as well as groups with whom you want to establish good relationships.

Say you're moving up the ladder to head an accounting office. Your first audience is the current roster of clients: You certainly hope to retain them and even better, would like to sell them additional services.

The 'What's-in-it-for-them?' question is best interpreted in this case as, 'What do they want to know?' That's a different question than 'What do *I* want *them* to know?' You may think about focusing on cross-selling additional services, for example, but that's not what's on your reader's mind. (I cover sales-focused communication in the following 'Creating Sales Letters'.)

Putting yourself in their shoes to brainstorm, you come up with factors such as:

- ✔ Will I receive the same level of service?

- ✔ Might it improve in any way?

- ✔ Will I be inconvenienced in any way?

- ✔ Are you qualified professionally?

- ✔ Where did you come from?

- ✔ Are you a nice person to deal with?

People want to know how a change affects them. An introductory letter is not, in fact, an invitation for you to talk about your accomplishments and qualifications at length. Most people overestimate others' interest in credentials when trying to sell them something. People usually take credentials for granted, if you provide a minimal grounding.

So supply the bare bones version of your history and incorporate some high points as relevant – a personal or professional honour, for example. Your content list as the new head of an accounting office may include:

- ✔ Show respect for outgoing chief (whom clients presumably liked)

- ✔ Assure clients of service continuity – absolutely no inconvenience

✔ Introduce yourself:

- Previous role, plus most impressive affiliation and a few clients

- Specializations

- Work as board member of a government accounting department

✔ Plans for improving client service, such as new technology to keep better records, expanded services requested by clients, personalizing service further

✔ Maybe: your work as active member of their community

✔ Maybe: a line about why you love your work or want to know your clients personally

✔ For important clients: offer to meet with them one-on-one soon

Use the same process for thinking through a letter introducing yourself to any group: the staff members of an office you're newly in charge of; suppliers you're dealing with in a new role; or present and past customers of your company. If you recently joined a consulting firm, an intro letter is a good way to tell clients and prospects about the company's expanding capabilities. If you work for a non-profit organization you may use letters to reach out to other agencies that work with yours or grant-giving organizations.

In every case, ask yourself what you would want to know if you were standing in their shoes. Few people want radical change in the amenities and customs of their lives. You want assurance that things will remain just the same – or maybe become a little better.

Make sure introductory letters are in line with your organization's culture and that the contents won't surprise your higher-ups.

## Creating Sales Letters

Writing 'cold call' letters is a staple assignment for professional copywriters and for good reason. Selling a product or service in writing is a tough challenge. So much competes for attention today that people are automatically sceptical, impatient, and bored with the piles of 'buy me' mail that arrives in every form including actual letters, emails, videos and social media.

The overabundance of marketing materials nowadays doesn't mean that you can't write a good sales letter, just that you can't expect to do it off the top of your head. If you're aiming for a slick, graphic-intensive print mailing piece, it's a good idea to get professional help with the writing as well as design. But today's online environment offers extraordinary opportunities to create a word-based marketing message and deliver it by email.

To accomplish a strong message for prospective customers, donors, or other groups you want to reach, first understand the core value of what you offer, the problems your prospect wants to solve, and how to connect the two. Then you need to figure out how to pull your reader in and make your case – in five seconds. (For advice on identifying and articulating your core value, check out Chapter 9.)

The step-by-step system that starts with analyzing your goal and audience I introduce in Chapter 2 works for this challenge. I focus on the one-on-one situation, where you want to convince a specific individual that your product or service is of value to him.

Begin by *defining your goal.* Generally don't expect someone to respond to a letter by putting a check in the mail. When you introduce something a reader is unfamiliar with, aiming to pique their interest is usually more realistic. The situation might call for referring your audience to your website for more information that might convince him to buy. Often your goal is a meeting so you can present your pitch in person, or at least via a telephone appointment.. So your letter should say just enough to interest your reader in a conversation by showing him why he should care.

*Understanding your audience*, in this case, involves thinking about the person's problems and the various audience characteristics I talk about in Chapter 2, and also, looking for a personal connection to give you a natural lead-in. For example, perhaps you talked with a company representative at a trade show, maybe you specialize in working with the same industry, or you read a news story about a new program at the target company.

Also, research the organization as well as the person well enough to anticipate its challenges and explain how you can help. Writing a good sales letter is much easier if you genuinely believe in the prospective match.

Sometimes you can combine both a personal connection and your problem-solving capability in a single opening sentence, such as:

'Chuck Smith suggested I contact you to explain how I solved his most pressing problem, one you share with him: Reducing government audits of overseas investments.'

You don't necessarily need to start from scratch when you write each letter. You can develop a strong basic core, but you must customize it as much as possible for every target.

Fortunately, almost every organization tells you everything you need to know on its website. When you don't know who to write to, dig a bit and you can find the exact person as well as the organization's explanation of its goals and values. In particular, you can discover a lot about style and tone. Is the company formal? Casual? Cheeky? Reflecting the company's tone and style in your own communications goes a long way toward suggesting that you're in synch with it.

When you're addressing your marketing message to a group rather than an individual – prospective customers for your service, for example – follow much the same process as you would for a specific person. The section on 'Writing to groups and strangers' in Chapter 2 shows you how to 'imagine' a composite audience and write for it effectively.

Shape a sales letter with these sure-fire strategies:

✔ Plan the letter from a 'what's-in-it-for-them' viewpoint. Assume most decision-makers care about making money or saving it, so figure out how what you offer relates to that.

✔ Frame the entire message in terms of 'you' – not 'I' or 'we'.

✔ Lead with something catchy but relevant – a story, a hot button, an unusual benefit, an offer. Or just say why you're writing.

✔ Incorporate any personal connection you can and your knowledge of the target company.

✔ Explain who you are *very* briefly and what your product does.

✔ Use relevant, brief case histories and/or testimonials.

✔ End with a clear, specific call to action. What is the next step?

✔ Provide multiple response channels: email, telephone, social media.

Always remember 'the ask.' If you want a face-to-face meeting, say so. It's smart to set a time frame: offering to establish your value in10 minutes, for example, is more attractive than requesting an open-ended commitment and suggests you're focused and won't waste the person's time. Also show flexibility – suggest several timeframes or scheduling the meeting at the reader's convenience, rather than saying 'I'll come at 4 p.m. on Thursday.'

Good salesmen advise that you should always be prepared to follow up with a phone call.

Do all the above in one page maximum, three to five paragraphs. Be sure the letter looks good (see the sidebar 'Formatting your letters'). And do not allow yourself a single spelling or grammatical error. Just one kills your credibility in an instant. Ask a buddy to proofread for you, and ask her for a personal opinion on how well the letter works, too. Chapters 4 and 5 offer loads of editing and proofreading advice.

Use your judgment about attaching available marketing materials. If they're well written and designed, they provide excellent backup in many cases. Keep in mind that interested recipients will almost automatically check out you and your company online, so your website and LinkedIn profiles, among other accessible material, should be in good shape to support your marketing message. (I talk about websites and online profiles in Part IV.)

A good sales letter evolves over time and takes considerable thought, not to mention trial and error. The good news here is that the basic message you create on how to present yourself is readily adapted to your website, print and online marketing pieces, 15-second 'elevator pitch', and more.

# Formatting your letters

If your letter is being delivered by post, use a standard business format, whatever its nature. If delivery is electronic, take pains to make the message look as much like a letter as possible so readers take it more seriously.

Lots of books and websites run through letter-formatting details, but here are the essentials:

✔ **Use block style.** Start every element flush left, but run it rag right (uneven rather than a straight line).

✔ **Eliminate indents.** Instead skip a line space between paragraphs.

✔ **Choose clear, simple fonts.** Try Times Roman in 11 or 12 point or a sans serif face like Helvetica if the message is short and need not look conservative.

✔ **Add graphic elements judiciously.** A headline, subheads, and color and type variations can be appropriate for sales letters; include just a few or none for other letters unless helpful for clarity.

✔ **Utilizse letterhead with your logo if you have one.** You can create the look of letterhead on your computer; you need not use pre-printed stationery. Incorporate a small digital file of your logo in messages you send electronically.

✔ **Supply contact information.** Make it full and complete utilizing the letterhead and signature block

✔ **Pick proper paper.** Stick with white, or a light color paper, that doesn't interfere with reading.

✔ **Sign your name preferably in blue, which looks formal but also makes your signature stands out rather than looking mass-produced as part of the letter.** When writing letters to businesspeople in other countries, take cultural preferences into account. I tell you about these in Part V.

# Part III
# Writing Business Documents, Promotional Material and Presentations

## Top Five Paths to Promoting Your Business with Writing

- ✔ Create executive summaries that decision-makers act on.
- ✔ Use persuasion techniques to energize reports and proposals.
- ✔ Develop a core value statement for your company – and yourself.
- ✔ Craft stories that bring your business and ideas to life.
- ✔ Script yourself to present well.

For more help on writing promotional material for your business, visit http://eu.dummies.com/how-to/content/write-a-company-and-purpose-description-for-your-b.html.

# *In this part . . .*

✔ Brush up on your document writing and produce more effective reports, proposals, business plans and executive summaries.

✔ Home in on your core business values and publicize these with profiles and resumes.

✔ Be prepared! Plan pitches, scripts and presentations to perfection and have answers ready for challenging situations.

# Chapter 8

# Building the Biggies: Major Business Documents

● ● ● ● ● ● ● ● ● ● ● ● ● ● ● ● ● ● ● ● ● ● ● ● ● ● ● ● ● ● ● ● ● ● ● ● ● ● ● ●

## In this Chapter

▶ Leading with the Executive Summary

▶ Ratcheting up reports

▶ Planning proposals, both formal and informal

▶ Building better business plans

● ● ● ● ● ● ● ● ● ● ● ● ● ● ● ● ● ● ● ● ● ● ● ● ● ● ● ● ● ● ● ● ● ● ● ● ● ● ● ●

*D*epending on the type of work you do, you may need to create a constant supply of proposals, reports and business plans. Or you may need to do so occasionally. Either way, these documents are often make-or-break.

✔ When vying for a contract or pursuing project approval, you must present your best possible case to win.

✔ Reports are rarely trivial. They're usually read by people you report to and often by others further up the ladder, decision-makers with whom you have no other contact.

✔ Business plans in which you ask for funding, support or action are in many ways the ultimate challenge because they ask people to invest in your vision.

Perhaps you can get what you want with poorly written business documents. But I don't know why on earth you would want to court that risk. When you work to write your best, you end up thinking your best.

This chapter gives you a wealth of tools and techniques to support your ability to create persuasive major documents. The following strategies apply equally to grant applications, white papers, training plans, technical reports, client reports and more.

 I lead off this chapter with composing an executive summary because you can use it to make every important business document more interesting, valuable and relevant.

# Writing the Executive Summary

Readers are all summary-mad these days. Whether perusing the capsule-size rundowns at the beginning of articles, or digesting multi-page intros to complex content in reports and proposals, people – you included – love summaries.

And no wonder: summaries save so much time. They tell you quickly if you need or want to read the actual material. Even if major decisions hinge on a report or proposal, many people may never read the entire document. CEOs make untold numbers of decisions based on executive summaries alone.

 So when a piece of your future hangs in the balance, make the effort to write first-rate executive summaries. Always reserve time to think them through as documents on their own. Never treat them as an after-thought you dash off after writing the larger document. Write them as original, complete, logical, and interesting statements. See them as a way to get people on your side with your best expression of what's important and, perhaps, what you recommend.

As with everything you write, begin your work on an executive summary with goals. Every summary has its own set of goals, but first know its role and what it needs to accomplish. (See Chapter 2 for more on goals.) Almost always, aim for summaries that:

✔ Generate interest – excitement, if possible – to lure readers into reading the full document.

✔ Integrate the document's main points into a cohesive story that readers can easily understand.

✔ Put the larger document in perspective for your target audiences so that they know why it matters to them.

✔ Say everything that matters most with energy and lively language.

> ✔ Use a reader-friendly format (NOT based on bullets).
>
> ✔ Create a call to action, rather than a pile of passive information from which readers are left to draw their own conclusions.

## Giving long documents perspective

Good reports, proposals, and other business documents are read, and often acted upon. Bad boring ones are trashed faster than yesterday's fish. They may even be used to wrap the fish.

A strong executive summary makes the difference between getting traction or ending up in the trash. It starts you off on the right foot with your audience and can keep you there by establishing interest in the rest of your material.

One good sequence is to write your document, then write the executive summary, then review the main document to ensure that it lines up with the summary and thoroughly supports it. Or, you can write your executive summary first and then back it up with the full document.

Both processes work because developing the summary helps you figure out your real story. This truth applies to a range of reports, whether you're relating how you spent your time for the past month, what your department or company achieved, the results of a study you conducted, what you accomplished for a client, or your research on a given subject. It also applies to white papers, grant applications, business plans, and all the rest.

Your aim in the summary is to predigest the information and give the reader a meaningful perspective. You accomplish these goals by understanding your own material in depth.

Suppose the task is to write a report for your boss on the last month's work. Two quick tricks can help you begin:

> ✔ Without looking at the already-written report, ask yourself: what settles out as important, interesting, provoking, promising, or enlightening this past month? Write that down.

> ✔ Imagine your partner or a good buddy was away for the last month and upon return asks, 'What happened in your work while I was gone?' What would you say? Write that down.

If you're following a report format that your company or department prescribes – with pre-set categories (trends, new projects, profits and losses, and so on) – try one of these shortcut processes for each category. But also take time to determine what matters with a bigger-picture brainstorming so that you know what perspective to give the report.

## Determining what matters

Your executive summary should not march through a series of mini-versions of the larger document's sections. After the opening statement – think of it as the summary of the summary – follow the document's sequencing and integrate the material and ideas for a cohesive, meaningful statement.

Figure out what's important – what is most worth sharing – especially in terms of your readers' interests. (See Chapter 2 for ways to get to know your audience.) Beyond trying the quick tricks I suggest a few paragraphs earlier, spark your own big-picture thinking in a systematic way by filling in answers to questions like:

> ✔ The most important thing that happened this month was_____.

> ✔ What my bosses and colleagues should know about is_____.

> ✔ My core message about the ups and downs of the last month is_____.

> ✔ The problem I really need help with or support for is_____.

> ✔ The good news is_____. The not so good news is_____.

> ✔ As a result of reading this report, the decision or action I want is_____.

> ✔ What I want most for myself is _____.

If you struggle to complete status reports, hang a copy of the preceding questions in your workspace or near your computer. If another kind of report challenge looms regularly, invent your own questions for guidance.

For models of how to handle an executive summary, check out the best. Warren Buffet, the financier, is justly famous for his crystal clear communication of tough material. Here's the opening of his 'To the Shareholders of Berkshire Hathaway' letter back in 2007 when the U.S. housing market was beginning to implode.

> *Our gain in net worth during 2007 was $12.3 billion, which increased the per-share book value of both our Class A and Class B stock by 11 per cent. Over the last 43 years (that is, since present management took over) book value has grown from $19 to $78,008, a rate of 21 per cent compounded annually.*
>
> *Overall, our 76 operating businesses did well last year. The few that have problems were primarily linked to housing, among them our brick, carpet, and real estate brokerage operations. Their setbacks are minor and temporary. Our competitive position in these businesses remains strong, and we have first-class CEOs who run them right, in good times or bad.*
>
> *Some major financial institutions have, however, experienced staggering problems because they engaged in the 'weakened lending practice' I described in last year's letter. John Stumpf, CEO of Wells Fargo, aptly dissected the recent behavior of many lenders: 'It is interesting that the industry has invented new ways to lose money when the old ways seemed to work fine.'*

Buffet goes on to explain the housing crisis in a paragraph, then moves on with sections titled: 'Turning to happier thoughts,' an acquisition; 'Finally our insurance business,' and 'That party is over', warning investors to anticipate lower insurance earnings, and more.

The whole introduction occupies seven paragraphs. It sets readers up to read the full report, with all the statistics, charts, and financial detail – in the frame of mind Buffet chooses.

Notice how Buffet's quoted statement aligns with ideas about good writing as shared in this book. His goal is obvious: to present a balanced picture but reassure his investors that his company is on solid ground despite very troubling financial events. Understanding his audience – Hathaway investors – makes obvious why he chose a fact-rich lead as his first paragraph. While not catchy, the numbers are nevertheless riveting to those whose eyes are glued to his bottom line.

Further, Buffet's use of colloquial language helps everyone relate to his subject. His assurance that 'we have first-class CEOs who run them right, in good times or bad' is both conversational and confident. The 2007 letter ends with a paragraph about how lucky he and his partner feel: 'Every day is exciting to us; no wonder we tap-dance to work.' You're never too successful or sophisticated to share your passion and enthusiasm. In fact, it's essential for getting where you want to go.

Check out a bunch of Buffet's letters online at www.berkshire hathaway.com. Even if you have no interest in the financial details, you can appreciate his clear, concise word choices and organized presentation style. Notice how he creates each letter's tone, and spend ten minutes analyzing what makes him such a credible writer and how he conveys trustworthiness, even when reporting bad news.

One more recommendation on executive summaries: Don't call it 'Executive Summary,' which is sleep-inducing. Give it a real headline that says something concrete about your content, positions it, and promotes interest. You can still use the words but add to them:

Executive Summary: How the Audit Shifts Company Priorities for Next Year

For more on writing headlines, see 'Putting headlines to work' later in this chapter.

# Shaping Successful Reports

As with every piece of writing, know your goal and your audience before diving into a report (see Chapter 2).

Think beyond the obvious reasons for writing reports. Consider *why* someone wants the information you include in your report. If you're told to file monthly or quarterly reports on your activities or your department's efforts, for example, the reasons may include:

- ✔ Your supervisor needs to keep a grasp on what's happening in her department.

- ✔ Your supervisor needs to draw on your material to, in turn, report to her boss, and on up the ladder, perhaps all the way to the CEO or Board.

- ✔ Decision-makers consider your ideas valuable because you're closer to the action, whatever that is, and speak for that piece of reality.

- ✔ Decision-makers want early alerts to problems, opportunities, things falling between the cracks and the general business climate.

- ✔ Your colleagues need to know what you're doing so that they can coordinate their efforts and invest their own time better.

Don't treat reports as time-wasters that take you away from your 'real work'. They're important to those you work for and offer excellent chances to show off your capabilities and prove yourself. Take the trouble to make them well organized, well written, and well strategized.

Target them to your readers. (I cover audience characteristics in depth in Chapter 2.) Think about your specific readers' preferences and what they want: the kind of information, the level of detail and style of writing, the types of evidence, and their probable attitude toward your subject. Consider what they already know about your subject and what interests them the most.

## *Focusing reader attention*

You can easily get lost in detail when reporting on an activity period, experiment, or event. You need to center your readers' attention on what you believe matters most. To figure out what's important and worth sharing, ask yourself a series of questions.

If reports are a regular part of your work take the time to develop a set of questions that are most relevant to what you want to accomplish and the nature of your reports. Start with the following list. Cross out those that don't relate to your own situation, adapt others as necessary and add more questions so you end up with a customized list that leads you to know your story and helps you present it.

Remember to take company culture into account.

- ✔ What's important to your company about what you're covering in terms of immediate goals? In terms of long-term goals?
- ✔ Were any milestones achieved?
- ✔ What's changed from previous month(s)? The impact?
- ✔ What has progressed, or regressed?
- ✔ What comparisons are relevant – last month, last year, or another timeframe?
- ✔ What initiatives did you take? What resulted? And will you take those initiatives again?
- ✔ Did you put any new systems in place? What progress was made on these?
- ✔ What strategies did you use? What were the results?
- ✔ What challenges did you experience? How did you solve them?
- ✔ Where did you see opportunities? Did you act on them or refer them to someone else? Did you achieve any results?
- ✔ What surprised you?
- ✔ What frustrated you?
- ✔ What occurred that should be taken into account in the future, or bears watching?
- ✔ Did the general climate of the past period offer challenges or advantages?
- ✔ In your opinion, is the department moving in the right direction? How/what would you change if you could?
- ✔ What would be fun or thought-provoking to share?
- ✔ What do you recommend based on what you're reporting?
- ✔ Do you see opportunities for collaborative action?

# Shaping the report

Unless you're following a prescribed format, after you've figured out your story, choose a format and sequence. Start by logically listing the categories that you need to cover. A project report may follow a sequence such as:

> Executive Summary
> Problem (or mission)
> What we did
> What happened
> Conclusions (recommendations, ideas, problems, next steps, and so on)

If you're reporting on activities for a week, month, quarter or year, the categories may be more like:

> Executive summary
> Old initiatives, progress
> New initiatives
> Staffing changes
> Unexpected challenges
> Environment scan – big-picture situation that's relevant
> Profits/losses
> Projections
> Resource or assistance needs

If the categories for your reports are predetermined, or you inherited them through long company traditions, honour them, but don't turn into an automaton. Even though the powers-that-be may insist on a given format, their eyes glaze over fastest. Nothing makes for a duller report or application, for example, than filling out each section of required information as a rote task, in the number of words that seem called for. Doing so produces a lifeless litany that makes you look like a hack.

After you have a reasonably organized set of categories and spend some time thinking about your overall message, start working with one category or section at a time. Do this in sequence or not, according to your personal preference. Some people like to start with what's easiest for them. The beauty of sectionalizing the document is that you can choose your working method while knowing in advance how the pieces fit together.

A good report or other major document doesn't happen overnight. Don't position yourself to start from scratch when the deadline is tomorrow. Consider collecting information gradually in a folder, on your computer or desk (or both), for each section. Add to the folders over time so you're not overwhelmed at the last minute and desperately trying to remember what happened, where the figures are and what it all means. Before you draft, give yourself time to read through all of the material you gathered and decide on your message, as I describe earlier in 'Focusing reader attention.'

## *Drafting the report*

When you're ready to pull the whole report together, begin at the beginning with the first section after the executive summary. For each section open with a good summary statement – the *lead*. As with the lead for many kinds of writing, aim to capture attention and explain what information is coming. For reports and other business documents, a good generalization that puts the information in perspective works well. A section on staffing changes in a quarterly report, for example, may begin:

> *The department successfully added three new highly-qualified specialists in high-need technical areas this period, while losing two mid-managers by attrition. This improves our positioning and enables us to better accomplish our goal of upselling technical services to current clients. Only one of the managerial jobs needs to be refilled.*

Then go on to fill in the details on the level you deem appropriate. To stay organized painlessly, try identifying subsections for each major part. To follow up the preceding lead, your subsections might be:

> New technical hires
> Expanding service capacities
> Manager attrition
> Overall staff situation/outlook

Stay conscious of how each section contributes to your overall message, as well as how you're relating to the company's problems and priorities. Know thoroughly how things fit together and make sure you clearly communicate that to your readers.

Don't bury what matters. To avoid overwhelming people with information, analyze what you can leave out. Providing too much detail may trivialize the important things you want people to absorb. If you don't provide a strong perspective, you can leave readers drawing their own conclusions. Lawyers routinely confound the other side by dumping tons of unsorted documents on them that they are forced to wade through. Don't information-dump your readers, especially if you work for them.

# Fast-tracking Yourself through Proposals

If the futurists are right, you may have more proposal writing ahead of you than you suspect. Every year many companies and not-for-profit organizations cut staffing and hire more consultants and independent contractors. Even if you stay in-house, you may find a growing need to pitch for new assignments or responsibilities, in writing.

Sometimes you may need to prepare formal proposals in a format either prescribed by an organization, or the occasion – if you're aiming for investment capital, for example, you need to meet your audience's expectations of content and style. In many cases, however, a far less formal proposal can succeed and may even be preferred by your target reader. More and more consultants I know use the much shorter and easier kind of proposal to sell their services. Accordingly, I show you how to write both kinds,

## Writing formal proposals

Most RFPs (Request for Proposals) are formal and standardized. This is true in most big-business situations, and also for many grant applications. You may have a list of specifications to meet and a prescribed format. Follow any RFP to the letter, especially if you're bidding for a government contract. At other times you may have more leeway to organize your document as you like, or to interpret a set of guidelines.

For help with preparing a long-form, high-stakes proposal, check out Internet resources and business management books. You can find abundant good advice on formatting and specific buzzwords, but you don't find much about the process of writing the proposal itself. So I focus on presentation tips that can make the difference between winning and losing:

- **Tell a story:** Even if the prescribed format makes storytelling tough, use the space to communicate a cohesive picture of what you recommend, what you'll do and why you're the best person or company to do the job. True, specialists may scrutinize only a few sections, but key readers review the whole document and want it to make sense cumulatively – with as little repetition as possible. (See Chapter 9 for storytelling tips.)

- **Know your audience's goal:**If you're pitching for a complex contract, take the time to understand the company and its problems. Read the RFP between the lines and research to see how the requested work fits into the company's overall needs – and by extension how you can fit in.

- **Give your audiences what they need**: Include content and details that specifically match audience expectations. Remember that most businesspeople want to increase profitability or efficiency, while a grant giver may be more concerned with how your project aligns with an organization's mission or generates change. All reviewers want to know a project's timetable, how you measure success, the budget, who will do the work and their credentials, your track record, and more depending on the nature of the need to be filled.

- **Write simply and conversationally.** But use a slightly more formal feeling than for everyday communication – only a few contractions, for example. Writing in the third person, with the company as an entity, is generally best, unless you are the central or the only person involved. A two-person organzsation can use 'we.' Make your language lively but jargon-free. See Chapter 4 for more tips.

- **Speak their language:** In order to echo the RFP's language, read it many times to pick up its voice. Respond in a similar tone. Notice any statements that are emphasized or repeated. These are clues to the organization's hot buttons and perhaps sensitivities honed by experience. Incorporate key phrases and ideas in your responses to show you are on the same wavelength, but don't come across as if you're parroting back their words and not providing substantial answers.

✓ **Remember the decision is about you:** Whatever you're proposing, you're asking someone to choose you and your team. Never skimp the biographical section. Show why each team member is right for the role, how the team works together, its accomplishments, and why you in particular can be trusted to deliver: on time, within budget, and to specification.

✓ **Go for the proof:** Don't say 'the team is creative, reliable, and efficient.' Cite examples, case histories, statistics and testimonials that demonstrate these points, as appropriate. Impress with substance rather than empty claims.

✓ **Edit and proof:** After writing, edit and proof several more times (see Chapters 4 and 5). One error costs you your credibility. Ask a friend with sharp eyes to proof for you too. If you fail to showcase your ability to communicate well and correctly within the document itself, you lose ground regardless of what you're trying to win.

✓ **Make it look good:** Your competitors will. Use all the graphic options to help your proposal read well and easily. Give your readers opportunities to rest their eyes, and entertain them with visuals that are relevant, never extraneous. (See Chapter 3 for advice on using graphic tools.) If a lot rests on this document, ask a friend with design ability for guidance. Or find a good model and adapt elements of its design or the whole layout.

✓ **Ask questions as you go:** Often the people in charge of the RFP or grant-giving process provide a way for you to ask questions. Don't be too proud to do so. If you're not sure whether you're eligible, better to find out first. If you don't understand a requirement, say so. If you don't know what supporting materials are welcome, ask. Take care to sound intelligent, listen, follow up on the clues – and do some relationship building during the process.

Always do a big-picture review before sending out a proposal. Check yourself by asking:

✓ Did I demonstrate my understanding of the problem or goal?

✓ Did I explain who I am (or who we are) and why I'm the best choice?

    ✔ Did I clearly state what I will do to address the problem and the expected outcomes?

    ✔ And if different people worked on the proposal, has the whole piece been edited to read consistently and well?

Many candidates focus proposals on *process* and short-sell *results*. For example, a training proposal to update staff technology skills should talk less about how many workshops the program includes and more about the gains that result in efficiency, problem-solving, and error-reduction after the training.

And, remember the professional proposal writer's mantra: Be SMART: Specific, Measurable, Achievable, Realistic and Time-sensitive.

## *Writing informal proposals*

In fast-moving times, few consultants or contractors want to do more than is necessary to win the job. If you're vying for a government or big-industry contract, or a grant, you usually have no choice other than to follow the given specifications. But in many other situations, you can save yourself a bundle of time.

One way is to build the proposal into the selling process and make it a simple agreement – confirmation of a plan already discussed. You can use a letter format (see Chapter 7) or just create a logical sequence to cover what's necessary. This approach requires a different selling process because it builds on a personal discussion of the job at hand rather than analysis of a written request. So the first step is to achieve that conversation. As any sales professional can tell you, aim for a face-to-face meeting with your prospect. Then write the proposal based on what you discover. Proposals based on phone conversations, or even less, are harder sells. Ideally, you want to gain a second appointment to present your solution – that is, your proposal.

At the meeting, rather than aggressively selling your qualifications, hold a conversation. Encourage the prospect to talk – a beginning that often works well is, 'I'd love to know how you came to this position.' Listen very carefully and use friendly prompts to keep the person talking and gently steer the direction. Ask open-ended questions:

> ✔ What problem would you most like to solve?
>
> ✔ How is this problem affecting your business?
>
> ✔ What difference would solving it make for you?

Watch for clues as to how you really can help the organization and how much they'll value having you fix their problems. It's unlikely that you'll be told the problem you (or they) identified is after all not important, but it's perfectly possible that exploring the fit between you and the prospect will reveal that it's not a good fit. It's better to find this out before you're highly invested!

If the conversation indicates a mutually beneficial arrangement is possible, you can move on to preparing an informal proposal. This can take the form of a simple, logical agreement that covers:

> The problem you propose to address
> Why that problem is very important
> What you recommend
> How you will carry the program out step-by-step
> What will result
> Mutual obligations, timeframe and so on
> Fee

At the end of this simple letter-like format, you can add, 'Agreed to by . . .' with room for signatures and date.

Adapt the thinking behind this strategy to your business and situation. If a meeting can't happen, use a phone conversation to find out about the company and its needs.

Here's an example of a simple proposal to pitch for an opportunity in my business of teaching practical writing.

### *A Workshop Proposal for Company XYZ*

### *From ABC Writing Workshops Inc.*

> I am pleased to propose a series of writing workshops to help XYZ customer service representatives handle customer complaints more effectively and actively build customer relations through email and letters.

### The Problem: Alienated customers

Your recent review of 24 representatives' interactions with customers showed:

• A growing number of complaints from customers unhappy with how their original complaints were handled

• An abrupt, sometimes rude tone in many outgoing messages

*(I can add a few more specifics here to define the problem.)*

### Impact of the problem on XYZ

The situation is affecting your company adversely and in your own analysis, is a major factor in the recent 8 per cent decline in your customer base.

### ABC Workshops proposes:

*(I include a step-by-step outline of the proposed workshop series here – specific but very concise.)*

### Program goals

The workshop series will achieve . . .

*(I list the outcomes that correspond to the problems and note how results will be measured.)*

### How we will work together

*(I describe collaborative planning, timeframes, obligations of each party.)*

### The presenters

*(I detail who will deliver the program, their credentials and so on.)*

### Fee structure

### Agreed to by_____

The entire document should be a few pages at most. Some more standard sections, like the 'presenters' section that describes staffing and credentials, can appear as a separate add-on.

Your tone and language for an informal proposal are even more important than for a formal one, which I talked about in the section before this one. After all you've spoken personally with the individual who might hire you. You've also seen how he presents, what his office looks like, how he communicates, what sparks his interest and concern, how important the problem is to him. Be alert to all these clues and picture him in your mind as you write. (Chapter 2 gives you ways to consciously analyze your audience so you can resonate with it in your writing.)

# Creating Business Plans

You write a business plan for two basic reasons: To obtain investment funds (or the equivalent if you're pitching an idea in-house); and to give an existing or prospective business a roadmap for growth. You may want to accomplish both goals.

Advice on business plans is everywhere: government offices that exist to help entrepreneurs and small businesses, business management books, online templates, software with ready-made formats, and plenty of companies that want to help you, for a fee. Check out *Business Plans For Dummies* by Colin Barrow for more information on writing business plans.

Business plans have much in common with proposals, and the two formats tend to blur into each other. So the foregoing advice on proposals – and also reports (see 'Shaping Successful Reports') – applies to business plans as well.

Analyzing audience and goal is especially helpful in creating a business roadmap. If your goal is to raise capital, ask yourself what your readers – the possible investors – demand to know. Your plan needs to effectively answer these universal questions:

- What's your mission, or idea – what exactly do you want to do?
- How do you plan to accomplish that mission?
- What are the risk factors?
- What's the profit potential and timeframe?
- How much will implementing your idea cost?
- What milestones are you setting?
- Why are you and your team especially qualified to succeed?

Professional investors often complain that too few business plans pay enough attention to the last point. As with proposals, you're asking someone to invest in *you*. If you want them to risk their money, logically, you must show them you are reliable, resourceful, resilient, not easily discouraged, and fully equipped to succeed.

Tell the story of *why* you're undertaking the venture. (Note the phrasing of the final question above.) Present your track record. Show you have solid business sense as well as a good idea. Communicate total conviction in that idea and in the team. Come across as confident, sincere and down to earth.

As with many forms of communication I cover in this book, when writing a business plan, *don't bury the lead*. Articulate your mission and business advantage in a single sentence and put that right at the beginning. At the same time, you must make what you want clear. Readers don't bother to figure these things out for themselves.

Building a good one-liner isn't easy. Marketers call it the *core value proposition*. You need to write it, and say it, to inspire yourself and your team as well as investors. A few examples of how your core value proposition may read, incorporating statements of what the writer wants:

> *JZ Pizzatoria Inc. plans to open the first pizza concession inside a federal penitentiary, with a customer base of 3800 inhabitants weary of bland food. We seek a capital investment of X million to fund this model.*

> *Jane Marvel, the Boot Queen of Alaska, seeks investment partners to upgrade manufacturing capacity for high-fashion boots made from recycled snow tires and bottle caps.*

> *PHD Company seeks to capitalize development of its original, patented software that identifies computer hackers, repels their attacks, and feeds a destructive virus into their own computers.*

For an in-depth discussion of creating core value statements, see Chapter 9.

# Writing Tips for All Business Documents

For your own line of work, you may need business materials that differ from the specific types I cover in the preceding sections of this chapter. Most of the ideas still apply, but some general writing guidelines and techniques are helpful. Establishing the tone, writing headlines and building in tactics of persuasion benefit all your business writing, from proposals and reports to business plans, white papers and RFPs that you write, rather than answer.

## Finding the right tone

Important business communications must come across as authoritative, objective, credible and confident. You're trying to persuade someone to do something, so you don't want to sound ponderous and dull. To the contrary, the more lively and engaging your document, the more responsive your audience and the more likely people are to respond with what you want. Given the mounds of boring material your readers face, they may actually be grateful for giving them a good read.

If anyone tells you that to compete for a lucrative contract you must write expensive-sounding, verbose, grandiloquent prose, don't listen. You want a transparent writing style that showcases your thinking, not fancy language that calls attention to itself. Employ all the good writing techniques at your disposal. Chapter 5 covers a bounty of useful strategies, but the following are core.

**Minimize use of:**

- ✔ Stiff, pompous tone
- ✔ Arrogant or self-aggrandizing atmosphere
- ✔ Passive, indirect statements
- ✔ Long, complicated words and sentences
- ✔ Jargon, acronyms, and buzzwords
- ✔ Long meandering sentences that demand two readings
- ✔ Abstractions

✔ Empty hype, including flowery adjectives and unproved claims

✔ Hedge words and qualifiers: *might, perhaps, hopefully, possibly, would, could* and the like

✔ Extra or extraneous material that doesn't support your point

✔ Mistakes in grammar, punctuation or spelling

**Maximize use of:**

✔ Conversational but respectful style

✔ Low-key, quiet confidence

✔ Straightforward clear sentences, average 12 to 18 words, with action verbs

✔ Short, basic words

✔ Short paragraphs of three to five sentences

✔ Expressions that are easily understood by anyone

✔ Short sentences with rhythmic flow

✔ Concrete, graphic words and comparisons

✔ Proof/evidence: facts, statistics, images, examples

✔ Positive language that doesn't qualify or hedge

✔ Story line: have one and stick to it

✔ Very correct spelling, punctuation and grammar

## Putting headlines to work

To make all your business documents more engaging and reader-friendly, adapt some good journalism techniques. One instantly energizing approach is to stop thinking of section headings as labels and to start writing these elements as headlines.

The difference is that labels are static, dull, and uninformative. Headlines, on the other hand, tell readers what's happening right now, in what they're about to read. They have a feeling of action and at best, provoke curiosity.

You can use headlines to begin sections in reports, proposals and business plans. They are easy to write when you think about delivering information rather than naming a category. Here are some labels transformed into headlines:

**Label:** *Admissions: Results compared to forecasts*
**Headline:** *September admission results exceed forecast*

**Label:** *Overall financial results*
**Headline:** *June starts disappoint – collaborative action needed*

**Label:** *XY Program case history*
**Headline:** *How the XY program turned an oil company's image from black to green*

If you're responding to given categories and must use them, simply add a headline after the label. Adding a colon at the end of the standardized label line can help:

*Admissions Performance:*
*This year's enrolment up 19 per cent over last*

Most reports, proposals and business plans benefit hugely from working in subheads as well as headlines. Try this method to solve organizational problems. As I suggest in Chapter 4, write a series of subheads before drafting the material itself and then add the appropriate information and ideas under each.

Breaking long sections of big documents into sequences of smaller sections with subheads pulls readers along and helps them make sense of what you're presenting. Planting guide-posts helps you focus your audience on what is most important for them to know and what you want them to know.

If you have a multipage section on financial indicators, for example, write a headline to capsulize the whole picture, and then a set of action subheads for each topic. For example:

**March Indicators Promise Much, Prove Little**

*Skilled worker recruitment loses traction: down .5per cent from plan*

*Stock price climbs to 126, up 2 per cent*

*Sales jump to 2012 levels, led by Jumex breakthrough*

*Company economists express cautious confidence for April*

You may question whether the preceding headlines and sub-heads are too specific, encouraging readers to not look past them. Your concern may be justified but realistically, you must allow for skimmers. This is all the more reason to present a fair, honest and balanced picture through these mini-statements.

The more clearly you signal where you've located specific types of information in your document and why they matter, the better the response. Helping people choose what to read is an excellent technique, given how selective people are about investing their energy and time.

The headline/subhead technique makes your material look more interesting and helps you look like a more take-charge, action-oriented leader. This is true even when the news you're delivering is bad!

## Incorporating persuasive techniques

Persuasion is a big topic that obsesses psychologists, communicators, marketers, and even neuroscientists today. Digging into some material on the subject and absorbing core ideas into your writing is definitely worthwhile. *Persuasion and Influence For Dummies* by Elizabeth Kunke is a good place to begin.

In the meantime, try implementing the following strategies into your writing right now whenever you want to persuade someone to your viewpoint, change her mind, introduce a new idea or make a convincing case :

- ✔ **Write with conviction:** Nothing is more persuasive to other people than your own strong belief in whatever it is you want them to agree with.

- ✔ **Provide evidence.** Always give people substance rather than vague generalizations about your product, proposal, or idea. Needless to say, always be honest.

- ✔ **Key in to your audience's viewpoint:** Connect to its concerns, problems, ideas, level of knowledge and so on (see Chapter 2). The best argument is useless if your reader doesn't care about solving that problem.

✔ **Focus your message:** Know it thoroughly and make sure every word, sentence, and paragraph supports it. Cut out unnecessary details and distractions.

✔ **Sound in command of your material:** Be positive in tone, never wishy-washy. Don't hedge. Look for ways to be engaging and interesting – anecdotes, examples, stories are good; jokes, probably not.

✔ **Don't dismiss opposing ideas:** Take them into account, and you're more credible. For example: 'Some scientists believe that eating more sugary products is good for children. However, the evidence shows. . .'

✔ **Take special pains with transitions:** Know how each piece of your story connects to the rest. Make these links clear with strong transitions between every sentence, idea, paragraph and section. Good transitions contribute to a mesmerizing flow and makes your argument feel logical and inevitable (see Chapter 5 for more on this technique).

And, keep in mind that scientists and economists are finding more and more proof of what marketing gurus have always believed: People make decisions based on emotion rather than facts. Therefore, when you want to persuade, paint pictures, tell stories and offer visions. Spark your readers' imagination.

All these tools and techniques for creating reports, proposals and other business documents are valuable for promotional and marketing materials, too, which I cover in Chapter 9.

# Chapter 9

# Promoting Yourself and Your Organization

• • • • • • • • • • • • • • • • • • • • • • • • • • • • • • • • • • • • • • • •

## In This Chapter

▶ Uncovering the core of your business message

▶ Digging deep for your true value

▶ Telling stories with power and purpose

▶ Publicizing with profiles, résumés, and email

• • • • • • • • • • • • • • • • • • • • • • • • • • • • • • • • • • • • • • • •

*I*f you're an employee of a business, non-profit, government agency, or any other type of organization, presenting a positive interface with the world is part of your job. If you're in business for yourself, success demands that you present your best case in every situation.

Despite the myriad communication channels available, you only have two basic ways to deliver messages – writing and speaking. Everyday media like email and letters are critical to company and personal image, as I talk about in Chapters 6 and 7. But just about everyone needs to create specific marketing and promotional materials to advance his or her cause.

This chapter gives you the essentials you need to write these materials well. It shows you how to create strong messages about your business and about yourself. As every part of this book stresses, good writing demands that you know *what* to say as well as *how* to say it. Substance rules, style follows.

# Finding the Heart of Your Business Message

The key to everything from marketing campaigns to sales pitches, proposals and résumés comes down to crafting your core message.

The *value proposition* or *unique selling proposition,* as marketing and sales people call it, is the central statement that tells people what benefits your product or service delivers and what distinguishes your business from its competition. I prefer the term *core message* because it makes the concept clearer and more practical rather than jargonish.

Often *core messages* are internal documents, but smart companies invest in their creation and stick with them as the essential frames for all communication and pivotal decisions. Done well a core message is the all-purpose touchstone for an organization, whether staffed by one person, or thousands around the world.

I will not kid you – crafting your core message is real work. But I can't think of anything more productive for everyone who sells a service or product or aims to establish a business. And even if you're an employee who's not directly responsible for selling – surprise! – you need a core message too, for yourself, your department, or both. Later in 'Stating your personal value' and 'Representing your department,' I show you how to adapt the core messaging process to focus on yourself and your immediate work group.

A good core message tells your audience what you offer in that audience's own language. It instantly shows that you're on the same wavelength. You can't communicate your message successfully through clichés like 'state-of-the-art' or 'most innovative' or 'best buy in town'. Dig down and scan wide. Figure out your truest value to those you want to connect with.

After you do this, creating any marketing material you need becomes a relative snap. You already know the essence of what you want your readers to know – and how to relate to their interests.

At one point in my career I worked for a large educational agency that creates and sells services to small school districts – co-operative purchasing, technology support, technical schools and 100 more programs. In creating marketing materials for the various services, I found producing good videos, brochures, or websites for some of them was much harder and sometimes impossible. I realized these programs had something in common: lack of mission and message clarity.

 When an individual company or a program doesn't truly know its goals and capabilities, it can't measure its success, nor share its commitment with stakeholders or business prospects. Many businesses have general ideas of what they do and their strengths, but haven't done their homework to objectively assess and articulate it. They may fail to take customer viewpoints into account. As a result they probably fail to communicate their best selling points – or worse, they may not even know what they are.

That's why you need to figure out your core value and build your core message upon it. This gives you a central, individual theme that connects your work to those you do it for. See 'Searching for true value' later for more details on how to dig deep and discover core value.

As an example, suppose I own a consulting firm that helps businesses create their core messages. I can say:

> *Keystone Message helps you tell your story to the world so it resonates with customers. We find the right words to liven up your sales pitches, website, networking messages, and more. We save you time and bring a full set of creative skills to this challenge. The results energize your sales team, make your website more popular, and brighten all your presentations.*

Or I can try something like:

> *Keystone Message guides you to state your company message in terms that relate directly to your customers' bottom lines. Your core message will communicate the benefits that only your company offers.*

> *International research shows that organizations that are highly effective at communications are 1.7 times as likely*

> *to outperform their peers. Our clients in industries similar to yours document that when their core message is put to work, they find a significant increase in inquiries from their websites, telephone call-backs, and response rate to their advertizing campaigns.*
>
> *Employee relations are also improved. One client's survey showed that sharing his company's keystone message increased employee engagement 18 per cent and commitment to company goals 22 per cent.*

The first message reads okay but it's just words: 'resonates', 'livens up', 'creative', 'energizes', and 'brighten up'. These are *process* words rather than results words, and customers don't care about them. They don't want to know what you do – but what you can do *for them*.

The second message addresses your customers' basic agenda: improve things that contribute to the bottom line. The first statement in the second paragraph about communication effectiveness is true but, I admit, I made the other figures up for the example. But you shouldn't and don't need to.

Your business may be less abstract than Keystone Message. A product may lend itself to quantifying results more easily than a service. Whatever your business, your customers may be able to give you real numbers for ways that you helped them. If not, or your venture is new, do some research and cite industry statistics. Or cite one outstanding example of how you helped a customer. Or do all of these things. (For specifics on research techniques and more on core messaging, see *Competitive Strategies for Dummies*, Richard Pettinger.)

## Searching for true value

You can get in touch with your organization's true value in a variety of ways. Choose one or more of these processes based on what suits you and your business.

> ✔ **Ask your customers or clients what you have accomplished for them and what they most value.** If appropriate to your industry, ask for specifics, especially in bottom-line terms. They may be more prepared to

deliver this information than you think; if you're a repeat or long-term supplier they may be quite aware of their ROI (return on investment). For ideas on how to frame good questions, see the sidebar 'Questions to ask your customers'.

✔ **Brainstorm with an internal group.** Working with your department or representatives from different departments gives you the advantage of advance buy-in from different stakeholders. Or work with a business-savvy person or two who you trust. The sidebar 'Questions to ask your team and yourself' gives you material for this process.

This 'inside route' to identifying your strengths can expand and solidify your ideas about what's important and what to concentrate on. It also gives you a broad foundation for a communications program. Additionally, the answers can give you a head start on storytelling for your business, which I talk about later in 'Finding, Shaping, and Using Stories'.

If you choose to use the inside team approach, consider supplementing it with at least a few outside opinions. Doing so gives you a reality check on whether you're moving in the right direction and staying aligned with your clients.

✔ **Do it yourself.** Ask yourself probing questions – or create a small circle of colleagues who can also benefit from exploration within a group setting. CEOs from top companies meet this way to share problems and solutions, and you can too. Focus on building a core value statement for each of you, one at a time.

✔ **Work with a business counselor.** If you're a one-person operation, a trained business counselor can help you reach productive conclusions. Seek out business development service agencies in your town, or county. Your local library has information about available services which are free or low cost. Local colleges often house business guidance centers or resources for entrepreneurs. If you want sustained, individualized support and are willing to pay for it, a growing number of business advisors and coaches offer such services.

# Questions to ask your customers

Seek out insights from customers to help craft your core message. Use written questionnaires, have telephone conversations, or conduct in-person meetings. Whatever your method, interpret these questions, add some and subtract others to align with your particular operation.

In addition to a base for your core message, plan to emerge with great testimonials for your website (see Chapter 12) and other materials. (Only use this material with your customers' permission, of course.)

And while you're at it, pay scrupulous attention to any performance shortcomings that emerge and be prepared to follow through and improve.

- What do you most value about our product or service? Why?

- Have we helped you increase profitability? How? Can you quantify that?

- Have we helped you increase market share? By how much?

- Have we saved you money? How much?

- Did you use the money saved another way? What resulted?

- Did we help you cut costs? How?

- What problems have we solved for you?

- Have we helped you reach new markets or audiences? Which?

- Did we increase efficiency? Systems?

- Did we help you reduce mistakes and errors?

- Did we improve relationships between staff members? Does this prevent conflict? How does that matter?

- What do you like about working with us? What don't you like?

- Did anything surprise you while working with us?

- When would you call us in the future?

- What would you say about us to a colleague?

- Did we meet your expectations? How can we improve? What can we do better?

- Should we add to our services in any way?

If you approach clients in the spirit of checking on their satisfaction level and seeking input on how to improve, they're almost certain to respond positively. Don't see the research as an imposition, but as a relationship-building opportunity. And don't be surprised if what you discover differs from what you expected.

# Questions to ask your team and yourself

Uncover insights that can contribute to your core message by brainstorming with partners or collaborators and if your organization is large, with representatives from different parts. Or work with a business counselor or a team you create – colleagues, partners, friends – who can amplify your perspective. Without outside input you risk reinforcing a misdirection.

Only some of the following questions may be relevant to you and your organization. That's fine. You're trying to tease out what makes *your* organization unique and how to position it powerfully. If questions don't apply, skip them, but spend some time adding ones that do.

✔ What makes us special?

✔ What do we do that's different from our competitors?

✔ What sparked the idea for this enterprise?

✔ What's unusual, interesting or surprising about our history?

✔ Do we feel a sense of mission in what we do? What is it?

✔ Do we have a philosophy or company culture that distinguishes us? What is it?

✔ What are we most proud of? (achievements, problem solving, creative thinking, collaborative skills, industry leadership, reliability, and so on)

✔ Does a particular person epitomize our history and values? How?

✔ What does our total body of work say about us?

✔ What's the best example of our extraordinary service?

✔ What is special about how we work with clients or customers, volunteers, or donors?

✔ Do we have a high satisfaction rate? How many of our clients come back?

✔ What was our toughest, most complex project so far?

✔ How do we help clients solve the problems that keep them up at night?

✔ How can we prove how successful we are in carrying out our mission?

✔ How might the world (or industry) change if everyone used our product?

✔ Has our growth pattern been steady? What has affected it?

✔ Why are we better than our competitors and should be chosen?

✔ Where would we like to be in a year? Five years? Ten years?

## Making your case in business terms

Reaching business people in their own terms is not rocket science. It's often about dollars and cents. Use this truth to make your core message more powerful.

Start developing your core message with a thorough look into work your company has done. Look for ways to show that you can:

- ✔ **Increase revenue and profitability**. For example: grow market share, retain customers, find new markets, reach a wider audience

- ✔ **Cut costs and streamline**. Examples: reduce expenses, increase efficiency, cut redundancies, reduce mistakes, redeploy staff, reduce turnover, minimize returns, cut red tape

- ✔ **Improve positioning:** build the client's or product's cachet, improve public or customer perception, raise company profile, minimize complaints, increase customer satisfaction

- ✔ **Change behavior**: train staff to work, team, or communicate better; promote adoption of organization's core mission and values; shift unproductive systems and behavior to productive ones.

Important as it is, money isn't everything. Identify your clients' pain points and think about how you address those, especially in different ways from your competitors. Perhaps you have evening office hours to accommodate those who work; wash dogs in their homes; train those who buy your equipment; or provide free 10-year warranties. If you're in business you probably offer such amenities. The idea is to think about value more systematically so you can communicate about it and sharpen your focus.

Every industry is different but they share the same imperatives, though they may take different forms. Increasing revenue for a non-profit may mean upping donations, sponsorships, or grants rather than selling more products. A government agency typically wants a larger share of the government pie, which may be achieved by better articulating the need for its service, demonstrating new efficiencies, or increasing client satisfaction.

## Stating your personal value

Creating a personal core value message benefits you in a number of ways. It clarifies your sense of identity and keeps you on target to your goals. Just as a core message guides a business or organization, a personal one helps you always know who you are and what you're doing.

Imagine going into a job interview with a solid conviction of what makes you valuable. You own an effective message about you. Knowing and believing in this message gives you the confidence to deliver it well. You're prepared to answer interview questions without floundering.

Or imagine, if you are employed in a job you want to keep, that a new department head takes over and calls you in for a chat. You know (or suspect) he's looking for people to cut. How can you justify your salary? If you go in with an internalized core value statement, you're certain to fare much better than your colleagues.

To develop your own value statement, think of your department or company as your customer. Analyze what you actually contribute in your role – not a set of responsibilities like in a job description. Read through 'Questions to ask your customers' in the sidebar and find ways to apply them to your circumstances. Can you say that you came up with new ideas or ways of doing things that saved money? Made systems more efficient? Solved a problem? Reduced mistakes? Fostered collaboration?

If you can quantify anything, do it. Imagine the power of being able to state, 'I found a new paper supplier and cut costs 18 per cent' or, 'I hire and train the interns, and we have a 98 per cent retention rate.' Soft skills count too, such as: 'I'm the go-to technology guy solving problems for my group' or 'I make sure that all communications going out from our department are correct and well written.'

The process of creating a personal core value message can pay off particularly well for job seekers. A young man I know was looking for a foothold in the art world and was interviewed for an administrative job in a major museum. Before going in he took some time to think about the prospective employer and his qualifications. He framed his core message like this:

> *My background and interests make me completely comfortable with the museum world and its people. I bring training and experience in archiving, preservation, and photography.*

> *My special skill is applying technology. I can assess technology systems quickly and create better ones to get the work done. Recently, for example, I did a project for a photo archive company, and in the process designed a computer-based system that does in minutes what used to take hours of handwork.*

> *I also like training people to use new technology in friendly ways that make them feel good about using it.*

The idea is not to recite a set of memorized words, but to crystallize what's real and speak from that basis.

The challenge is to match your abilities to the key demands of the job you want, or want to keep, and articulate that. Like a Boy Scout, you need to be prepared. No one lives in a job-secure world. Currently it's estimated that most people will have 11 jobs during their career. So be able to communicate your value in words: being 'good' is not enough. I've seen many people splutter when asked to justify their value. It's not a pretty picture and it rarely has a happy ending.

## *Representing your department*

In coaching groups of public relations professionals to sharpen their writing, I sometimes give them this challenge: write a memo to the powers-that-be asking that your department be represented at a top-level strategy meeting to which it was not invited. I'm always surprised by their blank stares when asked to write this message. And I've found marketing professionals no better prepared to make the case for their profession.

Just as you need a personal statement of core value, you need to create or buy into one for your department. This applies whether its function is accounting or testing or tech support. If you meet the CEO in the elevator and he asks what you do, the occasion calls for one line about your role, and the rest about what your department or office contributes. Even if you don't run into the CEO, you're guaranteed to do a better job if you're clear on your group's bottom-line goals and contributions and how they relate to the overall organization.

It's legit to ask your supervisor to share her perspective on the department's value. If she can't offer a value message, or if you're in charge, use the same process I outline for personal statements in the preceding section. Look at the larger organization as your department's customer and figure out what makes your area essential. If you have a supervisor who gives you a confused look when you ask about this but is open-minded, you might try out a statement you devise and ask whether it's a fair representation of your department's purpose.

Unless your boss shows interest in developing a core message for the unit, however, it's usually best to keep any statement you put together for your personal guidance. Many supervisors might regard your initiative as circumventing their authority.

Whatever the work you do, be able to tell others it's the most important in the world and why. This helps you succeed because nothing is more persuasive than sincere belief.

## Putting your core value message to work

You might use part or all of your core value statement in your marketing brochures, networking messages, website, company communications, and more. You can edit down to a good *boilerplate statement,* the paragraph you add to the end of press releases explaining what the company does.

The most important purpose of the core value statement may be as a background theme or infrastructure. When it's shared and accepted, a team – whatever its size and nature – is stronger, more focused and more powerful. The entire company's communications have good bones to build on.

Moreover, knowing core value gives you direction and inspiration. It tells you not only what to say to audiences, but *who* to say it to. The Keystone Message example earlier in 'Finding the Heart of Your Business Message' may lead the business owner to look for companies that want to increase website traffic, raise employee engagement, or help salesmen build messages that increase the call back rate. The art-world job seeker who created his statement for an interview (see 'Stating your personal value') now has a much better idea of other employers to approach.

Better yet, when you believe in your personal statement, you believe in yourself. You have a compass for decision-making. And you have the best tool for measuring your own performance against a standard you can trust.

You also have the seed for a good story, which I talk about next.

# Finding, Shaping, and Using Stories

Today's modern technological world, perhaps ironically, has come full circle to value storytelling, the oldest communication art, as the best way to deliver messages. Experts in marketing, branding, advertizing, public relations, and sales now advocate stories to communicate ideas, values, aspirations, and competitive advantage.

The idea makes perfect sense: Human beings have told each other stories for millennia, and as neurological researchers now demonstrate, we're hard-wired to respond to them. Specific areas of the brain process stories and when vividly told, these tales excite the same circuitry as actual experiences, making us feel we are living other people's actions and emotions ourself.

For children, stories make sense of a complicated world and at best, are inspiring. They serve the same purposes for adults. Given the chaotic and random environment we find ourselves in, it's no wonder we crave good stories that put things in perspective and have a beginning, middle, and end.

Stories bring presentations alive, stay with an audience and create a bond between teller and listener. They can make abstract ideas real and vivid. They offer endless opportunity to individualize and humanize an institution or leader. And stories reach people on the emotional level where, many economists and psychologists agree, decisions are made.

So naturally you want to harness story power for yourself and your enterprises. The problem comes in applying the idea. Where can you find a good story that embodies your mission? Can you buy one from a store? Should you take a fiction writing course? Or hire a novelist to create one for you? Not necessary.

Here's a simple and practical way to think about stories for business messaging: A story tells what happened. Sometimes it tells what *can* happen. Your story is implicit in the way you built your business, the reason you chose your career, the way you've helped other people, and much more.

The New York Times does a series – now morphed into an online video feature – called 'One in 8 Million,' based on the idea that 'New York is a city of characters.' But of course, outside New York, too, there's always a story. True, some are more interesting than others. You can develop a good one if you identify a story line that relates to your message, understand its meaning, and work to tell it well – all topics I address in the following sections.

## *Finding your story*

You can use stories in many ways, including as anecdotes to spark a speech (see Chapter 10) or blog (Chapter 12), but I focus here on the *lodestar story* – one that epitomizes your business and guides how you think and communicate about it. These stories often evolve over time and must embody the core value idea I explain earlier in 'Finding the Heart of Your Business Message.'

Keep in mind four basic types of stories that work for organizations:

- ✔ **Discovery**: How I started my business, discovered my talent or passion, found my mission, found a way to match my values to my work.

- ✔ **Bumpy road**: Obstacles I faced, mistakes I made, weaknesses I encountered, how I overcame challenges and grew the business.

✔ **Success story**: How I used my skills, product or service to help someone else achieve what they wanted or solve a major problem.

✔ **Big vision:** How much better the world will be when everyone reaps the benefits of my service or product – or when a disease is cured, a needy group is helped, and so on.

All four story types basically revolve around people. Good stories generally do. And of course your story must relate to the specific people you want for your audience. If you're explaining why you're passionate about your work, it must be work that relates to your readers. A bumpy road story must have a message your audience cares about – perhaps how you equipped yourself to solve their problems. A success story should center on somebody just like your audience so they can relate. A big vision should connect with your audiences' needs – perhaps by promising a solution to an important per-ceived problem.

Framing your experience and practicing selective memory is legit when you build a story, but *never* tell a story that is not fundamentally true. First of all, you're unlikely to tell it well, and moreover, you kill your own authenticity at the outset. Trust that the materials are there.

A good way to build a story is to start with the core message you want to deliver and scan your experience for a piece of history that illustrates it and lends itself to one of the story formats. If you've not yet created a core message, this is another good reason to do so.

## Building your story

For fiction writers and playwrights, just as for journalists, the hard part is the lead: where to start. So don't be surprised if your story presents the same challenge.

A good beginning is not usually a chronological one. When you start at the first event and proceed forward in time a story lacks suspense and doesn't provoke the curiosity that keeps people reading or listening.

Look for an interesting in. A surprise or a built in contradiction are good ways to start. The fact that Steve Jobs dropped out of college and built Apple fascinates. Similarly, the story of how Facebook was born in a college dorm, XYZ startup began with £20, or a 17-year-old sold his software for $37 million all grab people's attention.

You don't have to blow away your audience. Discovery and turning points in your own life or career make good lead material too.

> *One black Tuesday I sat shivering in my 45-degree basement room, looked at my almost empty jar of peanut butter and listened to my cat wail. I realized that next week I wouldn't be able to pay the rent – or feed the cat. I knew I had to come up with something.*

In effect, with this story you're starting in the middle of your personal saga. You might then speak to what got you to that low point and then how you moved on and overcame all those obstacles. The same approach works when you're telling someone else's success story:

> *The first time I saw Joe, his shoulders slumped. His clothes hung. His eyes were red pinpricks. He looked like he'd been up all night – and he had. He was trying to do his corporate taxes himself without losing his shirt or his sanity. At the end of his rope, he dug out my card and called me.*

Recounting a Eureka moment where you or a customer discovered or learned something vital can work. A colleague who teaches presentation skills workshops opens by sharing her first day of teaching, an awful experience until a student gave her the magic clue – just be yourself. Then she briefly recounts how she learned to be a speaking expert and is now equipped to help others become their best selves as speakers.

## Story-writing tips

The following ideas come from the fiction writer's portion of the writing spectrum, but they can help the business storyteller too. Use these approaches with both written and oral communication.

✔ **Show, don't tell.** Rather than sticking to straight narrative or piling on the descriptive adjectives, put readers right into your scene so they can draw their own conclusions. Paint a detailed picture of the situation, event, place, or person.

✔ **Engage the senses.** Use graphic language that activates people's sense of smell, hearing, sound, touch, as well as sight. Research shows that specific areas of the brain light up if you say hands are 'leathery' for example, rather than 'rough'.

✔ **Use dialogue.** Rather than, 'My sixth grade teacher told me I would be a failure', say, 'I remember the day that Mrs Dim, my sixth grade teacher, said 'Jeremy, when I look at you, I know I failed to teach you – and that you will fail in life." But be sure the dialog adds something meaningful.

✔ **Be concrete and specific.** Take time to pin down details and the right words. Abstractions don't resonate with people. 'I teach people to improve their writing' accomplishes less than 'I show entrepreneurs how to create messages that win more hearts, minds, and contracts.'

✔ **Use simple, say-able language.** Rely on short words, short sentences, and plain structures. This especially applies to written stories because you're tapping into an oral tradition that generates its own expectations. Who doesn't listen up when you hear or read, 'Once upon a time. . .'? Think about that natural story cadence and try echoing it. Or try using the words to spark your brainstorming, and perhaps even keep them in your delivered message: 'Once upon a time I put on my first suit and went out on my first sales call. . . '

✔ **Stay positive:** Highlighting your mistakes and setbacks along the way is effective; people relate to this sharing and may even mentally cheer you on toward success. But be sure your story has a happy ending – one that leaves the audience with a very good impression of you. Park any ironic jokes, told at your own expense, at home.

✔ **Know your point.** Be sure you know why you're telling your story and that this moral aligns with the core message you want to get across. In fact, many people write the ending first and then build the rest of the story toward it. You might bring the point home, as in 'I know now that

> following those side roads is what prepared me to set you on the right track'. Or you may decide to let the story make the point on its own. A big-vision story might end, 'I see a world where no one has to struggle for clean air and all children are healthy' or 'My idea will solve the industry's data storage problem and save millions.'

Stories are everywhere around us. Develop your awareness of good storytelling techniques in presentations you attend, what you read and what you listen to. NPR and the BBC both have storytelling programs and it's especially illuminating to hear well-crafted stories read aloud well.

## *Putting stories to work*

*You* may be your own most important audience. A strong story tells you where you've been, where you are now, and where you're going. It solidifies the relationship between who you are, what you do, and where you want to go. That's why therapists use story-building to help people understand and reframe their life experience. Stories as shared history or vision serve as the glue that unifies an organization.

Your own story gives you a versatile tool that can be adapted to:

- ✔ The 'About Us' section of a website (see Chapter 12)
- ✔ Website pages that focus on good-cause accomplishments or needs
- ✔ An elevator pitch (see Chapter 10)
- ✔ A job application cover letter
- ✔ Online profiles (see 'Writing online profiles' later in this chapter)
- ✔ Pitches for investment or other support
- ✔ Brochures and marketing materials
- ✔ A speech or presentation opening
- ✔ A media feature about your business
- ✔ Special event promotions, like a company anniversary
- ✔ Posting in your office as a framed piece

✔ Exhibit handouts for tradeshows and other public events

✔ A blog

I recently saw several good stories told on restaurant place-mats. Each basically relates who the founders were, where they came from, how the restaurant was born and evolved, which descendants are running it now, what makes it so great. These sorts of stories are hard not to read while you're waiting for food! Look for suitable opportunities to share and tell your own stories.

For non-profit organizations, stories can provide the entire key to fundraising, volunteer recruitment and more. They can make the mission real and important, even exciting. Some non-profits do this through the 'founder' story, effective when that person is famous or charismatic. Often charitable causes tell moving stories about the people who need their help and/or success stories about those they have helped. The most effective ones revolve around very specific individuals.

Many non-profits are very good at embodying their sense of purpose and accomplishment in stories. Companies can learn a great deal from them about humanizing abstract ideas to touch people and make their organizations memorable.

And, stories can be prime tools for carrying a corporate message about its good works, such as charitable causes it supports or efforts with sustainability, green building, and conservation. Demonstrating corporate responsibility is a must for all businesses today, and telling stories is a great way to do that.

# Using Value Messages and Stories to Promote

After you develop your core message or story – preferably both – you've done the basic work to kick-start your communication products, whatever they are. Whether you're writing a brochure, newsletter or website, draw on these tools to guide you and perhaps provide ready-made copy. Adapt messages and stories with imagination to the medium and to the particular audiences you're writing to.

Consciously aim for a consistent message across all the platforms you use. You can tell different stories in different media and at different times, but they should reflect the same underlying themes. This is referred to as integrated marketing, and it's essential to branding yourself or your organization.

Following are some of my favorite ways to apply the principles of value messages and stories to specific promotional projects.

## *Writing better résumés*

To guide readers to review your qualifications in the light you want, begin your résumé with an *overview statement.* Rather than telling readers what kind of job *you* want, tell them why you match what *they* want. Aim for a narrative that summarizes your capabilities in three to five lines. Doing this well can take a lot of thinking. But you can easily adapt your core message to the purpose.

For example, my young friend applying for the arts administration job (see 'Stating your personal value' earlier in this chapter) can say:

### *Jim White*

*Artist, art historian and administrator with experience and advanced training in archiving, preservation, and photography. Special expertise in designing computer systems to accomplish administrative work more efficiently and economically. Excellent interpersonal skills, adept at training people to use new technology cheerfully.*

What could have been a formidable task becomes simply an editing job here.

A few more tips for effective résumés:

- ✔ **Don't depend entirely on bullets to tell your story.** Put those bullet points in context with, for example, brief narrative overviews of each job. Bullets are disjointed statements and don't give a broad picture.

- ✔ **Write clearly, concisely, with short words and sentences.** You don't need full sentences; you can be somewhat telegraphic, as with Jim White's preceding summary statement. But don't distil the thoughts down to mysterious fragments.

✔ **Use action verbs everywhere.** Launched, streamlined, originated, chaired, generated, instituted, rejuvenated, mobilized. Avoid phrases that start, 'Responsible for...'

✔ **Translate responsibilities into accomplishments.** Employers want to know how you improved things and took initiative, not just that you were there and had responsibilities. This is a good place to quantify when you can: 'Created and introduced a new computerized system to automate work previously done by hand, cutting task time by 80 per cent.'

Unless you're creating a social media or other 'new media' résumé, stick to standard résumé formats, chronology and fonts. Edit and proof obsessively. One mistake and you're probably out. See Chapters 4 and 5 for more editing insights.

## Writing online profiles

Online professional networks, such as LinkedIn, XING, and Ryze are good business connectors for many people and are generally considered the 'professional' social media. My tips apply to profiles for LinkedIn and similar sites.

To adapt these ideas to other media, just read a batch of profiles on the site or service that you're interested in joining and see what approach you feel works best. Use that style and the guidelines of the medium.

In general, an online profile is a chance to communicate more of your personality than in a résumé. Writing in the first person often works well because you automatically take a more personal tone and genuine feeling comes across.

Write with a sense of where you want to go, not just where you've been and are now. Align your profile with your big goals. You can use the headline area to list what you do and appeal to search engines with search terms, for example

> *Business Writing. Magazine Features. Writing Workshops.*
> *Publication Project Management.*

Then create a strong opening statement that instantly tells people what you want them to know about you. Surprise! You can draw this from your core value statement or your story. For example:

> *When I realized how terrified most people are of sitting in the dentist's chair, I decided to find ways to make the experience more positive – something people would look forward to. Or almost.*

If you're trying for a career transition or new job, take advantage of the chance to say so:

> *I'm a public relations professional with a great background in the entertainment industry, and my special love is hip-hop culture. I'm looking to connect my two passions.*

Successful online material doesn't follow a formula. So experiment and scout for profiles you like, both in and out of your own field, and draw your own lessons from them. A few tips and possibilities:

- ✔ Share your enthusiasm and passion for what you do
- ✔ Include the achievements you're most proud of
- ✔ Skip empty rhetoric and get down to brass tacks; what you actually do and what it means is always more interesting
- ✔ Know what you want to achieve with this profile – find new customers? Connect with an industry? Showcase creative skills? Establish expertise?

As always, write to specific audiences, to accomplish goals.

## Writing email promotions

Emailing messages to groups is in many cases an efficient way to reach many audiences at once. The in box is where many of us live. But so much competes for people's attention that your messages must be crafted with care and thought.

Email campaigns work well for promoting events, seminars or other opportunities that your targets may want to know about. Especially challenging are messages about yourself, such as those that introduce or reintroduce you to an online networking group.

Probably like you, I get dozens of these messages every week. I find most uninteresting. But here's one that got my attention. The subject line included clear identification of the writer's business (law) and the message said:

> *Small business is like hopscotch played in a minefield: one wrong step and you can be destroyed! My job is to protect you from those dangers and help you grow your business into something enduring.*
>
> *My name is Todd Kulkin and I act as corporate counsel for small- to medium-sized businesses, start-ups and non-profits. I do it at a fixed cost: whether on an individual project basis or as your 'in-house' attorney for a fixed monthly retainer. I don't bill by the hour because my clients are served best when they don't have to watch the clock!*
>
> *I take a proactive approach to helping my clients recognise dangerous situations before problems arise. Unlike most attorneys, I also actively network on my clients' behalves and strategize with them for future growth through strategic partnerships. At the negotiation table, I focus on creating a win/win scenario for all parties while protecting my client (instead of killing the deal).*
>
> *If you are interested in what I can do to help your business, or just to see how we can help each other in a networking context, please do not hesitate to contact me.*

What I like is that Todd clearly identifies his prospective clients and their pain points, and then focuses on what makes his own service special: his willingness to work on a project fee basis rather than billable hours, mutual networking support, and help in strategizing for growth. He reminds readers of the legal dangers lurking and creates a sense that under his wing, you're safe.

You, too, want to build your messages about yourself or your organization on solid ground. Developing the substance for good communication empowers you to reach the people you want to reach more effectively – and at least as important, inspires you to review and improve your own work, service or product.

# Chapter 10

# Writing for the Spoken Word

● ● ● ● ● ● ● ● ● ● ● ● ● ● ● ● ● ● ● ● ● ● ● ● ● ● ● ● ● ● ● ● ● ● ● ● ● ● ● ● ● ●

## *In This Chapter*

▶ Constructing a powerful elevator pitch

▶ Drafting and delivering presentations

▶ Planning and scripting video

▶ Planning what to say in challenging situations

● ● ● ● ● ● ● ● ● ● ● ● ● ● ● ● ● ● ● ● ● ● ● ● ● ● ● ● ● ● ● ● ● ● ● ● ● ● ● ● ● ●

*Y*ou need to know two main things when writing speeches, presentations and scripts:

✔ They need to be written

✔ They need to be spoken

That may seem ridiculously obvious, but take these rules seriously and you're way ahead of the game, whatever yours is. Most people assume they'll rise to the occasion and wing much of what they say when they're on stage or just introducing themselves. Or, they write a speech as if it were a piece of literature and then are surprised at how hard it is to deliver it well.

Whatever the length or stakes of your spoken piece – from an elevator speech that lasts just a few seconds to a formal presentation – the planning and writing process I cover in this chapter gives you the foundation you need.

## *Elevating Your Elevator Speech*

The *elevator speech,* or *elevator pitch,* is an indispensable business tool. The name derives from the concept of giving a speech in the time it takes to travel in an elevator (lift). Think of it as a speech in miniature to introduce yourself in networking and other professional situations. Take it everywhere. If you don't think you need an elevator speech, you're not getting out enough!

The challenge is to create a super-concise spoken statement that tells the person you're talking to who you are, what you do, and what that means to him or her.

Not that long ago, the typical recommendation was for a pitch up to 30 seconds long. Then 20 seconds became the preferred norm. But things keep speeding up. My best current advice is to aim for 10 to 15 seconds. You can have an additional 10 seconds or so in reserve and use it if you sense a good audience reaction, but the 10 to 15 second version must stand on its own.

That short space leaves a lot unsaid, no matter how much you drill down to a core message. But brevity is good. Effective elevator speeches are conversation starters. If you can provoke a little curiosity and generate a question, you hit the mark.

If helpful, think of your elevator pitch as an oral tweet. A 140-character length message actually produces about 10 seconds spoken aloud.

To create a new elevator speech or improve an existing one, use the same framework that works for emails, proposals and blogs. The following sections tweak the process to suit the style and demands of spoken communication.

## Defining your goal

Every person and every situation may differ, but essentially, aim to connect your elevator speech with someone you don't yet know – or even more importantly, *someone who that person knows* – who may share an interest or link you to an opportunity you want.

Take a broad, relationship-building view of this idea. Trust that there is nothing you can say that will land you a job or consulting offer on the spot. Rather, aim to explore mutual interests. Your goal is to identify meeting points that may be purely professional, or more personal (like a common interest in antique cars); and if the outlook is promising, to find an opportunity to follow up later and build a relationship.

Expert networkers always listen to the other person very carefully and look immediately for ways they can benefit him. And they are alert to signals that the other person can connect them to someone else they want to know.

## Defining your audience

You can't do a good job on an elevator speech unless you think through your audience's perspective: what interests them, what they want to know, their pain points, and why they'd want to know you.

Of course generally with elevator pitches, you don't have a single specific person in mind, so think in terms of groups rather than individuals. (See Chapter 2 for pointers on audience analysis.)

Just because you're defining a group, however, doesn't mean you can be vague or general. Different groups have different characteristics. You can easily anticipate that lawyers have very different interests than painters, for example. But both may be interested in accounting strategies or intellectual property law.

 Analyzing your goal and potential audience gives you a big bonus: it shows you where to show up – the places, events, and occasions in which to invest your time, network and find the people you want to tell your story to.

## Strategizing your content

After you work on your core value statement (which I discuss in Chapter 9), you may be almost ready to launch your elevator speech. Scan through your core message to find a statement that comes close to expressing the single most important thing you want to get across. Then re-imagine it in words that work for the ear. (See the sidebar '10 Essentials for producing video' later in this chapter for specific writing tips.) For example, consider a value statement from Chapter 9:

### Jim White

*Artist, art historian and administrator with experience and advanced training in archiving, preservation and photography. Special expertise in designing computer systems to accomplish administrative work more efficiently and economically. Excellent interpersonal skills, adept at training people to use new technology cheerfully.*

If Jim went to a meeting of museum administrators, he might choose to say:

*Hi, I'm Jim White. I'm a technology specialist for the arts. I create computer systems that save museums a ton of money by handling administrative work more efficiently. Right now I'm looking for a staff opportunity.*

Jim's work here was to recycle the content into a conversational, easy-to-say, and somewhat memorable statement that centers on his most important asset.

The first imperative of a good written speech, whatever its length, is to *write* it – on paper or your computer. This lets you look at, edit and refine it. The second imperative is to *say* it. There's no substitute for speaking it aloud because it's ultimately an oral product and must be further edited based on sound.

Of course you want your speech to sound spontaneous, especially if it's an elevator pitch, so there's a third imperative: *practice.*

But you don't necessarily need to recite what you crafted word for word. More important, you need to completely absorb your message so without stress, you can adapt it to the occasion and the person you're talking to.

If you haven't worked on a core value statement and are starting from scratch on your elevator speech, think intensively about who you help. Whatever your product or service, ultimately someone benefits. Figure out how and what those benefits are. Think also about what in your work you're passionate about, and what makes you feel proudest.

Tailor elevator speeches to the person, or group. A search engine optimization expert may tell this to an audience of marketing directors:

> *I'm Marian Smith, and my mission is to get businesses right on top of Google search results. I'm the marketing department's secret weapon.*

While to a roomful of entrepreneurs, she may say:

> *I'm Marian Smith, and my company is a one-stop shop for online marketing, websites and social media support. We level the playing field for you – and do it affordably. And we're whizzes at SEO.*

Here are a few more representative elevator pitches to stir your thinking.

> *I'm a personal trainer who specializes in working with older women who feel out of shape. I give them custom programs they're comfortable with and can learn to do on their own. A few sessions with me can make an amazing difference in their lives.*

> *I'm a financial planner. I believe financial planning shouldn't be a service reserved for the super-rich, so I work by telephone to make good advice very affordable. I show people how to handle everything from paying for college to financing retirement and buying what they want.*

Develop your own mini-pitches with these sure-fire strategies:

- ✔ Be as specific as you can; generalizations make you sound like everybody else

- ✔ Use short words and sentences, and craft them to sound like natural speech, not a memorized statement

- ✔ Make it memorable, easy to repeat

- ✔ Rev up your spirits and voice to sound positive and enthusiastic and lively

- ✔ Infuse your words with your passion for what you do

- ✔ Support your message with good body language and facial expressions

- ✔ Practice it to the point where you sound spontaneous

Good elevator speeches encourage the listener to ask a specific follow-up question: 'How do you do that?' 'How can you consult effectively by telephone?' 'What kind of opportunity are you interested in?' 'How does it work?'

And elevator speeches lend themselves to closing with a direct question yourself. To any of the examples I cite above, you can with suitable variation say, 'Do you know anyone who needs that?'

## Representing your organization and yourself

When you introduce yourself as a representative of your company or other organization, you speak for it. Often focusing on yourself isn't appropriate when you're talking to potential customers or industry groups. But do identify your role. For example:

> I'm John James and I'm COO of Dempster & Dove. We're a local company that builds miniature tractors for suburban homeowners . . . My role is . .

Your description of the organization should ideally be a 15-second expression of core value created in much the same way as a personal elevator pitch. It should meet the same criteria as a personal pitch – memorability, sharp focus, enthusiastic tone. Your company may have a ready-made pitch, a way of explaining the organization that you can adapt.

If you're the owner of a one-person enterprise, you can speak in your own name or the company's and use the editorial 'we' if you wish:

> I'm Jean Leonard, and my company is Amateur Aerodynamics. We help airplane hobbyists increase their flying range . . .

If you're looking for a job or a career transition, it's fine to say so clearly. Help your conversation partner by being specific about your need. 'I'm looking for a marketing job' is far less likely to gain a nibble than:

> *I'm a 10-year veteran of the financial services industry and I'm working on an extra degree in marketing because that's what I really want to do. I'm looking to move into marketing now at a place where my experience would be valued. Can you think of anyone I might talk to?*

No guarantees, but if you're in the right place, the person you're speaking with is likely to glance around the room to find you a match.

Don't forget that in an elevator speech situation, the people you talk to are just as eager as you are to make a new connection and to be heard. Act as an attentive and responsive listener. If you can help someone else in even a small way, take the opportunity. Great networkers follow up an introduction by sending a relevant clipping or link, or information about a travel destination or something else that came up. Or if the exchange is mutually promising, an invitation for coffee.

Aim to be the last person to introduce yourself. Listen with total concentration to what the other person says without thinking about what you're going to say when it's your turn. (You don't need to – you're prepared.) Active listening creates a bond. It empowers you to find common ground and adapt your own self-intro to the other person.

# Preparing and Giving Presentations

As presentation coaches often point out, many people view public speaking as literally worse than death. I've never seen the research on this, but it does seem that the prospect of presenting terrifies most people. But effective presenting is more and more essential to today's business culture, so you need to get over it!

Here's the tried and true way presenting well and comfortably: preparation followed by practice.

Many books are written about presentation skills (notably *Voice and Speaking Skills For Dummies* by Judy Apps and *Presentations For Dummies* by Malcolm Kushner), so I focus on ideas to put the process into perspective as a writing challenge and make it easier to succeed.

## Planning what to say

Just as for an elevator pitch, make decisions for your presentations based on your goal and your audience. What do you want to do? Motivate? Inspire? Sell something? Share information? Impress with your expertise? Change behavior? Each goal calls for different content, whatever the subject.

The more closely you define your goal, the better the guidance you give yourself. For example, when you want to share information, think through *why* you want to share it. Wanting your audience to work harder and smarter is different from aiming to sign audience members up for one-on-one coaching. The first goal demands that you motivate the audience and deliver practical how-to information. To accomplish the second, you calibrate how much information to give away to entice audience members to want more.

*Who* you're giving the information to is the other half of the planning equation. If you're a scientist, you naturally present different material to other professionals as opposed to a lay audience interested in something useful or fun. Give real thought to what your audience wants to know, worries about, and cares about.

Unless you are a technical professional talking to people just like you, presentations are not usually the medium for deep, detailed, complex material. Despite how most teaching is still done, oral learning by itself is not very effective. And onscreen visuals and video in the way that most people use them don't help much.

Always the best rule of thumb: Keep it simple. When you plan a presentation, start at the end. What do you most want your audience to walk away with and remember?

Try to crystallize a *theme* for your presentation. Framing all material with a point of view, and putting things into perspective, is far more effective than giving them 'just the facts'. Most of us feel we're already drowning in information. We want to be told what the data, or product, or idea means.

Try the Hollywood approach of expressing your theme in one sentence. Billion dollar movies are funded based on sentences such as, 'Boy robot and girl robot fall in love and want a baby' A business equivalent? Perhaps for an audience of talent managers, 'Invest in cross-cultural experiences because it produces better managers for tomorrow.' For a new product, your theme can be as simple as 'Invest in this gizmo because it shaves 11 per cent off production costs.' Build your theme with the classic, simple structure – beginning, middle, end.

### Beginning well

Use an opening anecdote, provided it's relevant and you're sure your audience will receive it well. Your personal story may provide an idea. If not, try what many professional speechwriters do: ask all your friends if they have a good anecdote about the subject, the venue, or your audience's profession. But never tell a joke that can be interpreted as laughing at the audience. It's okay to laugh at yourself. See Chapter 9 for much more on the power of storytelling.

More essential than an anecdote is to use your opening to tell your listeners *what* you're going to share and *why* it's important to them.

### Middling well

Just as for an email or other document, brainstorm the solid middle content that will accomplish your goal with the specific audience. Keep to your theme and organize the material in a logical, easy-to-follow sequence. Easier said than done, I know. Remember that you don't need to deliver the universe – just one small focused asteroid is plenty.

One organizational method that works well for presentations is to create a list of the areas that relate to your subject, much like you create a list of subheads for a written piece, as I explain in Chapter 8. If you were introducing a medical device, for example, you might list:

*1. What the discovery is, briefly, and why it matters; who it will help*

*2. How the discovery was made*

*3. What collaborations were involved*

*4. Interesting surprises or challenges that arose during the process*

*5. Where things now stand*

*6. Next steps*

*7. Future vision: Why it's important, who it will help, and how; if relevant, the audience can participate*

For many subjects, a numbered approach works well and keeps you organized: 'Here are the six most important changes that will affect your future in the advertizing industry.' Or 'Here are four ways this new software will change how you handle conflict.' Most audiences love this strategy because they can tick off the items as you move along. Numbering gives them a sense of accomplishment and is easier on the brain. Staying attentive is hard work!

### Ending well

As appropriate, state your grand conclusion, sum up what you said, and reinforce the takeaway you want. You might bring home to your audience why your subject matters to them and, if relevant how to take the next step or put it to work in their practical lives. Sometimes it's appropriate to close with an energizing vision of the future as it relates to your talk. But don't rehash the entire speech and bore your listeners. Keep your ending brief.

As the saying goes, it ain't over 'til it's over. A good ending often requires that you prep for questions. Preparing for the Q&A helps you deliver more confidently, too. If you inspire tough questions, see that as a plus. But have answers ready. Politicians and CEOs do this and so should you. Brainstorm, with colleagues if possible, to figure out the likely questions. Especially try to anticipate the one question you hope no one will pose and know how to respond.

## Crafting your presentations with writing

Other than rocket science and brain surgery, perhaps, no thought is so complex that you cannot express it in clear, simple language. If you find being simple and clear a challenge, you may need to re-think your subject and ideas.

Writing helps you think through your presentation content and approach, so start with a piece of paper or your computer screen. Depending on how you work best draft a full script or create an outline that covers all your main points. Neither the draft or outline should accompany you to the event. Aim never to read a speech unless you must. Maintaining audience contact is much more important than remembering every word, or even every thought. Do aim to:

- Use basic, natural language as you do in conversation: short words, short sentences.

- Build in natural pauses – the oral equivalent of white space – between ideas, sections, and important sentences to help people absorb what you say.

- Say your words aloud as you write and listen for an easy cadence; when you find awkward hard-to-say patches, or you run out of breath, rewrite and check the sound again.

- Avoid using too many statistics or numbers because they dull the senses and numb the brain.

- Use metaphors and other comparisons to make your point: 'The applicants could have filled a football field' is better than citing a figure.

- Use graphic language whenever you can to engage the emotions and paint pictures. Check a thesaurus for alternative words to spark things up.

- Time your presentation to fit the probable space, allowing for introductions and Q&A as applicable. Identify areas to skip should you run on too long so that you don't short change your close.

- Have a few content options in mind: when you see your audience losing interest, speed on to something else.

## *Integrating visuals*

Notice that I've not yet mentioned PowerPoint, Prezi or their cousins. And for good reason: visuals should always be treated as support for your message, not the main show.

Don't use PowerPoint or any other presentation system to plan and write what you'll say. Your message becomes distorted when you try to jam it into a limiting, structured format. Don't make decisions about what to include or omit based on pre-allocated pieces of space or flashy templates.

Plan and write your presentation and then think about supporting visuals. Or jot down notes on possible slides as you go. When you prepare the slides, don't cut and paste onto them the editorial content you wrote: Treat each slide as an individual communication and figure out what (few) words should be included and what visuals help make the same point. Avoid throwing your whole speech onto the screen.

You are the central focus when you speak. People are there to see and hear you, not stare at a screen. Never read from your slides. And never distribute your handout before you speak because it distracts your listeners, who leap ahead to the end and then wait impatiently for you to finish.

Much more detailed information on using PowerPoint awaits you in *PowerPoint ForDummies* by Doug Lowe, but here are a few principles to guide you:

- ✔ Keep every slide simple and easy to absorb at a glance: no long lists of bullets and sub-bullets, no complex charts and graphs, no sets of statistics.

- ✔ Use visuals to translate those statistics or ideas into graphic form – for instance, if you're trying to explain the size of a nanometer, show comparisons such as a human hair and other objects.

- ✔ Keep fonts simple and LARGE so that people at the back can read the material. How large depends on the size of your room and audience.

- ✔ Keep graphics simple and consistent in style and colors. Check for legibility *before* you present to an audience to be sure the text projects well and is easy to read.

- ✔ Use the 'action' feature of presentation systems for dynamic visuals to show, for example, how one element of a graph line moves over time. But use animation features sparingly so they are not distracting.

- ✔ Incorporate brief video clips as available to liven things up, but be sure they're worth the watching time and support your theme.

- ✔ Test everything out before show time to make sure the technology is working, especially if you emailed the deck. Video clips in particular can come undone. The savviest presenters stand ready to deliver without PowerPoint and Internet access altogether because you just never can absolutely depend on them.

Don't drive yourself crazy by getting absorbed in the mechanics of presenting your material. Focus on the substance. In fact, a good way to stay grounded during a presentation is to use your slides as an organizational tool. Set up headlines and subheads that key you to remember important points. This keeps your audience with you, too. For example, use a succession of slides that just say things like: The Problem, What We Did, How it Worked, Our Conclusions, What's Next – each with maybe just a few lines of copy.

## Standing and delivering

The most important strategies for delivering powerful presentations are preparation and practice. When you do your homework and shape your message to audience expectations and your own goals – first in writing and then by practicing the message to internalize it – you have the right content and confidence to boot.

Practice is how dancers, musicians, actors, and athletes remember what to do when they're on stage or in the sporting arena. Rehearse as many times as necessary to feel comfortable and master your own sequence.

Generally, speaking without notes is ideal, but it's fine to use cue-notes as reminders, provided you don't stare at them for minutes or rustle through them to find your place.

There are a great many angles to creating and giving effective presentations, which you realize if you know an actor, have worked with a voice coach, or have experimented yourself with even a short speech. Practice won't make perfect, and doesn't need to. But awareness of some useful techniques can go a long way. Following are my ten favorite ideas for feeling professional and confident.

✔ Warm up: many professional speakers have an easy exercise routine they do before presenting; and many warm up their voices as well.

✔ Stand, don't sit – even for giving an elevator speech when practical.

✔ Keep your posture straight and balanced, but not stiff; no rocking or fidgeting or pacing (but natural hand gestures are excellent).

✔ Breathe deeply, from very low in your diaphragm.

✔ Radiate positive energy and pleasure at being there.

✔ Vary the pitch and tone of your voice.

✔ Maintain voice energy: don't trail off at the end of sentences or end with an upward inflection that sounds like you're asking a question

✔ Focus on one person at a time, perhaps for five second intervals.

✔ Notice how people react. If eyes glaze over, or half your audience is looking at their smart phones, move in a new direction.

✔ Don't sweat what you forget: even if you skip a major point, you're the only one who knows. Just focus on saying the rest with conviction.

TRY IT

# Just relax already!

Try any or all of the following techniques to help you relax and project enthusiasm.

✔ **The I-like-you trick:** Remind yourself before going on that you like the people you're about to address and that they are eager to hear the information you'll deliver.

✔ **A hypnotherapist's trick:** Right before you are to speak, imagine you've already delivered your talk and it was hugely successful. Imagine how that feels – how you'll stand, smile, walk, hold your head. See it and feel it. Then glide into actually speaking, carrying that feeling with you.

✔ **An actor's trick:** Just before beginning, or at key points, say to yourself, 'I'm about to share something exciting with you.' Your enthusiasm grows, and it shows.

If public speaking is important to you professionally, perhaps as an excellent way to grow your business, give yourself some solid grounding. Many good speakers value their experience with Toastmaster's International. Courses in voice or presentation techniques are often available through local colleges, universities, and other educational institutions.

## Scripting for Video

I recall hearing a communications professional report that, after finding that his company's expensive, beautifully produced videos drew only a fraction of the YouTube viewers who watched his mailroom clerk's videos, he put the clerk in charge of production.

Are production values – good picture, sound and scripting – dead? In the name of authenticity, do people prefer rough amateur quality-free video made on smart phones?

Certainly people have become sceptical of slick promotional material, both print and video. Digital technology makes video easier to create as well as less expensive and more accessible every day. But the fact that almost anyone can produce video means that to reach people and accomplish goals, yours has to be better and better. This may require some supplementary equipment and an awareness of production values. But fortunately, it doesn't mean unaffordability, because the everyday technology keeps radically improving.

Writing is one of the key ways to produce successful videos. *Scriptwriting,* however, encompasses not just writing words that someone speaks, but planning the *visuals* – what appears on the screen.

The need for good visuals is quickly apparent the first time you write a script. For every instant of narration, something must be up on the screen. During my first experience, I came to the editing room with 15 pages of carefully written and recorded voiceover and a few days of on-site shooting. The editor laid down the first two minutes of sound and said, 'OK, what's the picture'? We had only 10 seconds worth of relevant footage. Out went the script.

According to the nature of your project (and budget), content can include talking heads (people speaking directly to the camera), live action (such as demonstrations of a process or something happening), cutaways (close-ups of models, charts, or details of the scene), still images, on-screen titles, animation, and more,

I assume you don't have a production company on hand. My strategies in this section focus on basic ideas that you can apply to your social media résumé, website, or YouTube-bound videos to spotlight your product, service, idea, or anything else.

With video, keep it simple. Pick subjects that support your goals and that you can handle with the equipment and know-how on hand.

## *Introducing yourself with video*

Video is a powerful way to liven up a website or social media page. Someone – perhaps you – talking on camera about your business, product, service, or career dream is a much more personal introduction than written copy. You and your business become real to the viewer.

However, not everyone comes across well in living, speaking media. Video is especially high-risk if you plan a talking-head speech with the camera focused fully on you the whole time. You can work out a simple version of a Teleprompter, such as cue cards or pages with notes outside the camera's view, rather than reading. Or try for spontaneous. But coming across as warm and natural without some talent or training is very difficult.

So record yourself for a few minutes speaking directly to a camera and then take a hard look at how you come across on video. Ask colleagues for honest input. If the piece doesn't show you off to advantage, either:

✔ Scrap the 'here I am' video for the time being

✔ Do a really short version

Twenty or thirty seconds of video is usually enough for an intro. Think of it as an elevator speech with a camera. Your actual elevator speech, as I cover earlier in 'Elevating Your Elevator Speech', may give you the core of your video message. Also consider drawing on your personal value statement, or your personal story, both of which I talk about in Chapter 9.

What often works best is to talk about something that ignites your own genuine enthusiasm – for example, your passion for your work. I once reviewed a script for a travel agent that began, 'Hello, I'm Viola Smith, and I run a full-service travel agency.' I suggested instead, 'I'm Viola Smith, and what I love about my work is rescuing people from the travel adventures they didn't expect.' After your lead is in place, the rest falls naturally. Viola went on to give a few examples of extreme rescue, like finding a flight from Afghanistan for a family at 4 in the morning, and replacing a traveller's stolen money and documents in time for him to get home for his daughter's birthday. In less than a minute she demonstrated her problem-solving know-how, showed how far she goes for clients, and connected with prospects. Who hasn't had a disastrous travel experience and doesn't anticipate another?

A simple line or two introducing yourself is fine for a video opener – you don't need a flashy intro or magical words. But use your best writing-thinking skills with core value and story techniques (see Chapter 9) to come up with the right words you can say with conviction.

## Sharing expertise

Most people go straight to the internet to learn things: how to fix a computer problem, how to treat a pulled muscle, how to make a quilt. If you're good at something or have specialized knowledge, you probably already possess excellent subject matter for how-to videos.

If you think disseminating such videos is worth your while for establishing expertise or authority, concentrate on communicating your knowledge or advice as clearly as possible. If appropriate for your subject, create a step-by-step set of visual-plus-narrative instructions.

How-we-do-it videos are also good enhancements to your organization's website or blog. Whether you make boots or art glass or fix machinery, how-to tips can interest your target audiences. They can also communicate what makes your product unique and perhaps expensive: special materials, a demanding process, expert knowledge.

Video offers a lot of potential for service businesses, too, by providing glimpses of what you do and how. A training company can show clips of its workshops in action, for example, which is far more effective for marketing than endless descriptions. A non-profit can use video to showcase its accomplishments, focusing on specific people who its work has helped. A corporation can use this technique too, for sharing their contributions to good causes, or highlighting how employees give their time to volunteer work. With staff members alone this use of video really helps amplify a team spirit makes excellent material for customers via websites and social media, too.

## *Writing the script*

Even if the subject is 'you' as the sole talking head, don't expect to set the camera up and wing it.

The most important principle for business videos is to script before you shoot. Otherwise you won't know what you want to record and are likely to end up with a random assortment of material that doesn't add up to the message you mean to deliver. You may succeed if you shoot first, think later, but the process will be far more expensive and time-consuming than shooting to script. Production is typically the most expensive part of the video-making process, so strive for minute-by-minute efficiency.

Preparing you for video production is beyond the scope of this chapter. (See *Digital Video For Dummies* by Keith Underdahl or *Digital SLR Video and Filmmaking For Dummies* by John Carucci.) But I do give some basic grounding from the writing/planning perspective in '10 Essentials for producing video.'

# 10 Essentials for producing video

The following guidelines assume your project is a marketing-type video that includes some live action, talking heads, and narration because that combination works well for many business needs. But you can adapt the ideas for something simpler – or more complicated.

1. As with all business writing, start with a clear idea of why you're producing your video, whether it's mini or maxi in nature. What do you want to accomplish? Who do you want to see it? What exactly is your message? See Chapter 2 for more planning insights.

2. Decide on your production style or treatment before writing or recording anything. Plan, for example, for a narrated piece containing one or more interviews, live action, animation and so on. Brainstorm the content possibilities that the treatment suggests, decide which are realistic and worthwhile, and sequence them.

3. When you're ready to write, use a sheet of paper or electronic equivalent divided vertically down the middle. Label the left-hand column 'Picture,' and the right-hand column 'Words.' Word's Insert Table tool works nicely for creating simple grids within word-processing documents. A split page keeps you focused on your video's parallel needs and timeframes. (You can also use a storyboard like professionals sometimes, but not always, create. And you can use specific screenwriting software, but it's expensive and not necessary.) It's also smart to leave a narrow column on the far left to record time codes, essential to the editing process; and a narrow area on the far right for notes to help you remember things.

4. After you have a rough, preliminary script that includes the words and your picture ideas, create a shot list that covers every scene you need. Ultimately the shot list should include all the logistics the camera crew (or you) needs to set up, shoot and move on, in a strict timeframe. Be sure to prepare the people you're shooting! Recognize that you'll shift your script as you shoot, and juggling between words and pictures is a continuing process right till the end. Note that even if you aim for a documentary-style video, you still need to know what to shoot and what you basically want onscreen people to say.

*(continued)*

*(continued)*

5. After videotaping everything on your shot list, totally familiarize yourself with the video footage and other materials, such as stills or charts, so you know what's on hand for the 'Picture' side of the ledger. You can never have a blank screen. If it's just you-the-talking-head, just write 'me' in the Picture column. On the other hand, if you're incorporating live action, those segments may contain all the sound needed you want and narration may be unnecessary.

6. Find a really good lead, something intriguing or interesting about your subject. Make sure it has a good visual to carry the words. Or just start with the strong visual. Sometimes a startling fact or statistic or quote works well as an opening graphic, and it can be shown onscreen without words for a powerful opening.

7. Work your way through your script section by section, matching up picture and words. Aim to narrate or explain as little as possible and let the picture tell as much as it can. Don't repeat orally what's self-evident visually. Use the narration to keep things in perspective, explain or amplify as necessary.

8. For narration, distil the essence of the idea or fact into as few words as possible, but don't overlook chances to use graphic, evocative language.

9. Use short sayable words and simple sentences. Break grammar rules freely. Fragments are fine, as are one-word sentences, if the result sounds good and meaning is clear. Avoid complicated literary or other deep thoughts.

10. Edit, edit, edit until the narration reads like liquid. Have someone else read it; listen and edit and rephrase. If you record narration before editing, listen carefully and rewrite again if your narrator stumbles or sounds awkward. If you're working with professional editors or other specialists, listen to their suggestions too.

As the video takes shape and picture combines with words, look again to see if you have more words than you need to carry meaning. Or the opposite may be true: you may need some or more narration to ensure clarity. If you have the opportunity to add music, graphics, and titles, see contributing to those processes as part of your writing job too, if possible.

Video ideally *is* a team endeavor, and an exciting one. Even if you're a one-person operation and plan to accomplish everything with a smart phone or small digital camera, knowing how to develop a larger team effort with specialists is still helpful.

If you don't have a team of specialists to work with, build one with colleagues who have good ideas and a willingness to experiment. Ingenuity and imagination can to some extent make up for specialized technologies.

If you're basically your own crew, rely on the following production essentials:

- ✔ **Lighting is the big difference between interesting, clear video imagery and indifferent visuals.** Invest in a light you can position and adjust. Take the time and effort to light your subject carefully.

- ✔ **Sound quality counts hugely.** The biggest technical complaint about video is poor sound. People can apparently forgive not-so-good picture but hate having to strain their ears to catch or interpret the words. Look for help on recording sound. Seriously consider investing in a good, versatile microphone. The ones built into cameras and computers are not good enough.

- ✔ **When interviewing people on camera, frame really good questions.** Pose open-ended questions – not 'Did the program work well for you?' but 'How did this program change your life?' And ask with the tone you want the person to take: a bored routine sounding question earns an answer that matches.

In addition to using the books recommended a few paragraphs earlier, look for free help from camera or video stores. Tell them what you want to do and how you see your needs and ask for options. You will probably get some good advice and a bit of education.

# Scripting Yourself for Practical Purposes

Writing, with the planning that goes along with it, gives you a practical advantage in many spoken-word situations. Depending on spontaneous interaction when the stakes are high is risky. But using your writing skills to pre-plan your responses can help you outpace your competitors. Following are two scenarios where self-scripting is particularly effective.

## *Composing talking points for fun and profit*

If you ever wonder how CEOs and politicians equip themselves to win debates, be good interviewees, and prepare for press conferences, the answer is likely *talking points.* Large organizations also use talking points to ensure that all the executives, or everyone in the company, are on the same wave length in what they say about the company to the public.

Talking points give you a beautiful tool for any kind of confrontation, or any situation where you may have to think on your feet. The idea is to make a list of the things you want to get across. This demands thought.

For example, if you're preparing for a job interview, think through your best matching points and examples. Then write them out, preferably just a line or two for each, limiting yourself to a single page. Someone applying for a sales manager job may list:

> *7 years' experience in a similar industry, know many people*
>
> *Achieved 14 per cent increase in my territory's sales over previous person*
>
> *Appointed assistant sales manager a year ago*
>
> *Named 'Salesperson of the Year' three times*
>
> *Train new sales recruits*
>
> *Leaving job because of limited upward opportunity*
>
> *Hold business degree from XX*
>
> *Board member of local Heart Association*
>
> *Former board member of local school district*

Of course you have more to say on each point, and must think about each in depth, but the idea is to *know in advance what you want to get across* during the course of the interview, or other situation, and crystallize it in a statement you can remember. Then you can draw on this mental material to answer questions effectively. You also create a checklist of your 'advantage' points and gracefully add all or some at the interview's end ('You might also like to know that . . .').

You can also use a politician's trick to 'bridge' to something you want to say or to avoid putting yourself in an unfavorable light. ('I don't have direct experience with that strategy, but I did work with YYY, for three years and came to find out . . . '). Take care not to appear evasive if you use this technique, however. It's important to convey that you are straightforward and honest.

The talking points approach is equally useful in preparing for any confrontation. When you ask for a raise, express disagreement, air a problem or recommend an unpopular course of action, planning gives you confidence and underwrites your success. You'll know the important points to make and be ready to respond with answers when questioned or challenged. Create talking points for your sales presentations, too.

## *Scripting telephone messages that work*

Good salespeople script their telephone and in-person pitches and give more thought than most to crafting telephone messages that prompt call-backs. The key, according to my favorite sales coach, Jeff Goldberg, is to provoke curiosity. Long detailed messages that explain exactly who you are and why you're calling don't generate interest. Better is a short message such as:

> *Hi Jack, my name is Lynn Barrows. My phone number is . . . Jack, I'm calling you regarding IBM. Once again, my number is . . .'*

'IBM' in this instance is a current or past client and the link when Jack returns the call is that Lynn has helped IBM in a way that will also benefit Jack. Of course, the relationship with the well-known company must be genuine.

The actual sales pitch, when Jack calls, keys off Lynn's elevator speech: short, benefits-oriented and memorable. Which could be a good general guideline to inform everything you write.

And my last word on speaking your script: *Smile when you say it.* You can write the best elevator speech or presentation or sales pitch in the land, but if you deliver it without conviction and enthusiasm, you won't succeed. Write what you believe – and believe in what you say.

# Part IV

# Writing for the Digital Universe

## *Top Five Things to Do Well When Writing for Digital Media*

- ✔ Strategize all elements of your online presence to advance your goals.
- ✔ Adapt your writing to on-screen readability guidelines.
- ✔ Give target audiences content they value.
- ✔ Build blogs on your personal strengths.
- ✔ Cut all empty rhetoric and deliver evidence.

For advice on applying good writing principles to your website, check out this free online article at http://eu.dummies.com/how-to/content/applying-good-writing-principles-to-your-business-.html.

## In this part . . .

- Strategize your online goals to guarantee your business's digital presence.

- Find your online voice and swat up on website-building, blog-keeping and social media updates.

# Chapter 11

# Evolving Your Writing for Online Media

*In This Chapter*

▶ Reworking your words for today's wired world

▶ Strategizing your online program and goals

▶ Adapting good writing techniques for the Internet

*N*o question, the digital revolution has changed how we communicate – and even how we *think* about communication. Snail mail turns into email. Newspapers and magazines morph into online formats, marketing brochures into websites, advertising into social media word-of-mouth. Even telephone use declines as texting grows.

Mass media campaigns still exist, but the old top-down model – where professional communicators fuelled by big money organizations tell others what to buy and think – is fast being replaced by an 'everyman' model in which the digital universe gives every person who can access it a voice. At the same time, organizations must become more adept at harnessing the new tools to reach their audiences in more personal ways.

One key element remains constant. Everyone still depends on words. Delivery systems evolve and speed up but communication is inescapably language based. No matter how effectively visuals supplement your message, you need words to transmit all but your simplest thoughts. Good writing is in greater demand than ever.

## Smart searching

*Search engine optimization* (SEO) Is critically important to online writing because you want people to find you. Search engines such as Google rank material by its degree of value to users. Engines continually refine their criteria and algorithms to achieve this goal.

Rather than try to beat the system, work with it. Always provide value to your own audiences in your website, blog, and other electronic communication by contributing real substance that reflects their needs and interests. Keep posting new, fresh material. Check out online resources for how to use keywords well. Incorporate them into your blogs as well as website pages. However, don't try to game the system by cramming a ton of keywords and search terms into your material. The search engines do not want you to do this, and Google, for one, will penalize you for such trickery.

Other SEO strategies include growing the number of your *in-bound links* – the number of other sites that cite yours, and the number of times your material is referred to. For much more, see *Search Engine Optimization For Dummies* by Peter Kent.

In fact the single word that drives marketing, advertising, public relations, and social media today is *content.* The connected world is ravenous for written material: Information, ideas, tips, facts, entertainment. If you can contribute digital content people want to read, you're valuable. Moreover being a good content creator is to your personal and professional advantage.

Yesterday's question was: 'How can you persuade people to read what you write and act on it?' Today's question: 'How can you give people material that's so compelling, useful, and interesting that they come to you, want to do business with you or even become active members of your community?'

To use digital media to sell something, get your point across, influence, collaborate and inform, you must write well. In fact every channel is so flooded with messages yours must be especially well-crafted to succeed.

This chapter shows you how to adapt good writing techniques to digital media and use it to accomplish goals. The strategies apply to websites, blogs, online profiles and postings, social media, and even microblogs like Twitter, with some variation.

They're also relevant to podcasts and video which also demand well-planned writing,

And trust me, even if I don't address it specifically, my advice applies to the newest and shiniest online tool that's prominent as you read this.

# Gaining Perspective on Digital Media

The impact of the digital revolution on traditional media – and all business writing, in fact – has been so strong it's almost hard to see. Reader expectations have changed during the last 15 or 20 years because of email, websites, blogs, and social media. Established media venues have responded by revamping their techniques and strategies. Not always quickly or willingly.

## Changing significantly – and yet very little

The shift toward less formal, simpler and more concise writing is part of this picture. So is the trend to use graphic techniques to direct the reader's attention and clarify meaning: headlines, subheads, white space, color, and all the rest (I explore both topics in Chapter 3). Also, print formats are being made more interactive by inviting opinion and response and directing readers to connected Internet material.

On the other hand, all the principles and techniques of good business writing for traditional media apply to digital. The message delivery system has changed radically, but good writing has not and will not. The guidelines I present in the rest of this book apply to digital content, but in some ways more extremely, as I explain later in 'Shaping Your Writing for Digital Media'.

Don't for a nanosecond think that the ability to deliver a message with a flick of your finger justifies quick, careless online writing. People who read your websites, blogs, tweets, and posts on a screen, big or small, are the most selective readers of all (even if they're not fully aware of being so). You're competing for their attention with countless millions of other people. If your message lacks the right substance, they may not come and they definitely won't stay. If it's badly written, you lose all credibility as well as the power to engage.

## Leveraging your digital power

Online media offers you so much access to the universe – and so much exposure – that every bit of content you send out into it merits thought and care.

If you're in business for yourself or want to be, opportunities abound. The Internet levels the playing field in many ways. A small startup can compete with established companies and often, with much bigger ones. Just a smattering of what you can accomplish if you run a business or work on contract:

- ✔ Establish your expertise and authority in a field, perhaps as a thought leader

- ✔ Make yourself findable locally, worldwide, or in the middle, to people who want what you offer

- ✔ Provide accessibility all week, every hour of the day, across international borders

- ✔ Promote your product or service in nearly infinite ways and find target audiences

- ✔ Interact in real time with customers and contacts

- ✔ Connect effectively with suppliers, collaborators, supporters, past clients, prospects

- ✔ Listen to and participate in conversations that enable you to understand your market and customers better

The virtual world is now so integrated with our life that you may forget that creating a new business with no office, perhaps no staff, and minimal resources is a new and amazing option. And this enormous shift is possible largely through the magic of words – supported by visuals, of course – but basically and most essentially by words.

Not-for-profit organizations have also discovered how to use the Internet to accomplish many of the same goals as corporate users, as well as additional ones: build support, maintain ongoing contact with audiences, generate understanding of issues, attract volunteers, and most of all, raise money.

If you work for a company or a not-for-profit organization but don't have specific responsibility for developing online media, the Internet gives you interesting opportunities nevertheless. You can:

- ✔ Build a personal support group internally and/or externally.

- ✔ Share or contribute your social media savvy to the common cause.

- ✔ Educate and train others about social media practices and uses.

- ✔ Blog or tweet on behalf of your company (with approval and in a positive spirit), showcasing your skills and insight.

- ✔ Scan your company's online presence and the environment to understand relevant issues, company goals, competitors and challenges.

- ✔ Listen and find good ideas to bring in, thus advancing your grasp of the market, customers and their problems.

You may belong to a generation that grew up with the Internet and find it an easy comfort zone. Your affinity for digital media may make you more valuable to your employer than you realize. The missed virtual opportunities you think obvious may be less obvious to the managers. Or they may not know how to implement a social media or blog program, or how to find the resources. If you can tie a digital idea to your organization's bottom line goals and offer to do the work – tactfully but enthusiastically – you may create a new role for yourself. I've seen more than a few people become official bloggers or social media coordinators for their organizations. This book gives you the necessary strategic thinking as well as techniques to hone your writing for new online opportunities. And because you already know your company better than any outside person does, you start with a big advantage over possible new recruits.

Don't forget how the Internet can benefit you personally. Your present situation may be secure and promising, but you're smart to always look to the future anyway. You may aim to build a personal following or a community, find collaborators, test the waters on a business idea, showcase your abilities, brand yourself, develop ways to turn a passion into a living, or secure your next job. Make e-media part of your individual career plan by using it strategically, starting with clear goals as I cover in the following section.

# *Strategizing Your Digital Media Program*

Using the Internet is so easy that most people totally fail to plan what they put on it. But today's connected culture works for you when you know what you want, select your target audiences, and figure out how to meet its needs.

Unless you want to use the various media purely for fun or to happen across new friends, invest your energy within a planned framework. Random blogging and tweets yield random results. A personal program that thoughtfully coordinates a website, blog, and other online networking can accomplish. . . almost anything. The following sections show you how to plan purposefully about where you want to go online and how to do it.

## *Thinking through your online goals*

In the earlier section 'Leveraging your digital power' I list a number of goals for both employed and self-employed people. Some may resonate with you, and you may have more of your own.

Start your online plan by deciding on your overall umbrella goal – for example, to amplify the number of leads in your pipeline by 20 per cent this year; or to launch a social media consulting service for small businesses.

Then establish a set of do-able sub-goals. To establish the social media service, your sub-goals, or action items, may include:

- ✔ Brand myself as an expert and problem-solver
- ✔ Make myself findable by people who need me in a 50-mile radius
- ✔ Build connections with business prospects
- ✔ Create relationships with people who can refer business
- ✔ Use online media to directly market and sell my service

Next, break down each sub-goal into specific activities that help accomplish it. To establish expertise and brand yourself, for example, you might create a website, blog about problems you solve, give advice through business networks like LinkedIn, tweet about industry events and insights, participate in relevant professional and interest groups where your customers may gather, and so on.

Of course, don't overlook all the options beyond the Internet, too. You can appear as a speaker in local venues, write a column for a local publication, or attend professional group meetings, for example.

No plan is accomplished overnight, and setting up a new business is an especially ambitious goal. Furthermore, social media campaigns and other online initiatives take time and sustained effort to work. But the central lesson holds: for business purposes, spend your online (and offline) time strategically within the framework of a defined mission. Make deliberate media choices and plan what you write about.

For example, if you're a visual artist, Facebook or Pinterest, a visually oriented social media site may be a better environment for you to show off your wares and share ideas than a business connection site. If you're building a career as a dance instructor, writing a regular blog about movies probably won't help as much as a blog related to dance.

Yes, you can make good arguments for expanding your circle of contacts and showing a more personal side. Just do so with purpose. Make thoughtful decisions, try them out and analyze the results.

One of the Internet's sterling qualities is how well it accommodates some trial and error. Plenty of books and tons of advice stand ready to help – but the truth is, none of the precepts are close to being set in stone. No one-size-fits-all formula exists. What works is to do first and evaluate results second.

Shifting direction or rewriting digital material costs pennies compared to what is needed to fix a publishing mistake or rework a multi-million dollar commercial. So innovate and experiment – but always without risking your long-range image. The online world is very public.

Think of ways to test-run your experiments past smaller audiences instead of entrenching yourself in an approach that may antagonize key audiences.

Ultimately, your online aim is to be consistent across platforms. Your website, blog, online profiles, Twitter feed and the rest of your online presence must all align for a unified image of the company or persona you choose to present. Your print materials should also reflect the same graphic look, including your logo and color choices, and the same basic representation of who you are (see Chapter 9 for ideas on how to identify yourself or your business). This consistency is what marketers mean by branding, and it is a perfectly affordable asset if you keep things simple.

## Attracting the online audiences you want

I talk in Chapter 2 about analyzing your target audiences and exploring all the factors that may affect the ways you reach them.

All the demographic and psychographic elements I suggest in Chapter 2 apply to traditional and electronic formats. You must decide on your ideal audiences and understand their needs. Your material must always answer the 'what's-in-it-for-me' question.

But the wired world has its own twists. Potential readers are infinitely more numerous online than with traditional media and yet also feel more abstract. And harder to envision. For online media the process is less *push out* – sending material to a defined group – and more *pull in*, earning readers who matter to you. These differences require new ways of thinking.

Imagine the entire Internet is spread out on an ocean as tiny outposts or islands. Flocks of birds fly above scanning for their own species' preferred food. To attract redheaded geese, if you so choose, you must offer them the right food. You must also send signals to tell them that you have what they want. You trust that if the first geese to land find the experience convenient and attractive, and the right food is there for them, they'll spread the word for you and more will come.

The analogy is simple: Choose your audiences, know what they want, give them the right product, and create good content, relevant to their needs. Send signals that you have the goods through appropriate social media channels, search engine optimization, email campaigns, and other means as appropriate.

Encourage word of mouth recommendations – always an important marketing tool but in the Internet age, the most powerful of all. Every study shows that more and more, people trust their peers for every kind of recommendation and advice. We look online to find advice and insights for just about everything we buy. In addition to keeping word of mouth in mind when you write your material, remember that you want to encourage others to blog about your product and share likes and dislikes. You can't really plan to 'go viral,' usually a random event, but your own activity in promoting other people with re-tweets, for example, can help stoke activity on your behalf.

Like the island that wants to attract redheaded geese, your business invariably faces competition, whatever you offer. So your product or service must not only be good, but the showcases you use – your website and supporting media – must be outstanding. That means well planned, well written, well designed, and user-oriented.

One of the biggest mistakes many business-owners make is to focus on finding one-shot buyers rather than building long-term relationships with those they already have. To sell more to an existing customer costs you a fraction of the investment demanded to capture a new one. Keep established customers coming back by:

- ✔ Offering new content that they value.

- ✔ Staying current with their problems and concerns; social media offers many ways to do this.

- ✔ Justifying customer trust with good service and fast response.

- ✔ Inviting input, comments, and sharing.

- ✔ Finding ways to stay in touch without becoming intrusive or annoying.

You're not, of course, restricted to a single audience in your online media program. If you make redheaded geese happy, you can also serve puffins, perhaps. They may show up as an 'unintended audience' so keeping an eye on your user analytics (a service offered by Google and others) gives you important insights to your best, as well as emerging, targets.

You can create separate website pages or other online content pieces for different audiences, but they can relate under one umbrella. Or maybe different sites are called for. Such decisions are yours to make, consciously.

If you're using the Internet not to promote a business but just to stake your place in the virtual sun, contribute to a hobby or passion or any other reason, the same principles hold. Know who you want to reach and create content that attracts and interests that audience.

# Turning Scanners into Readers

Today's readers and consumers enjoy an infinite array of choices. Whatever your purpose, you enjoy greater success if what you say you is clearer, more concise, and faster-moving than other people's material.

Your strategy for bringing in an audience and inspiring them to want more has two steps: Capture divers who are scouting for specific information by ensuring instant matches for their searches. Keep them by sustaining the momentum and providing a welcoming, convenient environment.

Search engine optimization is the most important tool for drawing in your audiences (see the earlier sidebar, 'Smart searching'). To keep your audiences with you once they've arrived at your site and meet their expectations, you can use a wide range of techniques. The following sections explore some of the top tools for giving your visitors a good experience.

## Adopting a share-it outlook

Finding ways to make money from websites and other Internet initiatives is an endless pursuit, but the medium's overwhelming tenor is to give away something valuable.

Many successful consultants and organizations have long found that providing their best advice online (or at least some of it) makes good marketing sense. People value genuine contributions to any field that interests them so this approach builds audiences. Your initial contribution may trigger high impact word of mouth response – achieving re-tweets is a prime example. Too much self-promotion, on the other hand, is quickly detected and avoided (see the later section 'Communicating credibility' for more).

Your best Internet playing card is to understand the value of what you know, no matter how esoteric or unusual it may be. Then decide on ways to share it online through blogging, tweeting, answering questions, participating in conversations, joining groups, or whatever other avenues you can imagine. (For a process to figure out your own best value, see Chapter 9.)

Be generous. Trust that what you give will be returned many fold.

## Clarifying your message

In addition to knowing your digital goals and understanding your audiences, you must know exactly *what* you want to communicate: your core message.

There's no substitute for creating a written statement to draw on for all your media ventures. Doing so enables you to identify the purpose of your website, blog, and other electronic ventures, guiding you through their development. Your statement informs your strategic use of social media and everything else you employ to promote a business or yourself, including your profile and elevator pitch.

In Chapter 9, I give you an in-depth list of questions to guide you through crafting a basic business message. In Chapter 12, I show you how to craft a mini-version of the message suited to websites. Investing time on your mini-message can pay real dividends.

## Communicating credibility

If you use the Internet to promote yourself or a business, the way you use the media must convey that you're authoritative, knowledgeable, trustworthy, reliable, responsive, open to input, and more, according to the case. Viewers look for clues to your credibility. Some tips for establishing trust:

✔ Write your best, and meticulously edit and proof (see Chapters 4 and 5).

✔ Deliver everything you promise – or better, over-deliver.

✔ Include only verified information and keep links updated.

✔ Use technical language sparingly and only as audience-appropriate.

✔ Maintain a positive upbeat tone.

✔ Provide clear easily found contact information and briefly identify your credentials.

✔ Invite input in specific ways, and respond to it.

And never:

✔ Criticize anyone on a personal level.

✔ Conduct personal arguments online.

✔ Reveal anything about yourself you don't want the world to know.

✔ Use offensive language or tone.

And above all: do not use Internet venues for blatant self-promotion unless it's clearly appropriate to the specific medium. A website, for example, can and should include product information and a purchasing pathway. A Facebook business page can focus on a business. But promotional material is not what readers look for in blogs, tweets, and most social media.

You can promote, but softly. For example, call attention to a presentation you're giving, a new post or an e-book. Some public relations specialists calculate that promoting something via Twitter is OK one time out of every four messages. The other three tweets need to share ideas, comment on subjects of interest, pose questions, and offer links to good material and other people's tweets.

Set your own rules and range, but keep in mind that Internet users want useful information and reward its sources over the long run. Even a blog devoted to a commercial product must contribute something genuine to fans – inside information and behind-the-scenes action, for example.

## Cutting the hype, maxing the evidence

A century of traditional advertiing and public relations has dulled sensibilities to highly promotional writing. Although most people claim to hate ads and marketing pieces, they can still skim through blurby printed material to find kernels of interest. But not on the Internet! Online readers strongly resist the clichéd, overblown, and hard to believe. Moreover, research shows that reading online is physically more difficult than print. Online readers have no patience for wordy, over-wrought presentation.

Cutting out the dross is even more imperative as more and more reading happens on tiny screens. People won't get past self-serving introductory statements and flowery language when reading on a tablet, smart phone, or other device.

Begin with this simple principle: make no claims you don't back up. Despite their huge presence on the Internet, nobody credits those empty statements like 'the most innovative breakthrough in the entire 21st century technology power-house' anyway. Tell readers as specifically as you can why and how your whatever-it-is improves their lives in some way.

Try to eliminate nearly all adjectives and descriptive words. Use statistics, facts, testimonials, case histories, and visual proof as appropriate. Cite benefits rather than features. Of course, you can include the features or technical specs if they're important to some readers; just place them so as not to distract from the core message.

## Using non-linear strategies

I once had an argument with a video producer about a story-line I scripted. The sequence was getting out of order in the editing process. 'It's A, B, C, D' I insisted, in effect. 'No!' he shouted. 'Don't you understand that there's no more *linear*? No more beginning-middle-end? That's *over!*'

I've since decided he was right, and he was wrong. In the context of the Internet, everyone has become an information diver. You may land on any page of a website or in any part of an online conversation, and you don't care about logical development of the entire site or interaction. You don't intend to read it through like a novel. Since the material probably won't be read as a sequence, it must be modular – presented as pieces that make sense on their own.

You must accommodate online reader behaviour with matching writing techniques:

- ✔ 'Chunk' information into easily absorbed units so that readers in motion can swoop in and grab what they want.

- ✔ Make sections self-contained so readers aren't required to read other material in order to understand the piece currently in front of them.

- ✔ Repeat some information as necessary so that readers can get what they need.

- ✔ Provide different access points to the material so readers can find and enter the site from different angles.

- ✔ Offer choices: links to other parts of the site with more depth or breadth, or different angles on the subject, and links to offsite information sources.

But don't take modular, non-linear structure to mean that you can present disjointed bits and pieces that add up to less than the sum of their parts. Every page of a website, for example, must make sense on its own.

Sustained narratives rarely work online, but I still recommend building a site – even a blog post – with a beginning, middle and end. You're not writing a novel, but you can still provide a strong headline or lead, a carefully constructed message or set of messages, and close with a call to action.

## *Incorporating interactive strategies*

The biggest difference between digital and print media is the ability to interact with readers. People are now so accustomed to giving their opinions and responding to what's presented that they expect you to invite input, and respond to it. Today's audience is no longer a passive one – if you're successful.

The wired world is all about creating relationships. Accomplish this by involving readers in every way you can think of.

- ✓ **On blogs,** invite responses and be specific. Do you vote yes or no? Did you have a similar experience to share? Do you have a solution to this problem? What else would you like to explore?

- ✓ **On websites,** offer tangible things for people to ask for: information, an e-newsletter, a discount. Invite them to buy something, join something, contribute something, or spread the word. Or ask people to rate a product or experience, send a recipe, or a photo of a common topic.

- ✓ **On social media,** such as Facebook and Twitter, encourage creative interaction. Companies that successfully leverage social media monitor customer conversations and participate in them, offering the latest news and inside views of their brands. So listen and respond to complaints, ask questions, run campaigns and contests, ask readers to contribute to a cause.

Organizations are especially excited about the idea of *user-generated content.* Rather than having to create all your own online material, try to draw customers into creating it themselves. Find ways for users to easily contribute their stories or images, participate in special promotions or games, write about favorite movies, books or travel experience, and so on.

If you incorporate any of these audience engagement techniques, be sure you're equipped to follow through – and do so. Send the freebie, share the results, pay attention to input, respond to comments (including the critical ones), maintain the forum, and prod it along. Yes, all this takes time and other resources. Mostly time.

# Shaping Your Writing for Digital Media

Imagine a formal, stiff, academic style essay – you may have written your share in college – with long complex sentences, weighty words, and a dense look that signals slow reading ahead. The piece may take a few readings to ante up its thought nuggets.

Now decide to write for online media in as an opposite way as possible. The following sections highlight some key differences.

## *Loosening up*

Online writing can ignore many formalities of grammatical correctness. Contractions are fine: *won't* rather than *will not.*

Sentences can begin with words like *and, but* and *or.* Or they can consist of a single word: *Never .Ask. Maybe. Why?* Sentences like these can effectively punctuate copy and make it feel lively.

What your computer grammar checker identifies as sentence fragments often work well too:

> *Why web surf? Because we like it.*
>
> *Too many choices, too few good ones.*
>
> *Better than excellent.*
>
> *Hardly ever.*
>
> *Well, you asked.*
>
> *Successful? Absolutely.*

But be sure that your incomplete sentences are clear in context and don't read as mistakes.

Many characteristics of good online writing sound like practices borrowed from texting and instant messaging – but only to a point. Keep away from texting shortcuts, and abbreviations in all digital writing other than texting. They look unprofessional at best.

## *Keeping it simple*

Much of the Internet is not geared to subtle, in-depth discussion full of ambiguities. People are generally reluctant to read large masses of challenging material onscreen and don't want to decipher its meaning. Moreover, online readers don't like scrolling or clicking through multiple pages. So keep your messages short and simple.

Of course exceptions abound. For example, you may pinpoint an audience that specifically welcomes technical material or sophisticated thinking. If you target a general audience, however, stash the complexities elsewhere or keep them in a separate section. Consider linking to the in-depth version or making it downloadable.

To support skimming and speed reading, look for ways to present information telegraphically, at-a-glance rather than as narrative. Descriptions and technical specs lend themselves well to this approach. Use introductory phrases such as the following to summarize long lists of information and help readers move more quickly through complex material:

> *Product suited to:*
>
> *Kit includes:*
>
> *Use contents to:*

---

# Digital writing checklist

Good online writing gets right to the point, reads fast, and reads well out loud. Strive to include as many of the hallmarks of good writing for digital media as possible:

- ✔ Informal, friendly and conversational style

- ✔ Warm, personal, positive and upbeat tone

- ✔ Ultra-concise: no excess words or thoughts

- ✔ Few or no adjectives and adverbs

- ✔ Lively action-oriented verbs, usually in present tense

- ✔ Short, simple, everyday words (many one syllable)

- ✔ No jargon, mystery abbreviations, or business-speak

- ✔ Short sentences: one to 14 words with few clauses (as signalled by commas)

- ✔ Short paragraphs: one to three sentences

- ✔ Varied paragraph length: some may be just one word

Bulleted lists work well too. But don't make those lists too long or present them without context. Start each item with the same grammatical part so that they read consistently.

What about humor? If you can write copy that has a sense of fun or surprise, terrific. Typically such material is really hard work that talented teams labor over for weeks, months and even years. If you're a writer or artist, make showcasing your creative skills one of your goals. But for most websites and other online content, good substance presented in a down-to-earth, easy-to-absorb way works better than risky humor.

If you have a gift for spontaneity and charm, use it. But try your experiments out on your friends before launching them into universal orbit.

## Keeping it global

Unless you're really disinterested in any readers other than a narrow group of locals, don't forget that on the Internet you write for international audiences. Even if you choose to address only British or North American readers, many of them are not native English speakers. So the simplicity I recommend for all writing is doubly important for the digital world.

Watch especially for idioms, clichés, slang and expressions that non-native speakers are unlikely to understand. Take special care that your tabs and links are totally clear and unambiguous. Cute and clever are bad qualities for navigational tools. Only use titles that say exactly what you mean and are not open to interpretation.

For more tips on adjusting your digital presence for an international audience, see Part IV.

## Keeping it short: Tweets and texting

If you think good writing guidelines don't apply to the 140-character tweet or to texting, which is typically about 160 characters, you're certainly not alone. However, *in business situations*, sloppily written tweets and texts often work against you:

✔ **Not everyone readily understands the abbreviations and shortcuts common to texting and tweeting.** Your message may be disregarded, or it may be misunderstood.

✔ **Some people just don't like the style.** Preferences are partly generational. Older people – many of whom are probably important to your prospects – may even resent receiving messages that appear to them disrespectful. And some younger people feel that way too.

✔ **Careless writing can cost you credibility.** Hastily crafted messages can make you look like a lightweight, not to be taken seriously, in some eyes. Smiley and frowny faces don't help your cause.

Of course, delivering a message in such a tight space is a challenge to begin with, and a tougher one if you're trying to follow traditional writing rules. The solution is to use your common sense on a case-by-case basis. If your boss or client is texting you with symbols and abbreviations galore, you can safely text the same way to them. If they're not, texting may not be the right medium at all. Again, the principle is to know your audience.

A tweet is a public statement. I suggest you make each one as clear and understandable as you can to the most people. You may choose to use the most widely accepted abbreviations and skipped words, but do so carefully.

Tweeting is a good way to practice the art of brevity. Yes, you should edit tweets! Steadily producing well-written tweets with interesting comments can take you a long way. Employers hungry for media-savvy help go hunting in the twitter world for such people.

Keep in mind that tweets and other casual-seeming posts are part of your public persona and can't be erased. As in *never*. Always protect your dignity and privacy. Write to give value, not just to share your favorite snack food. Never write anything that could embarrass you or anyone else. Look up 'disgraced politicians' online if you need a reminder of what can happen.

For more tweeting tips see Chapter 16, 'Ten Ways to Tweet Strategically.'

Chapter 12 digs more deeply into writing for websites, blogging and online profiles – the key content components of most digital adventures. I show you how to translate this chapter's ideas and guidelines into concrete examples of high-octane e-copy.

# Chapter 12

# Writing for Websites and Blogs

*In This Chapter*

▶ Finding your voice on websites and blogs

▶ Organizing and building a website

▶ Using online graphics and design to support your words

▶ Creating and growing a blog

*T*he Internet is like a magic door that democratizes communication. It empowers you to reach almost anyone, anywhere, and offers you virtual space to represent your own interests.

The price of entry for online action keeps coming down. You can post comments and images, tweet, connect with people through social media and invest only the time it takes to do the work. But you may also want a more stable presence that you can control, direct and develop: your own website, blog, or both.

This chapter gives you the tools and techniques to plan and write for your online presence whether you want to present your business, hobby, personal passion, or yourself.

# Shaping Your Words for Websites and Blogs

In the early days – meaning the last decade of the 20th century – you had to possess (or hire) sophisticated professional skills to create and maintain a website. A first-rate, multi-dimensional site still demands a team of specialists working together to plan, write, design, produce and optimize it as a pivotal marketing tool.

But thanks to online services such as Wordpress, Wix, Typepad and whatever is best and newest, you can now easily create a blog by doing all or most of the work yourself.

The distinctions between blogs and websites are blurring. You can plan a blog that looks like a blog: A page that leads off with a new posting on the subject of your choice with access to previous posts. Or it can look like a website: a multi-page platform representing your business (or you) that leads with a home page and observes some fairly standard conventions. This home page can connect to an array of additional pages, perhaps including a blog.

As do-it-yourself tools grow better, you can more easily build a site to your own satisfaction with little technical facility. Still, don't underestimate the power of good design sense or HTML know-how to help you engage audiences, appeal to them visually, and interact with them better. (If you relate well to technology, check out *HTML, XHTML and CSS For Dummies* by Ed Tittel and Jeff Noble.

And never ignore the value of good writing. It's the heart of every website and every blog. Studies show that while visuals entice and entertain, most visitors value the words far more. Even if your site ultimately uses few words, it must make sense in a way you can express to yourself, at least, in written language.

# Working on your writing style for websites and blogs

All the guidelines for online writing I present in Chapter 11 apply to blogs and websites. Use the following strategies to further hone your blog and website writing.

### Consciously adapt your writing style

You can write online in a variety of ways, but you need to pick your specific style in order to be successful. Figure out how you relate to your profession and to your audience, and then create the online persona you want to project.

A lawyer or management consultant, for instance, generally wants to be perceived quite differently from a social worker or artist. But you may be a lawyer who works with intellectual property and needs to connect with artists, or a consultant who wants to be seen as creative. Or you may be an artist who wants to be seen as business like. Of course, you want to be 'yourself,' but consider how the way you present will affect viewers.

### Keep your copy short, pithy, substance-focused, and straightforward

Don't just get to the point quickly – *make* your point and move on. Research says that online reading is 25 per cent slower than reading print material. Moreover, it tires the eyes, and your visitors are impatient for hundreds of their own reasons. All powerful reasons to keep text short and lively!

### Choose your keywords early on

The Internet has dozens of cost-free ways to help you identify the best words and phrases to include in your site or blog. Google's searchwords.com and adwords.com tools enable you to pick words and phrases that are most used by searchers looking for what you offer and also identify terms that your competitors use so you can choose those that are less common if you wish.

### Use your keywords in headlines, subheads and body copy

Put them to the top and left on a page, and lead with them in headlines and subheads whenever possible. Both readers scanning for what they want and search engines find them more surely that way. Researchers who track eye movement on web pages report that the top left corner is the most read territory, and the average viewer's attention tapers off as the eyes move down the page. Also, boldface your keywords when appropriate. This practice works well for blogs.

Be sure to use all keywords in fully natural ways. Loading the deck with numerous keywords draws penalties from most search engines. For more advice, see *Search Engine Optimization For Dummies* by Peter Kent.

### Break copy up into small chunks

Short paragraphs – one to three sentences – go a long way toward online readability. But don't use all one-sentence paragraphs, which also generates unenticing copy. Chop your prose into chunks by:

- ✔ **Adding lots of subheads.** They keep you organized and give readers an easy set of stepping stones to follow.

- ✔ **Building in white space.** Bullets and numbered lists are effective. But for online copy don't list more than six or seven items and be sure they have a context that makes them meaningful. (Just beware of listing more than five or six items.)

### Minimize scrolling

People really don't like to scroll. Many popular website home pages seem to continue vertically ad infinitum. I see this approach as highly counter-productive. An established site, or one featuring content that's updated constantly, can present a cascade of features, but most home pages are not the place for extended introductions or arguments. Instead, strive to develop strong leads that pull scanners to inside pages.

### Make every page self-explanatory and self-contained

People don't typically choose to land on a home page and then read through the site in your preferred sequence. If they're looking for one among five things you produce, they'll probably land on that page. So make sure they know where they are in cyberspace wherever they land on your site. On every page use your company name prominently, include clear headlines, and a call to action. Link to other parts of the site as appropriate.

### Go for clear (rather than clever) title buttons, icons and links

User expectations trump originality, but you don't necessarily need to stick to the cookie cutter. Naming your company's background page 'growing up' rather than 'about us' is a bad idea. But 'our story' can work fine.

### Frame everything in you, and we or I

Use these words to personalize what you write. Beyond connecting better with your site's users, writing in terms of 'you' helps you stay focused on reader viewpoint rather than your own. When it's natural to say 'I' or 'we,' don't hesitate. There's no need to write in an abstract third person mode. You can switch back and forth, too. General Electric says, 'GE is building the world by...' and two sentences later, 'We build appliances, power lighting systems...'

### Craft conversational, fast-reading copy

Use all the techniques I cover in Chapters 4 and 5 – contractions, simple sentences with few commas, a rhythm that moves the reader along. Cut all unnecessary adjectives and all empty hype – no grandiose statements, jargon, mystery abbreviations, and acronyms!

Use all the tools of engagement **available.** Ask questions, invite opinion, offer something irresistible to your audience. And whenever you can, show your passion and commitment to what you do. Nothing is more convincing.

In sum, find fun and value in drilling down to the heart of your own message and deliver it with conviction, tightly.

# Building a Traditional Website

Whether you do it yourself or employ production and design support, take website planning seriously. Don't plunge into your site as a visual exercise or technology challenge. It's probably your most important business document and deserves careful thought. Whatever you want to accomplish, first frame your site with a cohesive written roadmap. The following sections give you a step-by-step approach to planning a website. It's writer-centered. If you want to try a media-specific planning approach that's graphic or flow-chart based, try *Web Design For Dummies* by Lisa Lopuck.

If you already have a functioning site, it's smart to review it from the big-picture perspective that I cover in the following subsections. Among the online world's beauties is its mutability. Moreover, because you *can* easily make changes, you *must*. A good site constantly evolves, especially given today's bevy of analytic tools that tell you what's working and what's not. And of course search engines award higher rankings to those sites that update and grow. Change and expansion can reap real results.

## *Defining your goals*

Just as with every piece of writing – as I talk about in Chapter 2 and demonstrate in all the chapters on print communication and email – first think about your website's *goal*. What do you want to accomplish with your website, exactly?

Your initial answer may be to sell something or more broadly, to market something you produce or offer. Don't stop there! Push your brainstorming to specifics, especially if your venture is new and starts with the site. Additionally answer practical questions such as:

✔ How much of your products or services do you want to sell online?

✔ Are you prepared for large quantity orders?

✔ How far can you reach in the real world to satisfy global customers? Can you ship items long distances – or does it make sense to restrict your geographical thrust?

Once you clarify your marketing goals, brainstorm what website content might help accomplish them. Depending on your product or service the website's goals may include:

✔ Presenting yourself as the go-to problem solver in your field

✔ Establishing thought leadership

✔ Demonstrating your product's superiority or value

✔ Showcasing your originality

✔ Generating sales partnerships

✔ Supporting your search for financial investors

## Refining your audience ideas

Know as much as possible about your primary audience. Who do you want to market your product or service to?

Start by consulting the audience characteristics section of Chapter 2 and pull out all the demographic and psychographic factors that apply to your product or service. Then add all the characteristics relevant to your target market that you can think of.

If you want to reach consumers directly to sell a new tech gadget, for example, your list may include:

✔ Age and gender

✔ Occupation

✔ Hobbies

✔ Degree of technological savvy

✔ Economic status

✔ Buying habits (how they shop for such products, where they go for advice)

✔ Preferences for type and amount of information

✔ Related interests

✔ Problems: what keeps them up at night?

Brainstorm for multiple audiences that may be interested in your gadget, too. If you produce a high-tech wine bottle opener, for example, your research or experience may suggest that male buyers and female buyers don't value the same

benefits – one favors extra efficiency, the other ease of use, for example. Profile every audience individually.

If you want to sell your bottle openers to a business audience, such as wine stores, figure out who in these organizations typically purchases your type of tool and then profile these decision-makers using your knowledge, intuition, and research.

Your sub-goals may suggest secondary audiences. If you're marketing a product and also looking for financial support, you should consider investors and their needs. Should you want to align with other suppliers, know who they are and what they're looking for.

Don't interpret the advice to consider additional audiences as meaning you must create a website that serves all possible audiences and purposes. If you take this approach, you're likely to over-promise and not be able to deliver. Rather, invest in making deliberate, thoughtful choices in online content that benefits specific individuals or groups. Aim to work with a niche market and gradually deepen your reach, or carefully extend to new markets over time.

Mountains of marketing knowledge exist in books and blogs. If you establish a new business and start with a website, but have little marketing experience or knowledge, it's a very good idea to take advantage of these resources. When big companies create or revamp websites they bring whole marketing departments and long experience to bear on the process. Learn to think in marketing terms and your website, and entire venture, will more surely succeed. (Check out *Marketing For Dummies* by Ruth Mortimer.)

## Structuring a basic site

After you're clear on your own set of goals and the audiences you want to reach, ask the what's-in-it-for-them question this way:

- ✔ What does my audience want?
- ✔ What interests them?
- ✔ What do they need?
- ✔ What worries them?

✔ How do I (or can I) help solve their problems?

✔ What will keep them coming back for more?

As an example, consider someone whose goal is to create a social media consulting business. He decides that his primary audience is **_entrepreneurs who work on their own and_** are over age 45, and time-challenged small businesses. Focusing on just the solo entrepreneurs, he characterizes them as being practical people in a wide range of businesses who want to promote through social media channels. They probably feel:

✔ Insecure and perhaps uncomfortable with using social media tools and techniques

✔ Short of time and over-burdened with multiple responsibilities and day-to-day operations

✔ Worried about losing to more tech savvy competition

✔ Conscious that they must keep their enterprises growing

✔ Aware they must offer responsive customer service

This rough profile, plus a second one for the small business audience, enables the consultant to position both his business and website more closely. He can start by defining his core value, what he does and his main competitive advantage. I talk about this in depth in Chapter 9. When the social media consultant applies the core value strategy to his website, he can write a statement for his own guidance in down-to-earth terms:

> _I'm a social media specialist who provides SM planning services, handles the mechanics for busy or fearful clients, educates them on good SM use, and trains those interested to do some of the work themselves._

Based on this premise, the consultant may then frame his website this way:

> _I need a website that showcases my skills and proves my credibility and expertise. It explains how I help my clients grow their businesses, save time, use social media, and become comfortable with its use._

The next challenge – how to translate this thinking into a website plan and structure – becomes easy to meet. The consultant can plan for the following content chunks:

> *Describe what I do from the customer perspective (Services page)*
>
> *Explain who I am and establish my credentials and understanding of their challenges (About Us)*
>
> *Cite evidence, such as stories about how my services have helped similar clients grow, save time, interact with customers, and so on. (Case Studies)*
>
> *Offer pieces of useful practical information site visitors can act on quickly and that will draw them back for more (Blog)*
>
> *Give readers helpful additional materials (Resources)*
>
> *Provide easy ways to reach and interact with me (Contact)*
>
> *Give visitors an enticement to get in touch or at least provide contact information (Special Offer)*

If you think I took a long way round to end up with a standard-sounding site structure, you're right! But you need a process to translate your own goals into a framework that serves your purposes. The basic site structure that has evolved over years works in many situations, though of course you can adapt it to your needs.

In most cases, inventing a totally new website architecture is not a good idea. Audiences come to websites with preset expectations and want to explore efficiently. They have no patience for figuring out what you mean or where you put things. Logical organization, clear wording, and easy access to information are essential.

Better to focus your originality on *what* you say within the framework, how you present it visually, how you engage people, and how you use additional media such as video to deliver your message with impact. See the later section 'Incorporating Graphics and Other Elements' for more detail.

## Assembling a home page

Your website home page must instantly tell people they are in the right place for the product, service, information, or whatever else they're looking for. Even though many viewers land on other pages first or never visit your home page, it must introduce your message effectively.

The following sections touch on the major elements common to smart home pages.

### Company names and taglines

Ideally, your company name should tell it all – capsulize what it does. Think of going to a lively trade or craft show: Would you rather exhibitors identify themselves with banners like 'Main Street Services' and 'Cutie Pie Products,' or 'Overnight Laptop Repair' and 'Toddler Puzzles in Wood'?

If your enterprise is new, coming up with a tight way to say it is worth a lot of thought. As an old advertising adage puts it, 'Don't be clever, be clear.' Take account of keywords (see the earlier section 'Shaping Your Words for Websites and Blogs') and keep what's most important as far to the left as possible (where both people and search engines more often notice it). Thus, you may be better off putting your name later in your tagline. For example, 'Social Media Support by Jane' may work better than 'Jane's Social Media Support.'

If you're anchored in a name that doesn't represent what you do, make up the difference with a good *tagline,* the phrase or slogan that follows the name. Don't be surprised if this is a tough task. Copywriters work very hard at this. Aim to be brief, transparent, simple and clear.

Taglines bolster the following less-than-crystal-clear names for two real companies and a non-profit, melding well to tell each story. (These are real organizations and if you look them up online, don't be surprised if their home pages are substantially different from what I present. Things change fast in the web world!)

> PERSUASIVE GAMES (www.persuasivegames.com)
> *We design, build, and distribute videogames for persuasion, instruction, and activism*
>
> COURSERA (www.coursera.org)
> *Take the World's Best Courses, Online, For Free*
>
> ACUMEN (http://acumen.org)*Changing the way the world tackles poverty*

### *The positioning statement*

This element of your homepage often follows the organization name and tagline. The positioning statement is where you want to distil the reason your organization exists, who it serves, and ideally, your competitive advantage. You may be lucky enough to have worked out a core value statement for your organization that you can adapt to your website (Chapter 9 shows you how to create one). Or you may be part of an organization that hands you one. Whatever the case, make sure what you use really works.

Your positioning statement is a plain language sentence or a bit more that says exactly who you are, what you do, and who should be interested. This is the heart of your central marketing message. Use it with suitable variations on all your materials – traditional and electronic – to tie them together for brand consistency.

If you work for an organization larger than yourself, resist the use of a pre-existing mission statement if possible. These typically are forged by committees and couched in exactly the kind of language to avoid online – formal, stilted, generic, and hollow. Better to think of your website's positioning statement as a new opportunity to immediately explain your role and relate to your audience.

Here's how Persuasive Games introduces itself after title and tagline:

> *Welcome to Persuasive Games.*
>
> *Games communicate differently than other media; they not only deliver messages, but also simulate experiences. Our games influence players to take action through gameplay. While often thought to be just a leisure activity, games can also become rhetorical tools.*

Here's how Acumen positions itself.

> *A bold new way of tackling poverty that's about dignity, not dependence and choice, not charity.*
>
> *Acumen is a non-profit that raises charitable donations to invest in companies, leaders, and ideas that are changing the way the world tackles poverty.*

When I looked at Coursera's site a month before writing this section, its approach was chatty and offered more context:

> *Once upon a time, the only way to take a course taught by a professor employed by a great university was to attend a great university. With Coursera, you don't have to leave your seat. Instructors from Princeton, Duke, Caltech and 13 other schools conduct online classes on everything from math to music, complete with video lectures, quizzes and homework. You might end up in a course with tens of thousands of classmates all over the world. And the site is free – no scholarship required.*

But when I checked more recently, I found that this gabby discourse was gone, replaced by a search box in which the site visitor can enter a subject of interest. These lines appeared under it:

> *Join 3,879,639 Courserians.*
>
> *Learn form 388 courses, from our 83 partners.*

As I watched, the first figure changed to reflect more 'Courserians.' The rest of the home page consists of upcoming course titles with interesting images to represent each. Coursera's copy shift is a good example of applying the 'show, don't tell idea' to a website – try to say less, show more. Website thinking shares a lot with video in this regard, which I talk about in Chapter 9: When you can use visuals to tell your story, you need fewer words.

Work at your positioning statement, over time if necessary. Yes, you can find sites that skip positioning statements and those that rely solely on images to tell their story. But unless you're as widely known as Walt Disney, or can use magnetic space images like NASA relying on a photo or news item to explain who you are and what you do is risky.

Here's one straightforward way our friend who's setting up a social media consulting business (see 'Structuring a basic site') can combine name, tagline and positioning statement to present his business.

*SOCIALMEDIA-IN-MOTION CONSULTING*

*Social Media Planning and Support for Small Businesses and Entrepreneurs*

*Social media is the way to grow your business – but it takes time, tools and techniques. We handle it all! We'll show you how to use the right media and take care of the mechanics. Imagine, online power in your hands.*

The name, tagline and positioning statement can generally be used in this sequence in descending order of importance – and font size. The name should be largest and preferably rendered as a designed logo, or at least look like a logo, with an interesting typeface. The tagline can nestle below it. Take some creative license with the positioning statement, but using it on the bottom half of the home page often works well, depending on the design.

## Calling for action

Most web specialists believe that every page should contain at least one call to action, certainly at the page bottom. Actionable activities may include links to other parts of the site or offsite resources.

Use simple declarative statements and hyperlinked words and phrases to tell viewers what to do next. Give thought to which words to make 'clickable,' indicated in general by underlining: *Call Jane today for your <u>free 15-minute consultation</u>*

*Sign up for our <u>FREE weekly newsletter</u>*

*<u>Question? Click here.</u>*

*Sign up for our <u>webinar</u> today!*

*<u>Free e-book!</u> (or article or white paper or tip sheet or template)*

*Find out more about our beancounting <u>service</u>*

*Buy now and get a <u>10% discount</u>*

Or just

<u>Buy now!</u>

Put some imagination into how to involve readers actively, start relationships, and build a mailing list for your future outreach. You may be able to capitalize on materials already on hand, or may decide to take the time to create them.

Check out *Web Marketing All-in-One For Dummies* by John Arnold, Michael Becker, Marty Dickinson and Ian Lurie for help.

# Writing your inside pages

View each section of your site as its own complete cyber world. On every single page, viewers should know exactly where they are and what they're looking at; how to find the home page and other key parts of the site; and how to follow through on the action you want them to take.

Following are some content ideas for various pages which are part of nearly all well-developed websites.

### About Us

This page is your opportunity to tell your story – the personal one, the business one, or a combination of both. You can use third person – *he, she, they, it* (for an organization) – or first person – *I* or *we.*

You can use first person for About Us and third person for the rest of the site if you wish.

Third person has a more formal feeling and you may have a reason for choosing it. But on the whole, telling your story in first person gives it more personality and is more engaging. Writing in first person leads you to think in warmer language, too.

When to use *we* and *us* is trickier. If you're a solo operation and want to give the impression that you have a whole organization behind you, why not? Millions of people say 'we' for this reason and in any case, you probably have a set of resources and specialists to call on if needed. So go ahead and talk as 'we' and at the same time feature yourself as the prime mover.

Your About Us page allows some creative thinking and expression. Some options:

- ✔ Tell the story of how you came to build this business and/or your expertise
- ✔ Cover a notable success that communicates the heart of what you do

✔ Include your key credentials, the ones most meaningful to your audience

✔ Incorporate third-part testimonials from happy clients

✔ Talk about why you love your work, why you feel passionate about the help you offer, or simply why you think it's important

Keep it brief and readable. This is not the place for a rambling self-indulgent bio. If you feel it necessary to list a lot of specific training or experience, try using a sidebar. For ideas about finding a story that epitomizes your business, see Chapter 9.

Include a good photograph of yourself or your team and give some thought to the emotional qualities you want to project. A female management consultant I know deliberately had a 'tough' portrait photo taken to show prospects she was capable of dealing with CEOs while a psychologist friend chose a warm, low-key welcoming look; she even wore unnecessary glasses to look more approachable.

### The Services page

This is a good place to exercise your chunking skills (see Chapter 11). Break out your distinct services and use strong subheads to introduce each. If you have a long list, consider a dropdown menu or links at the top to take readers directly to the service of interest.

The social media consultant I used as an example earlier in this chapter might begin with a concise overview of offered services and also include a section titled 'How we work with you.' Additional options for his social media consulting services page may include:

*Social media custom planning programs*

*Social media posting services: daily, weekly*

*Facebook campaigns*

*LinkedIn campaigns*

*Social media introductory workshops*

*Social media coaching and support*

### The Contact page

Provide complete information for how to reach you by email, telephone, even fax and snail mail, unless you have good reason not to. Especially if your site will be used by an international audience, bear in mind that businesspeople in specific industries and other countries have different communication preferences – a surprising number depend on fax, for example.

Never overlook your viewer's natural desire for 'real' contact information. No one wants just an email address that says 'info@' or a company name. Give your audience a live real person to write to or call. See your contact page from the visitor's angle; she'd have to be really determined to make a call and ask for an anonymous person. An 'info@' address makes the reader wonder if anyone reads emails sent that way. If you have different staff members to handle price quotes or answer questions, for example, give a name for each.

If you want to know which phone calls you receive derive from your website, make up a specific contact name. But always answer the call.

The contact page is a good place to collect information about your site visitors. Keep online forms short and simple to use. Assuming you do not intend to share the information with third parties – which in any case is illegal in some countries without permission – build in a brief, matter-of-fact statement saying you will only use the information to communicate with the person, and will not pass it on to anyone else.

### Testimonials

All the research says that testimonials are among the most-read parts of websites. We're predisposed to trust third-party endorsements by people who are like us. Testimonials enable you to say things about yourself that would be hard to write about yourself. What's more, testimonials add life to a site because they are written in different voices.

Group testimonials as a separate page of their own (called Testimonials, What Clients Say, or some other name) or scatter them around the site in a sidebar area. Or do both if you can collect a good number.

Don't try to write testimonials yourself! These always sound like you did. Ask clients with whom you have good relationships to write recommendations or endorsements. Help them by providing a few simple questions:

- ✔ What do you most value about the service (or product) I provide?
- ✔ How has it helped you?
- ✔ How has it changed how you handle X?
- ✔ What would you say in recommending me to a colleague?
- ✔ What do you like most about working with me?

Alternatively – and a better option in many cases – is to ask the person questions like these by phone and take notes or record the conversation (with permission, of course). Gathering testimonials in this way lets you explore more freely and ask follow-up questions. You probably come up with better answers than your prepared questions elicit. After your conversation, draft a good statement that retains the individuality and any interesting detail. Always ask the person to review and approve your version. See Chapter 9 for how to gather testimonials as part of a larger goal, developing a core value statement.

Needless to say, keep your ears open for constructive criticism and ideas for improving your performance as you collect testimonials.

# *Incorporating Graphics and Other Elements*

Graphic design is beyond the scope of this book but is so important to the way in which your words are read – and whether they're read at all – that I offer my viewpoint and some tips.

For online media, design and words are inextricably linked. But despite the way that art directors and web producers handle website creation, typically 'adding' the words last, the writing is what really drives a website. Your words deliver your message – or fail to. Graphics and design support the copy, make the site readable, entice and compel. They should help lure people in, please their eyes, highlight what's most important and show them how to find what they want. Ideally they embody the central idea of the site and make it visual.

This premise carries a number of implications that you need to consider when writing your copy:

- ✔ **Leave out the expensive glitzy animated intros.** Most only annoy people. Especially leave out the music or other sound that accompanies viewers through the whole site; they quickly tune out and click off. If you must include either the intro or music, provide a clear opt-out button.

- ✔ **Make the text easy to read.** This means a large enough type in a classic face: Arial and similar typefaces are favored. Printed material reads best in serif faces ('feet' on the letters), but onscreen, the clean look of sans-serif reads well and looks contemporary.

- ✔ **Avoid everything that can possibly interfere with easy reading.** Go with dark fonts against light backgrounds, and a simple color palette with no more than two or three main colors. Avoid or minimize dropout type (white against a dark background), copy in all capitals, and an over-variety of typefaces.

- ✔ **Avoid busy, overly complicated design.** A complex layout confuses the eye and provides no logical path to follow. Especially on the home page, keep the look simple and highlight the elements that are important to visitors. If you work with a designer, be sure he knows which components merit the most attention.

- ✔ **Never present long dense text blocks.** Break up anything longer than a few sentences with visuals, subheads, bullets, and lists. Build in plenty of white space.

- ✔ **Use good, relevant visuals.** Research, again, says that people don't like visual material that's not related to the site or message. Don't cheapen your message with crummy clip art or generic photos of happy smiling diverse groups of people. Use photos of real people with whom readers may have contact. Or invest some creative thinking in how to interpret aspects of your message into interesting visuals and find free or cheap image sources online.

✔ **Use video if and when possible.** People love the extra dimension that video offers and it can show off your personality, demonstrate your expertise or offer a sample lesson in how to do something. See Chapter 9 for more on video. (For more on incorporating video into your website, check out *Video Marketing For Dummies* by Kevin Daum, Bettina Hein, Matt Scott and Andreas Goeldi.)

Unless you have strong confidence in a specific video, don't make it play automatically right off the home page. Viewers hate that.

✔ **Find ways to avoid forcing readers to scroll.** First defense to endless scrolling is brevity. Another is to break pages into separate subsections – for example, give each different service its own page. Or, at least give people a way to choose what they want to look at with clear drop-down menus or links.

And finally, proof, proof, and then proof some more. Online mistakes undermine your credibility and may even kill your entire message. Proofreading online is notoriously difficult, so take the trouble to print out the pages for editing and proofing. Then ask a trustworthy person with a sharp eye to do it. Chapters 4 and 5 offer a wealth of editing and proofing insights.

To find out what's working and what's not, do your own usability research. Ask a few colleagues or friends to review your site from a user's viewpoint and watch them navigate the various pages. Pay attention to how they move around each page and between pages. Listen to their comments carefully and ask some questions. Did anything confuse or frustrate them? Did they stop reading at a certain point? Did they linger anywhere? Skip or speed past a section? Frown or smile?

## Creating Your Own Blog

Whether your goal is to support a business, build a platform to support a book or consultancy, stake a place in the virtual universe, make friends or influence people, the blog may be your medium of choice. Like all the media you use, a blog works best if you plan it and co-ordinate it with all your other communication channels.

Blogs can take many forms. Collect your own favorites and analyze what you like about them. Be aware of content choices, style, tone, length and all the other factors. Getting to know others people's blogs enables you to create your own guidelines for how you want yours to look and sound.

Comprehensive help is available from *Blogging For Dummies* by Susannah Gardner and Shane Birley. Here I present my own take on how to plan and write blogs.

The following sections give you a framework to think within as you develop your blog, as well as some ideas to try out.

## Planning your blog

If you want to use your blog for any purpose beyond the joy of self-publishing your own writing, invest some thought first. Some elements to consider and questions to ask:

- What are my goals? How can it support what I want to accomplish in my personal and/or business life?
- How much time is this worth – or, how much time do I want to spend on the blog? How often can I post?
- What should I write about?
- Who do I want to reach?
- How do I handle the mechanics of getting posts up?
- How do I promote my blog and let people know when I have new postings?
- What does success look like? How do I know my blog is helping me achieve the goals I set?

 Decide beforehand how much time you want to give a blog project and use this decision to frame your commitment and frequency of publishing new material. While there's no set rule for how often to blog, it seems sensible to assume that less than once every two weeks makes it hard to sustain audience interest. You can also decide whether to focus on short posts of a few paragraphs or longer, in-depth material.

Blogging is an unparalleled tool for marketing, especially when integrated with all your other marketing activities. Today content is king. And blogging is the main way to offer content that draws people to you (a process known as *inbound marketing*).

Write a plan for your blog, using a process similar to the one I recommend for websites earlier in 'Building a Traditional Website.' Think through your goals thoroughly and your target audiences. What do the readers you want need? What problems must they solve? What interests them?

Analyze what your intended audience is already reading and talking about. Research existing blogs that are similar in nature to discover specifics about the audience and pick up the conversational tone. Study the content of leading bloggers over time and see if you can identify some niche areas that aren't now covered. You may want to begin by posting comments on other blogs or actively build relationships with established bloggers who share your interests and who you like.

## *Choosing a subject*

As part of a recent writing workshop for communication professionals, I asked participants to create a plan for a personal blog and compile a list of 10 subjects they intended to cover. Some chose subjects with a deliberately limited audience – for example, an immigrant planned a blog about life in New York to update her large extended family on her activities and bring them into her world. Some chose a cause, such as eating nutritiously with prepared foods or high fashion dressing for overweight women. Each subject suggests its own niche and promotional strategies.

Another participant wanted to write a blog about his personal impressions of new films, books, restaurants and 'whatever.' That presents more challenge: Who will want to read it? Can the writer be so entertaining that readers will care about his opinions? How can you build an audience beyond the writer's immediate circles for something so amorphous?

Conversation about this blogger's interests soon revealed that he'd had a passionate hobby since his early teens; he was a part-time disc jockey and had educated himself in the tools and techniques used by professionals. Asked whether he could think of suitable DJ-related topics to write about, his eyes lit up and he enthusiastically came up with a long list of ideas on the spot.

The lesson: an ideal choice for your blog subject may be something you care about because it fascinates you, excites you, prompts your curiosity, or just seems important. Like the amateur DJ, you may have existing expertise on a particular subject and a lot to share beyond your personal opinion. Psychological research indicates that people tend to under-value what they know (and over-stress what they don't know or think they aren't good at). Great blogs stem from a focused passion of almost any kind, mated to knowledgability.

Another prime area to explore for blogging is any subject that inspires you to genuinely help people and for which you are equipped. How-to blogs are endlessly attractive and successful for many audiences. Ideally, you can provide something new, or at least a new angle on the topic, but people also appreciate round-up pieces that gather good ideas and information for them. Give credit as due by acknowledging the source, and linking to it.

When you're blogging to support the organization you work for or your own enterprise, use the same criteria to identify topics. Explore subject possibilities such as:

- ✔ The part of the work or service you care about most
- ✔ Things you have special insights about or access to
- ✔ Inside tips and behind the scenes glimpses into organizations (particularly effective if the business or non-profit boasts a fan base)
- ✔ Highly specialized information
- ✔ Announcement/analysis of new product
- ✔ Stories and examples of how customers have used or been helped by the product or service

# Writing for blogs

I offer general guidelines for online writing earlier in 'Shaping Your Words for Websites and Blogs,' but the following writing tips apply specifically to blogs.

If you're writing for your own blog, feel free to take liberties. Experiment. Be creative. Ignore the following guidelines at will and monitor what happens. If the blog's purpose is to support your enterprise, however, avoid jeopardizing its reputation and relationships. And don't forget that if you write a company blog, or you're blogging about company matters in your own time, more is at stake than how others perceive you. Criticizing the company you work for or its leadership can be career suicide. A blog is, after all, a public forum.

### Structure and organization

While a website can present pieces of information as separate chunks that don't necessarily relate to each other, and can use grammatically incomplete sentences for effect, a blog needs to be more cohesive and sequential. You're typically presenting directions, opinions or arguments. So your narrative in each posting needs to flow and be held together by good transitions.

### Tone

Aim for writing that's simple, straightforward and conversational.

Choose the tone most appropriate to audience and subject (see Chapter 2 for much more on crafting your tone). If you're writing about headstones, obviously a flippant tone may be taken badly. Lawyers and accountants have not yet lightened up noticeably as a group, so they probably require a more formal tone than soccer fans.

If you choose to limit your audience to those who are already knowledgeable or enthusiastic, like sports fans, is it okay to use jargon and terminology understood only by insiders? Yes, if you're sure you don't want to expand your readership to newbies.

Always be positive and upbeat when blogging – even if you're writing critical reviews of a film, book, product or idea. Be wary of criticizing anything or anyone personally, or at least be prepared for repercussions. And NEVER attack or slur anyone personally. Doing so is bad manners and hurts you every time. And you run an increasing risk of being sued.

## Length

The ideal length of a blog or blog post varies widely and depends on the subject, audience, and what you're willing to put in. Many e-media gurus recommend quick-read posts of a few paragraphs. But this keeps the material superficial and many readers find these limits frustrating.

As a rule of thumb, to contribute something solid, I say plan for 500 to 700 words. But if it's a quick tip or idea that doesn't call for elaboration, do a couple of paragraphs. If you write for a technical audience that thrives on detail, go longer.

Varying the length of your posts each time is absolutely fine – even preferred by many audiences.

## Headlines

Headlines are critical to getting your post noticed by readers and search engines alike (see 'Shaping Your Words for Websites and Blogs' for more). They're also critical for attracting readers to older postings, which you may choose to list alongside the new blog.

Start out with how the information benefits the reader: Will they find out how to do something faster, better, cheaper? Improve their lives in some way?

Free is always a great promise:

> *All-purpose business writing template to make you a star – FREE!*

Sharing secrets is great:

> *What nobody knows about X and why it can kill you!*

Saving money is appealing:

> *Buy monthly supplies of your favorite soft drink at 40% off*

A promise to teach readers how to do something is tempting:

*Teach yourself to play the piano like a soloist in 6 weeks*

A question can be compelling:

*Do you know what your girlfriend watches when you're not there?*

And headlines with numbers are always grabbers, which is why you see them so often:

*9 ways to save a fortune on your health insurance*

*Watch for the 7 signs of extreme dandruff before you're humiliated*

*Three easy arguments to get a raise*

Of course, a headline needs to be honest. Don't promise anything you can't deliver. And the rest of the blog post must back up your headline.

### Subheads

Subheads help you easily organize your own ideas, improve visual impact by adding white space, pull in readers, and keep them going. What's not to like? Even a short blog benefits from subheads. Make them active and informational rather than just labels:

Rather than,

*The new numbers*

Write

*New numbers show upward leap*

If you're using a numbered list as in the last set of headlines I cite above, bold the first phrase or sentence of each item to produce a subhead-like effect. This simple treatment makes your blog look easy to read and get through – important assets when you're competing for attention with such a wide virtual world.

Writing good subheads is also covered in Chapter 8.

# Categories and tagging

To help people find your blog posts, it helps to identify them with at least one category and at least one tag. A category is the larger descriptor – if you write about food, 'cooking,' 'appetizers' and 'desserts' are category options. A tag is a more specific label. If you're presenting a cheesecake recipe, categories could include 'dessert' and 'baking,' while tags might be 'cake,' 'cheesecake,' 'cheese,' 'low-calorie cheesecake,' and so on as appropriate.

The process is the same as for thinking of keywords and search terms: you figure out how members of your intended audience will look for what you're writing. You can tag internally, within the content itself; and/or externally, which relies on services like Technorati and Flickr.

# Part V
# Thinking Global, Writing Global

## *Top Five Ways to Communicate with an International Audience*

- ✔ Develop an awareness of your own cultural filters.
- ✔ Write simply without idioms, metaphors, ambiguous wording and passive tone.
- ✔ Establish a personal connection with your reader whenever possible.
- ✔ Respect formalities and take your cues from the other person.
- ✔ Ask the right questions to build insights into each culture.

To read up a bit more on doing business in a multicultural environment, why not visit http://eu.dummies.com/how-to/content/doing-business-in-a-multicultural-environment.html.

# In this part . . .

✔ Learn how to communicate with your international audience and ensure the global presence of your business.

✔ Understand and be aware of cultural courtesies in order for your business to connect with other cultures.

# Chapter 13

# Using English as the Global Language of Business

*In This Chapter*

▶ Communicating with other cultures

▶ Writing emails and letters to non-native English speakers

▶ Adjusting your online presence for international audiences

*E*nglish is the language of international business and shows every sign of remaining so for the predictable future. But that is very far from meaning that other countries have adopted British or American culture, values, and ways of doing business.

People of other nationalities don't think like you, even if they speak and write in your language – and even if they love American movies or British pop stars.

Business protocols and expectations differ. If you reach out to someone in another country in hope of doing business, you're more likely to succeed if you act knowledgably and with respect for their conventions and values. Heedless writing produces messages that they may misunderstand or even find insulting.

While the body of advice on communicating across cultures face-to-face is growing, relatively little of a practical or country-specific nature has been written about international writing. I sought out direct sources, generous-minded people willing to consider how cultural differences affect written language. Some of these contributors are corporate communicators, others are business people, journalists, or advisors who help new ventures connect with the countries where they've lived.

A few are *For Dummies* authors! I share this collected advice in Chapter 14.

In this chapter, with the help of these contributors, I present some general guidelines for writing to people whose native language is not English.

# Considering Native English in All Its Flavors

Before looking into the details of international English speakers, a note on the varieties of 'native English' – people grow up speaking English in Great Britain, the United States, Canada, Australia and New Zealand.

Significant differences obviously exist between spoken and written English in the Old and New Worlds. The ocean in between generated quite a lot of them over time. And the oceans between England, Australia and New Zealand fostered other sets of differences. But for practical reasons, I'll refer to two general categories of English, British and American, the latter including the U.S. and Canada, which differ minimally.

Some variations are obvious, such as various spellings and grammatical conventions that an American reading a British newspaper notices, and the reverse. More subtle are the many idioms that separate the two main styles of English, the language of American and British people.

However, writing good global English requires that you eliminate as many idiomatic expressions as possible anyway. There's no real reason for an American to adopt British spelling and expressions when writing for business purposes, nor do British speakers need to adopt American habits.

Actually, one major exception to this rule exists.

British English is customarily more formal than American. People in countries that use British English generally don't care if you write *honourable* or *honorable, sympathise* or *sympathize,* but they may well care about the degree of formality with which you write. Countries inclined to British English prefer that formality – and except for America, so do most countries that use American English.

Reflecting American culture, psychology and interpersonal patterns, American English is probably the most informal language in the world. Surprise! The entire rest of the globe doesn't necessarily appreciate that quality. People who deal with Americans a lot are often used to the informality, and certainly many younger people relate to it. But when you don't know either to be the case, your messages should err on the side of formality in order to be taken seriously.

Whilst British culture is changing, the British are still typically more reserved than Americans, less likely to wear their hearts on their sleeves, share feelings with new acquaintances, or bring up personal subjects. They're unlikely to start off on a first name basis with people they don't know and less likely to approach strangers. They value good manners more highly and pay more attention to hierarchy, origins, and titles. Overall, they communicate – in person and in writing – more carefully.

I realize that British people may dispute the characterization, especially because interactions are becoming less formal, in particular for the younger generation. But my point is that when you don't know the culture, age or disposition of your audience you're better off acting – and writing – in the British way!

At the same time, people in many non-English countries value relationships as a preamble to conducting business which most Americans are unaware of. They want to know who you are, who you know, and whether you can be trusted before considering a business arrangement, however beneficial the prospect.

Relationship building can take time. And it often requires your personal presence. You can make initial contact through emails, letters, phone calls, or even fax, depending on the country, but you need to show up, build relationships, and negotiate face to face. Invariably demonstrate respect, especially in regard to the variations in the way different people communicate. When people write to you in English you consider imperfect, stiff or overly formal, remember to feel fortunate that they are troubling to respond or reach out to you.

# Adapting Your Writing for Global English

Years back I was in Paris and found myself sitting next to another tourist, a Russian, outside the Louvre. We were both waiting for friends and to pass the time we talked – both using primitive French learned in school. As two non-French people with small vocabularies, we understood each other perfectly. Much better than when either of us conversed with French speakers.

The idea applies to written language as well as spoken. No matter what their native tongue, most readers who speak English as a second (or third or fourth) language do so in the same basic way. Therefore you can use some general guidelines to ensure being understood.

However, as I stress throughout this book, always know as much about your audience as possible. If you're writing to a highly placed multi-language sophisticate, the following global English rules do not apply. You don't want to sound condescending.

The rules do apply, however, when you write to any individual or group whose English language skills are not highly developed. Organizations that communicate with relatively uneducated employee groups and non-native English speakers follow similar guidelines. These ground rules are also useful when preparing material for translation. In fact, keep in mind that your readers may look up words as they go along.

To write global English:

- ✔ Use short, simple, basic sentences. Avoid multi-clause structures.

- ✔ Keep paragraphs short so there is plenty of breathing space between them. Dense pages look difficult to read.

- ✔ Avoid contractions. For example, write *do not* rather than *don't.*

- ✔ Keep to short basic words, but bear in mind that many short words in English have multiple meanings and may be used as nouns as well as verbs. *Run,* for example, can be either. *Look* has a number of meanings.

✔ Omit idioms, slang and colloquialisms that overseas readers are unlikely to understand. These words and phrases are rampant in written and spoken English, so develop an awareness of those you tend to use and find substitute wording.

✔ Avoid most metaphors, especially those based on sports that other countries don't understand and don't find interesting – for example, baseball and cricket.

✔ Avoid passive tense and indirect phrasing as much as possible. 'Our legal office prepared the contract' is better than 'The contract has been prepared by our legal office.' See Chapter 5 for more advice on active phrasing.

✔ Minimize 'stately' words such as those that end in –*ion* and –*ment,* which produce awkward wordy construc-tions. For example, 'The accomplishment of the build-ing's construction is planned for June' is better said as, 'We plan to finish the building in June.'

✔ Don't abbreviate words, including abbreviations borrowed from texting. Readers may not understand and/or like them.

✔ Don't use buzzwords and intra-company or industry insider acronyms and language.

Don't expect to transform your writing for global understanding on a first-draft basis. Plan to edit, edit, edit. Look for shorter words to substitute for long or ambiguous ones. Eliminate all unnecessary words and repeated thoughts. See whether you can simplify with more careful punctuation; more commas than you ordinarily use may help clarify meaning. Simply worded subheads can be very helpful. Proof scrupulously – an error your reader notices costs you heavily.

Adopting the right mindset goes a long way, but some of the preceding guidelines are easier to recommend than implement. You have to work harder than usual to make reading your messages as easy as possible for non-native English speakers. Becoming conscious of culture-specific idioms is a special challenge. Reread everything to look for this kind of 'insider' language. Enlist colleagues or friends in the editing process.

And almost universally: Do not employ humor. 'Funny' is open to cultural interpretation. You risk not only being misinterpreted but may come across as insulting. In particular, never make a joke at someone else's expense. Self-deprecating humor may be acceptable but may also present you in a bad light.

# *Writing Messages to Send 'Round the World'*

Thanks to modern technology and communication systems, as well as an increasingly global outlook, setting up business arrangements with other countries is within the grasp of even small companies today. But a lot more is involved than writing English-language messages to other business people and pressing send.

It's smart to do your homework and carefully adjust your writing. The following sections show you how.

## *Monitoring your assumptions*

Begin writing for an international audience by becoming aware of your own assumptions about other cultures. For example, as an American, you may love your work and think about it all the time. You probably check your email on the beach. But for many other people of the world, their jobs come second or even third. Family may be the main focus and leisure activities second. Work is seen as a way to support the more important parts of life. These deeply ingrained cultural norms can make a difference in how people interact with you.

Do your homework on practical matters as well as cultural. Scout the Internet, where you'll find useful information on doing business in some countries, but not all. Try to find someone to talk to who knows the country well from a business perspective. For insights on other cultures and general business interaction check out the latest edition of the classic *Kiss, Bow or Shake Hands* by Terri Morrison and Wayne A. Conaway.

Aim to know the 'normal' working week and working hours for the country of choice – they are not the same worldwide. In most of the Middle East the working week is Sunday to Thursday. In hot countries there may be a three- or four-hour break mid-day so you may not reach anyone from noon to 4. In other countries, like Japan, important business is conducted after hours, in restaurants, and bars. Some countries, like France, more or less close up shop for vacation in August.

Another very basic piece of homework: countries don't all rely on the same communication systems, so find out which media work best with the place you want to work with. Email or letters are not always suitable. If the postal system doesn't function well, as in Mexico, letters may take a month or may never arrive. And not everyone in the world sits by his computer or smart phone waiting for emails and rushes to respond promptly. A telephone follow-up may be necessary.

Don't assume that an email to the 'wrong' person will be forwarded to the right one. And in some places, a subordinate or other gatekeeper may not relay a message to a higher-up. Or vice-versa. Do your best to identify the right person and find out what you can about him or her, as well as the organization. Chinese businesspeople routinely do such research to a degree that astounds their counterparts and gives them a major advantage.

 Even though English is the global business language, you are still better off approaching some countries and individuals through their own languages. Invest in a good translation or get help from someone who writes well in that language – preferably, in the case of huge diverse areas like Latin America, someone familiar with the specific culture rather than merely 'Spanish'.

There can be distinct variations between regions of the same country as well. In many parts of the world, ethnic identity is hugely important. Writing to someone in the country of Georgia, for example, in Russian rather than his own language, can be a huge mistake, even though the business culture is basically Russian.

 Never assume business people you write or speak to, whatever the level of their English skills, are unsophisticated about business practice, negotiation technique or technology. That is not just unlikely, but apt to land you outside the door you're trying to enter – perhaps without your shirt. Many people, wherever they're located, are widely travelled today and those in the front lines of international business may have studied in the US or another English-speaking country.

## Connecting with other cultures

For people in many countries, relationships are all-important and must precede business. Simply appealing to mutual self-interest may not be enough. A cold call message may be ignored, or may be reviewed sceptically.

Begin establishing a connection by finding someone the person knows, or someone who can begin linking you with a string of people and ultimately the person you want to reach. If you can't come up with a start point and don't want to hire an intermediary, your country's embassy or a chamber of commerce in the country you're interested in may be equipped to help and be happy to do so.

A corollary of this idea: To conduct business in many countries, you need to *be there* – available in person immediately or very shortly after your initial foray receives a promising response.

All along the line when you meet business people in another country, be careful to act with polite regard and impeccable manners. Everyone in a specific business community probably knows everybody else, or close to it. Even in a very large country like Brazil, the middle class that runs the business world is still small, and people are very connected to each other.

Remember too that your counterparts almost certainly know far more about your culture than you do about theirs, even after you do some quick study. Still, make an effort to familiarize yourself with the cultural icons and passions of the country you want to engage with. These can range from sports different than those you follow to culture, historical events and milestones, economic achievements, monuments, and other things unique to the country. Working up your conversation so you can talk about things another person cares about is definitely worthwhile for in-person meetings and shows interest and respect. You may also find occasion to comment on something nationally relevant in written communication.

Prepare to be patient. While some cultures are characterized by quick decisions and fast processes, they tend to be the exception. The need to forge trusting relationships is one reason. More aversion to risk is another.

You may need to maneuver a mountain of multi-level government regulation and red tape, at least to western eyes.

There's no easy one-way-fits-all guideline here. If your exploratory communication is productive and you're proceeding toward a business arrangement, in many cases you need professionals to help you deal with government, legal, and business systems that may be totally unlike those you're used to. And in some parts of the world, even where there's an aggressive and welcoming business environment, you need to start with the government and follow a formal registration procedure. This is the case with the United Arab Emirates, for example.

## Writing first messages

Especially when you're writing to introduce yourself and your idea, follow this general rule for emails and letters – keep them short and simple.

Take account of the language's conventions, such as how to write out dates and times. Some countries write dates in the order, day-month-year, while others start with the month. Time in many places is measured on a 24-hour basis.

### Beginning well

For emails, invest thought into writing a good relevant subject line that explains why you're writing (see Chapter 6).

Take great care with how you address your reader. In many cultures, degrees and titles are taken very seriously and if you omit the correct ones, your message may remain unread. In some countries, like China, it's even important to know the relative age and ranking of the person you're writing to, because seniors on both counts are due extra respect.

**Never use your reader's first name for initial contact.** Every person I interviewed in researching this part stressed the point and found it a mistake that Americans often make. Their advice is take your cue from the other person and employ a matching level of familiarity, such as using the first name or mentioning a personal situation, only *after* the other person does so first.

Some countries use formal set openings and closings for business communications, and you need to know what they are.

In Chapter 14, I outline what is commonly expected in many countries.

If someone your recipient knows suggested you contact them, or you have a mutual acquaintance, say so immediately in your opening paragraph. If that's not possible, try to find some kind of connection – a school, for example.

The question of whether to begin a communication with small talk – and what kind of small talk – is complicated. For a Japanese correspondent, for example, referring to the weather or family (provided the latter has been mentioned before) is a plus, but in Germany or Russia, getting to the point is more valued. In all cases, err on the side of excessive politeness.

### Writing the middle and end

Aim in the body of your message for total clarity. It's usually best to stick to a single point or idea. Be very specific about your reason for writing and what you hope to accomplish.

One consideration is whether to use some phrases, words or sentences in the other person's language. In some cases it's taken to mean that 'you're trying,' but to other cultures – especially if you get the wording wrong – you end up looking insensitive.

It's especially hard to cutback or eliminate idiomatic ways of putting things. These words and phrases are completely ingrained in how you think and write. Here, additional eyes are usually necessary. Try to have at least two people review what you write from this angle alone.

If you're a woman, you can realistically expect that some cultures may not accord you automatic respect. Be especially clear on your role and positioning in your company and highlight the mutual advantages of doing business.

On the technical side, bullet points and lists are often useful because they're easily absorbed by people with varying degrees of facility with English. For the rest, follow the basic guidelines I give in 'Adapting Your Writing for Global English' earlier. If you did your homework and know you're writing to a highly educated person, however, write less simply. The same usually applies to high-ranking individuals in large organizations.

End, as with any good email as I cover in Chapter 6, by repeating *the ask* – what you want – and the next step you hope to take. As appropriate, use the formal ending common to the country (see Chapter 14).

### Maintaining the correspondence

Often you must usher a budding relationship along with continuing respect and politeness. Don't take offense if answers are very slow to materialize. In some countries, including some Western European countries, the culture does not put a high priority on the need to get things done quickly.

Follow up with emails or telephone calls as appropriate and don't show impatience. On the other hand, know that in many cultures business people avoid delivering a direct no. They may appear to be evasive and indirect, expecting you to interpret the meaning of what they say. If you have a friend or colleague familiar with the country, ask what clues to watch for so you know when further effort is not worthwhile.

As you've probably experienced yourself, reading a foreign language is usually much easier than writing in it. If you can read your correspondent's language, or have someone available who can, you may want to tell the person you're corresponding with that answering your letters in their own language is fine. The suggestion is usually appreciated, and results may be faster.

# Writing Other Materials

You always face competition in marketing your product or service, and your competitors may come from many parts of the world, including the country you've targeted.

Plan for support materials suitable to the culture when you want to connect anywhere. People all over the world check out you and your organization the same way you do, via the Internet and other research. They evaluate you on the basis of what you give them and what else they can find out by any other means.

If the connection matters to you, take the trouble and possible expense to effectively showcase what you offer.

## Translating promotional materials

Experienced global business people typically have the reverse side of their business cards translated into the language of the other country. Presenting business cards in person, by the way, takes a particular ceremonial form in many countries. In an Arab country, for example, presenting a card with your left hand is offensive. (Chapter 14 has some additional insights.)

Like business cards, prepare brochures and similar materials in your counterpart's language. The person you're writing or talking to may be comfortable reading an English version, but may share it with a number of people who aren't. Remember that especially when you're dealing with a substantial company, the best English-speakers may be delegated to work with you. They may or may not include the actual decision-makers or others with a voice, such as industry specialists.

To translate marketing materials, get professional help. While you can choose to use online translation services for a brief communication, doing so for a print piece is risky. Awkward language never helps your cause, let alone poor grammar or spelling.

And the possibilities of offending on a cultural level are limitless. You cannot possibly anticipate many of the boundaries without thorough knowledge of customs and values. In some countries, for example, showing a man and a woman together is unacceptable, even in an obvious business environment.

Guidelines for good presentation differ among countries, as well. Materials written in German, for example, typically look denser than English speakers are accustomed to; the paragraphs are long, the sentences lengthy and complex. However, a German speaker still prefers simpler writing and presentation when reading another language.

Be sure to ask a professional translator for advice on technical issues as well as cultural ones.

## Globalizing your website

If you're serious about engaging in international business, take a thorough look at your website and consider simplifying and streamlining it. Fortunately, if you follow the guidelines I present in Chapter 11, your online presentation is already clear and easy to navigate.

However, you must consider major issues when globalizing a site. If you're focused on doing business with one specific country, you may want to create at least a partial site in that language. At one time English-speaking companies faced less competition in marketing overseas via websites, but today most products or services have local providers with websites – and consumers naturally prefer using sites that speak their own languages.

Building a site that works for every culture and contains nothing offensive to any group can be a formidable task. One that's beyond my scope here. But for a limited renovation, include all the following:

- ✔ Copy based on short words, sentences of 8 to 14 words average, and short paragraphs

- ✔ Crystal clear headlines, subheads and headings that describe the content unambiguously without confusing cleverness

- ✔ Navigation that is as obvious and easy as possible

- ✔ Visuals that are relevant, tasteful and not distracting – and include no images or colors offensive to a culture of interest

- ✔ Plenty of white space

- ✔ No fancy animated intros and unstoppable music that may annoy people

- ✔ No humor that may be misunderstood and held against you

It's especially difficult to cut the catchy language and idiomatic presentation that you, or your website producer, worked so hard to create. But that's an issue that relates to most of what you write for an audience of non-native English speakers.

Effective cross-cultural messages are generally less colorful and individualistic than when you write to those who share your language, customs, and values. This is not a surprise: you're trying to produce culture-free writing without ambiguity or nuance. Naturally the result has little or no 'style'. However, as I state at different points in this book, simple language can communicate complex thoughts very well. But it does take more work.

## *Reviewing your Internet presence*

Everything about you on your own blog, Facebook, Twitter and other social media is accessible just about anywhere on earth. If that thought hasn't given you pause on the domestic front, it should do so for the worldscape.

If you reach out to international audiences, or intend to in the future, be doubly cautious about the information you post. Monitor what friends and colleagues say about you, too. Conservative readers from other cultures may be even less forgiving of questionable behavior and images than prospective employers.

In today's way of thinking, Google is your résumé. Try to keep it clean and respectable.

By the way, if you're applying for a job in a different country, the manner in which you present yourself may take a radically different form, even if it's a Western European culture. Find out how to do that in an appropriate résumé.

# Chapter 14

# Adapting Business English to Specific Countries

● ● ● ● ● ● ● ● ● ● ● ● ● ● ● ● ● ● ● ● ● ● ● ● ● ● ● ● ● ● ● ● ● ● ● ● ● ● ● ● ● ● ● ●

## In This Chapter

▶ Connecting across cultures

▶ Writing well to China, Russia, France, Japan, India, Mexico, Germany, and Brazil

▶ Avoiding mistakes and paying cultural courtesies

● ● ● ● ● ● ● ● ● ● ● ● ● ● ● ● ● ● ● ● ● ● ● ● ● ● ● ● ● ● ● ● ● ● ● ● ● ● ● ● ● ● ● ●

*I*t's a big world out there – full of countries developing their economies and, to varying degrees, eager to establish business relationships with other countries. Today's easy communication systems, together with growing acceptance of English as the world's business language, can disguise the deep gulches that still exist between cultures.

A first imperative when communicating with people outside your own country is to become more aware of your own values and the filters through which you see the world. For example, Americans aim to be concise and direct and value individualism. Many other cultures have different priorities – family, relationships, a society of consensus, perhaps.

In Chapter 13 I provide general principles of cross-cultural writing and the thinking behind it. In this chapter I give you some specifics for eight sample countries chosen to demonstrate different cultural perspectives, and because they are likely to be of interest. I also note the specific contributors at the end of each section, excepting several who preferred not to be credited. Don't read this chapter looking for comprehensive information or formulas. After all, a dozen different people in the US can come up with different ideas about what's important about writing business English.

# Tailoring Business English

Surprisingly little has been written about how to tailor business English to particular countries, I decided to seek information and ideas directly from people who are part of other cultures or have lived within them, write often in English, and are sensitive to language and cultural differences. I found sources through friends, business contacts, the *For Dummies* author network, professional associations and research. I first asked all my contributors whether they agree with the following basic writing guidelines:

✔ Use simple short sentences

✔ Avoid English-language expressions and abbreviations

non-English speaking native might not understand

✔ Avoid contractions

✔ Use basic words rather than long complicated ones

✔ Keep sentences and paragraphs short

✔ Avoid humour that may be misinterpreted

Most agree with all the points, and so they form the basis of my general guidelines for writing in English for a global audience (see Chapter 13 for specifics). Where they didn't agree or took exception, I note in the country's coverage in this chapter.

I recommend reading through the whole chapter to glean helpful strategies for communicating more effectively with other people throughout the world. Use the ideas to stir your own consciousness of how perspectives differ and figure out the best questions to ask to help you create successful interactions with people from any country.

The Internet levels the playing field enormously. While big internationally known companies may be more readily received than small players in many environments, the opportunities for small and middle-sized enterprises to build productive relationships are new and real. Writing by itself is unlikely to accomplish this. But the written word is often the best and most practical way to make initial contacts. Knowledge, thought, and above all, respect, helps open doors.

The advice I give here is in broad strokes, and I never intend to slip into stereotyping. Remember that the differences among regions and individuals in a non-native English-speaking country are often considerable – just like in your own native country.

All Russians or Brazilians do not think alike or have the same expectations. Always find out as much as you can about the particular person you're writing to, as I explain in Chapter 2, as well as her country, region or ethnic group. Her position, education, values, priorities and many more factors are important to shaping successful messages.

# Writing to China

The US is a powerful cultural influence in China, thanks to American movies, websites and books. The Chinese are comfortable with American-style English. In general, however, expect a warmer reception for messages written in Chinese.

A language difference: conjunction words are traditionally not much used in Chinese. Sentences are short and readers are left to figure out the relation between sentences themselves, which leads to ambiguity. Younger Chinese, however, are beginning to write long English-style sentences with conjunctions, especially when writing in English. To be clear, use words like 'therefore', 'because', and 'so'.

Find a good connection *before* approaching a Chinese business person. Non-Chinese business people are almost certainly best off seeking help for legal and registration issues, and hiring an agent to protect their technology.

### Practical tips for email and letters

The proper form of address depends on your relation to the reader. For friends, colleagues, or people you know, first names are acceptable. For someone important or of higher social rank, use Mr or Ms and the last name. Hierarchies must be observed: address those who are higher than you or older in a very self-deprecating and effusively respectful way.

Get to the point of your communication quickly – bottom line on top. But if you know the person or have been writing to him or her, include a brief introductory statement asking how the person is.

For a sales letter, make a brief introduction and then sell your product or service. If you're writing for informational purposes, go directly to the point, answering or asking questions.

Use straightforward English that is not convoluted: short sentences, clean and precise language. Avoid analogies or anything complex, especially relating to sports that Chinese people don't play or care about.

To end: 'I look forward to your reply.' 'Best regards' is accepted.

### Mistakes to avoid

When communicating with Chinese business people:

- ✔ Don't leave phone messages, they are often not relayed; instead, follow up and try again.

- ✔ Don't walk into meetings, negotiations or other situations without a mutual agreement on expectations.

- ✔ Don't take gifts you won't want to repay in kind.

- ✔ Don't forget to show respect: know and use all the titles a person holds.

- ✔ Don't forget to do your research, know what you want, and go into negotiations with a strategy.

### Cultural issues

China's economy is centrally controlled, and business is in large degree influenced by the state. The government fears too much outside influence and treats non-Chinese companies differently from Chinese companies. But despite strong centralised government, local activity is absolutely thriving. Many local governments act independently to interpret policies and trends in their own ways. However, not everyone on the local level speaks and writes English.

The Chinese are also famous for doing their homework. Expect that when you present yourself for business, everything about you and your organisation is already well known to those you're negotiating with.

Also critical to understanding Chinese business is the concept of *guanxi* – a network of far-reaching contacts that can include family members, school friends, colleagues, and more. Network members are under continuous and often lifelong obligation to grant each other favours. As Maneula Zoninsein notes, 'It's about relationship networks. Once they know and trust you, you'll be introduced to the right people.' If you don't have a starting point, Zoninsein recommends contacting your country's embassy for help. For various reasons, a 'cold' email to initiate a conversation may or may not be answered, especially if you are not highly placed in a well-known company. Or you obtain meetings, but they may prove to be fruitless. 'You can meet hundreds of people at a company but get nowhere if you're not talking to the right one,' Zoninsein says.

 Find a connection to introduce you to the right person. Then spell out your offering clearly and how you imagine you can collaborate, which may not be obvious to your prospect. Show you respect them and their role and that you have done your research.

Many Chinese business people are ambitious and move quickly when they wish to. Typically your presence is required. If you write and the response is, 'Let's meet tomorrow,' be ready to show up, and be on time! Remember that in China, there's always room for negotiation.

Thanks to the popularity of the Internet and instant messaging, younger business people may use less formal English when writing. Abbreviations like *ASAP* and *pls* are used. But always assume you need to be formal and respectful. When an important person holds several titles, use them all.

*Contributors:* **Manuela Zoninsein**, CEO, Smart Agriculture Analytics, China-based company that helps companies manoeuver China's 'smart agritech' market; **Weng Xunyu**, Project Manager, Tany Foundry, Zhejiang, China

# *Writing to Russia*

Russian business people study British English in school, and often read it better than they understand it when spoken. But they are very comfortable with American business practices. They may often appear rude in their communication. In telephone conversations, a Russian may say 'Speak!' or 'I'm listening,' rather than 'Hello,' and may end a telephone conversation with a bang of the receiver.

Their business writing tends to be dry and formal. It may to Western eyes look officious and somewhat discourteous. 'The polite forms in Russia are much simpler and often the business correspondence style is abrupt and takes the form of an order, rather than request,' Anna Shevchenko says. Accordingly, expect correspondence to use simplified polite forms – *can you* rather than *could you,* for example.

Always take into account Russian bureaucracy, company hierarchy, and general mistrust of non-Russians. Appropriate tone is difficult to balance. Russians find the British too polite and flowery, and Americans too informal. Generally, unless you have a good relationship with the person, write very politely and formally but not to the point where you challenge your reader's understanding. Not everyone speaks good English, so short sentences and simple language are key. Avoid sounding condescending.

The former Soviet republics, including Georgia, Kazakhstan, Armenia, and Ukraine, are Russian in their business practices but not culturally. While it may be beneficial to use a standard opening in Russian, do not do so if the person may not be an ethnic Russian. He may either not speak Russian, or not want to. When you don't know, stick to English, says Ilan Greenberg.

### Practical tips for email and letters

Email is the accepted way to communicate. Address people you don't know as *Dear Mr* or *Ms* and their last name (not the Russian-style full name of the father, which is considered stodgy). If writing to someone in a government position, a more distinct salutation may be in order, like *Your Excellency,* for a high-ranking official.

If you're beginning a business relationship with an email, get to the point immediately. State the reason you're writing and mention a connection in common when possible. If you have a relationship with the person you're writing to, begin with some personal information: 'How is your family?' or 'How was your son's birthday?' Or you can ask about the person's health. Expect in turn direct inquiries that may be a bit more personal than you're used to. But if you're writing to a higher-up, get to the point and skip such preliminaries.

To end an email or letter, thank the person for her time or mention the next steps in communication. *Best wishes* is a frequently used close. *Sincerely, Thank you,* and *Best regards* are all fine.

### Mistakes to avoid

When communicating with Russian business people:

- ✔ Don't assume a lack of sophistication among business people in Russia or the former Soviet republics; many are well travelled.

- ✔ If you're a woman, don't expect to be taken seriously unless you make it clear who you are, otherwise a lack of seniority may be assumed.

- ✔ Don't use emoticons.

- ✔ Don't misspell Russian words if you use them.

- ✔ Don't forget to be especially respectful to senior managers.

- ✔ Don't relax formality when dealing with government offices.

### Cultural issues

'It always helps to have a connection inside the country *and* within the industry you're trying to penetrate,' Daria Nikitina says. And it's always best to introduce yourself in person. To follow up a meeting, you can use Skype, and some Russians use it to stay in touch with employees who travel. However, different industries may frown on Skype and choose to communicate primarily by letter.

Although you may find your Russian correspondents rude and abrupt, be carefully polite yourself. Russians are not always good at replying, so if you don't receive a response, don't hesitate to send another letter.

Keep in mind that the Russians know a great deal more about you than you know about them. The more frequent their direct contact with British and American business people, the more sophisticated they are in dealing with them. The Russians are generally known for being very tough negotiators with an abrupt style. They want to win, so stay on your toes!

Some younger Russians are moving toward less formality, but this varies according to the company they work for. Government departments in particular remain very formal.

*Contributors:* **Daria Nikitina,** Media Specialist; **Anna Shevchenko**, Managing Director 3CN, cross-cultural risks consultancy; **Ilan Greenberg**, journalist formerly based in Kazakhstan and professor of foreign relations and writing

# *Writing to France*

British English is valued in France, mostly because of cultural attachment. But the preference is relative. If you have the impression that the French take great pride in their language and would rather be addressed in it, you're right. As Laura K. Lawless notes:

*I cannot stress enough how much better it is to write in French. If you don't speak French, hire a professional translator, through the International Federation of Translators (*www.fit-ift.org*), for example. Avoid uncertified translators and automatic translators. Poor translations would have a very negative impact on your business dealings.*

If you write in English, the guidelines for simplicity apply, but you must gauge your audience. 'Simple words show authenticity. But in English many of the hard, complicated ones are derived from French, so [the French] understand them. So you need to be not too basic, and not too complicated,' Jean-Philippe Schmitt says. If you write in French, more elaborate language is preferred.

Write with extreme politeness. Business relationships are very formal in France. The French are accustomed to respecting hierarchy and formal terminology. According to Schmitt, Americans come off as very direct, which the French consider rude. He recommends being 'less direct and more formal.'

## *Practical tips for email and letters*

Salutations for letters and emails should consist solely of the person's title, last name or honorific. Never use first names. Write *Monsieur Hollande* or *Monsieur le Directeur* rather than *Dear Mr Hollande.* For women, use *Madame Hollande, Madame la Directrice* or other appropriate title.

You can appropriately open with some background information about your company, any connection you have in common and/or your expertise, plus the reason you're writing – what you propose. Keep away from personal matters.

An email can end, *Meilleures salutations.* To close a letter, you may simply write *Sincerely.* However, it's usually best to use a formal closing that is particular to France. These can vary but follow very specific conventions, for example:

> *Dans l'attente de votre réponse, Monsieur Hollande, je vous prie d'accepter l'assurance de mes salutations distinguées*

Note that other French writing formats are similarly demanding. A French résumé or letter of intent has very specific requirements that you must know and follow.

### Mistakes to avoid

When communicating with French business people:

- ✔ Don't use *Cher* or *Dear* in salutations.

- ✔ Don't raise personal questions about family or health.

- ✔ Don't use humour, which can shock the French as inappropriate to an initial business relationship.

- ✔ Don't write carelessly, whether in French or English; pay attention to grammar, spelling, and vocabulary. In French, be sure to find the proper accents on your computer, and use them carefully.

- ✔ Don't use smiley faces.

- ✔ Don't use contractions, which look colloquial.

- ✔ Don't use the familiar word *tu* if writing in French; always use the formal *vous*.

### Cultural issues

The differences between French and English-speaking cultures comes through in the languages. English is very verbal, direct, and active whereas French is a nominal language. 'We use a lot of nouns,' Schmitt says, 'This makes us very passive. We beat around the bush and don't like to take responsibility. We use passive and indirect rather than putting ourselves as the actors.'

Thus, sounding direct may offend the French. Using less 'I' and 'we' constructions can help you appear more professional. Incorporating all the formalities is also recommended. Efficiency and friendliness are not generally valued, but outside business, people who communicate proactively and persistently can overcome the passive tendency of the French.

Cultural aspects make France a tough market for outside business people. The structures are rigid, and French people expect that rigidity to be respected, certainly in the way they write. The challenge is to be civil within the given structure.

Consider regional differences as well. Paris is multicultural but the south of France is more traditional and requires extra conservatism in how you write.

And, bear in mind that the French, like many Europeans, may not see their jobs as their highest life priorities. Indeed, careers may run third after family and personal pursuits.

*Contributors:* **Jean-Philippe Schmitt,** CEO, JP Linguistics, a consulting firm for French-American business; **Laura K. Lawless,** author of Intermediate *French For Dummies* and the about.com French Language Guide

## *Writing to Japan*

The Japanese prefer American-style-English for business purposes. However, a surprisingly small percentage of Japanese business people have been able to speak or write it. Japanese typically study English in school, but the teaching is academic rather than practical. One recent study showed that only 9 per cent of Japanese professionals had a facility with English.

The Japanese find English difficult, but the main reason for their lack of skill with the language is the insular view of their economy that prevailed until recently. Further, few young Japanese study in English-speaking countries. This situation is changing rapidly, however, and today Japanese industry assigns a new value to learning English and to truly joining the global economy.

Assume limited English skills and observe the guidelines for easy-to-understand writing I cover in Chapter 13: simple short sentences, basic words, and short paragraphs. Avoid colloquialisms, slang, abbreviations, and humour.

Fortunately the Japanese are very accepting of written communication in English and assume email and letters are appropriately written, provided they are clear. However, formality is essential, as is respect for elderly and important people.

A Japanese correspondent, or someone you meet in person, may ask questions in order to precisely 'place' you in the order of things. You should do the same and research a person's age, position and standing in the organisation.

### Practical tips for email and letters

Use last names with titles – Mr or Ms. – invariably if writing to someone for the first time. The Japanese customarily use honorifics to show respect for important people, often the suffix -*san,* which may be added to a first or last name. Never add –*san* to your own name.

Business cards are ritualistically exchanged in Japan, so be sure to bring a generous supply printed in English with Japanese on the reverse side. Treat every card you're given respectfully, read them carefully, and do not write on them nor put them in a back pocket. Place them gently in a card holder designed for the purpose.

Getting to the point quickly is preferred, so readers do not have to work to understand anything that is unnecessary. Begin by stating your message's purpose, such as to confirm a decision, suggest an idea, or present a report. Introduce yourself and any relationship with the recipient. Take care to write logically as well as clearly. To close, remind your reader of what you expect in reply,

End emails with *Best wishes* or *Sincerely yours. Regards* is often used for letters.

### Mistakes to avoid

When communicating with Japanese business people:

- ✔ Don't forget, ever, to acknowledge age and hierarchy in dealing with the Japanese.
- ✔ Don't embarrass anyone or criticise them publicly, causing them to lose face.
- ✔ Don't expect even important business people to speak or write English.
- ✔ Don't express emotions; the Japanese feel them too, but restrain from communicating them.

✔ Don't be surprised if you hear a lot of apologies, which people in this culture often express.

✔ Don't forget to bone up on Japanese rituals, such as presenting business cards when you appear in person.

### Cultural issues

For the Japanese, core values centre on pride, honour, trustworthiness, self-image, and being respected by others. Groups are owed paramount loyalty. Decisions are typically by consensus of all concerned parties.

The Japanese, and thus their language, value subtlety and ambiguity, rather than the directness that characterises American-English. They leave much unsaid and open to interpretation. They view truth as more relative, often involving group considerations.

Expressing 'yes' and 'no' is complicated in Japanese. In conversation, non-Japanese assume that when someone nods his heads and even says the word for 'yes' it means agreement, when these gestures are often only respectful signs that the person who nods is listening. The Japanese are highly aware of body language and non-verbal signals.

In both writing and in person, the Japanese avoid saying 'no' directly. If you receive a response such as 'We'll think about it' or 'We're interested, but the summer is not a good time,' you are being let down gently and are expected to understand that. In cases where you are the one saying no, be equally circumspect so as not to hurt the person's feelings. Aim to ask open-ended questions rather than those geared to producing a 'yes' or 'no.'

The Japanese require that relationships and mutual understanding be built before transacting business. They must first trust you. Their aim is to conclude with a win-win, rather than conquering an opponent, and to assume the relationship will be long-term. And, they are well-disposed to an outsider who writes with an appreciation of Japanese culture, showing an effort to understand it.

*Contributor:* **Kaz Amemiya**, corporate communications consultant, Cross-Media Communications, Inc., Tokyo

# Writing to India

English is the second language of India, which is fortunate because more than a dozen different Indian languages are spoken there. Style is strongly British in both speaking and writing. Communication with American companies has produced some acceptance of American style.

Commentators agreed with the six basic rules but noted that contractions are fine, and that the individual reader must be taken into account when deciding on whether to use only basic words. Using basic language when writing to the chairman of a company, for example, can lead to him underestimating you or feeling underestimated himself. At the same time, other non-English officers in the same company may not understand high English properly. 'One has to use more meaningful words at times. Language has to be impressive when writing to business houses, which does not mean the use of difficult words but conveying the message vividly,' Sewa Singh says.

## Practical tips for email and letters

Email and letters are good channels to begin and maintain relationships. Aim for clear communication without ambiguities.

When writing to someone you don't yet know, balance getting to the point with a formal/friendly greeting such as, *Hope all's well with you* or *Thanks for the prompt reply* or *This is with reference to.* If the relationship is a continuing one, you may go straight to the point.

When writing to top-level Indian people, address the person according to his status. Business people expect signs of respect. Use the surname unless you have already established a degree of informality. For a higher ranking person, you can use *Respected* or another honorific instead of *Dear* or *Mr.* Try to address your letter only to the concerned person so its importance is not diluted, and generally don't write to higher-ranking people than the one you want to deal with unless you must.

With a new acquaintance, introduce yourself with some concise background before getting to the point. One suggestion: break communication into three parts – background and facts, issues, and what is required from the recipient.

Important people do not want to waste time reading long letters, so make your specific requirement very clear.

Emails and letters may end as appropriate: *Looking forward to hearing from you* or *We look forward to a long and fruitful relationship with you.* The usual closings work: *Thanks, Regards, Sincerely, Faithfully*, or a variant.

Reply promptly to every email with a statement like, *Thanks for your email. I will attend to it shortly.* Send your full response as soon as is practical.

### Mistakes to avoid

When communicating with Indian business people:

- ✔ Don't use slang.
- ✔ Don't make grammatical mistakes. Indians pride themselves on being strict about grammar.
- ✔ Don't deviate from the content with irrelevant material.
- ✔ Don't combine two issues in one letter.
- ✔ Don't use first names if you don't know the people well, especially if they hold senior positions.

### Cultural issues

Every community has different customs and culture, so the safe approach is to keep the tone absolutely businesslike, unless you already share a degree of informality with the person and are knowledgeable about the community. Some of the well-established business communities like the Marwari, Gujaratis, and Sindhis for example, have specific social practices. Some reading about the historical background of the community you're dealing with can help cement a long-term business relationship.

Younger people tend to be less formal with each other, but not necessarily with outsiders. Approach all new contacts conservatively.

*Contributors:* **Sewa Singh,** Narangwal, Punjab

**Parthiv R. Kamdar, Deloitte, Mumbai**

# Writing to Mexico

Mexico boasts a thriving competitive economy, low unemployment and a large, growing middle class, making it a great market and resource for many companies. English is widely spoken, often well. High school students are required to be proficient, and moreover, many Mexican business people are highly educated and may have studied in the US.

Nevertheless, English-speaking business people may choose to write in Spanish via a translator or online translation, which needs careful review. Alternatively, using Mexican-style openings and closings is appreciated. Whichever language you write in, keep your style formal.

'Don't use slang and funny sayings they won't get,' Sandro Piancone says. 'They learn standard English in school and won't understand.' Keep paragraphs short, two or three sentences, to make documents easier to read.

Sending business letters by the postal service is not a good idea. Mail can take a month to arrive, or may never arrive at all. Federal Express or other commercial international shipping system works better; faxing is also an option. Email works, but responses may take two or three days. Most Mexican business people are not '24/7 plugged in, sitting by their email, and they don't all have Blackberries or smart phones,' Piancone says. 'Make a phone call after you send an email to check if your recipient has received it'

## Practical tips for email and letters

Write dates in the British style – day, month, year. Do not use first names. Remain formal until the other person uses your first name, in which case you may respond in turn.

Address people by their last names with a title. If you are fairly sure the person went to college, *Lic.* (for *Licenciado*) is appropriate for both men and women, as in *Lic. Lopez*. Other titles may be appropriate, such as *Ing.*, for an engineer. A full salutation can read, *Estimado Lic. Alvarez.*

You can also simply say, Sr. Alvarez (for a man) or "Sra." for a woman, without preceding these words with "Dear."

Be meticulous about spelling the company's name correctly. Mexicans take particular offence when you don't.

If you know the person, you can begin with cordial remarks asking about their children or the weather. But get to the point faster when you're writing to people you don't know. If you have a contact or common acquaintance, say so immediately. After a solid relationship is in place, you may find that correspondence devotes more space to reaffirming connections and common interests than the business at hand.

Closing in Spanish shows you're trying. One way: *Sin mas por el momento, le envoi un cordial saludo.* (Without more for the moment, I send you best regards). Or, just say *Atentamente,* equivalent to *Sincerely.*

### Mistakes to avoid

When communicating with Mexican business people:

- ✔ Don't be impatient for results; Mexicans work in a slower timeframe.

- ✔ Don't try to negotiate complicated systems of tax and labour law without help.

- ✔ Don't criticise Mexican business people in public, which undermines their honour and dignity.

- ✔ Don't write sloppy correspondence; Mexicans pride themselves on eloquent use of language.

### Cultural issues

Mexicans take rank and hierarchy very seriously, so be sensitive to status. Social and personal relationships are paramount. A Mexican saying translates, 'Without trust there can be no business.' They trust their family and connections, and you must demonstrate that they can trust you as well. Building trust usually takes time and your in-person presence. Mexicans are very proud of their heritage; they appreciate when you show an interest in their culture.

Doing business in Mexico also takes a connection. Find starting points through lawyers, banks, business associations, trade groups, or a consultant dedicated to helping manoeuver the Mexican systems.

Like the Japanese, Mexicans dislike saying 'no' directly. So watch for nuanced rejections.

*Contributor:* **Sandro Piancone**, author of *Discover the Secret Treasure Map to Selling Your Products in Mexico*, and CEO of Mexico Sales Made Easy.

# Writing to Germany

German companies and individuals may be more familiar with either British or American English, depending on their particular experience. Either way, the key guideline is *formal.* Never address anyone over age 16 by their first name. Germans are very respectful of hierarchy, so take scrupulous care to find out all the titles the person can claim – including academic – and use them all.

Avoid spelling and grammatical errors, which identify you as unprofessional. Germans may also take what you write or say more literally than intended. If you ask a German colleague how he is doing, for example either in writing or in person, he'll tell you. 'If you ask the question, you should wait and listen for an answer, not just skip on to the next topic. This will be viewed as rude,' Leesha Austin-Buehlmann says.

Recognise that Germans tend to be more reserved than Americans or British. They also tend to be well-educated, and well-informed about international matters and current events, and conduct such discussions both in business and personal settings. They may ask you for your opinions – especially about politics in your own country.

German is spoken in Austria and parts of Switzerland, and the business cultures are similar to Germany's. In fact, Austria is considered even more formal in style.

## Practical tips for email and letters

Give all emails good pertinent subject lines. You can address *Dear Mr Mueller* or *Dear Ms Mueller,* but must know any academic distinctions and credentials. *Dear Dr Mueller* is better if true, and if the doctor is also a professor, *Dear Professor Dr Mueller.*

Get down to business right away unless you know the person well. Write formally and correctly. Keep emails short and simple, focusing on no more than two or three points. Avoid emails that have no greetings and sound like you're issuing an order: *Johann, can you send me the monthly report?– Mike*

Generally, business letters should also move quickly to the point while being carefully polite. Keep them straightforward and simple. A suitable close can be *Best Regards* or *Kind Regards.*

Provide complete contact information. Note that by law, communications from German organisations include a detailed email signature with information about the company managing board, registered offices, and more.

Opinion is mixed on whether it's a good idea to include some German phraseology. Generally, err on the side of safety and stick to English.

### Mistakes to avoid

When communicating with German business people:

- ✔ Don't use slang, idioms, in-company terms, or lingo.

- ✔ Don't use smiley faces or other emoticons.

- ✔ If you're including German words in the text, find the correct special character letters on your computer.

- ✔ Don't use humour at anyone else's expense.

- ✔ Don't use the familiar for you, *du,* if writing in German; use the formal *sie.*

### Cultural issues

Germans tend to be more averse to risk than Americans and British and value thoroughness, accuracy, and planning. 'They approach tasks/projects with the view that all possibilities should be carefully thought through and analysed before jumping in and moving forward,' Leesha Austin-Buehlmann says.

Germans at times think that North Americans especially want to launch projects without planning effectively and fully thinking through potential consequences. They also criticise them for not carefully reading messages and documents, and in their eagerness for action, not listening to the problems and concerns voiced by European colleagues.

Germans also are put off by North American business people who appear to believe that Europe is a single country.

In general, younger people in Germany are becoming more informal in their communications style, but a very conservative approach remains best.

*Contributors:* **Leesha Austin-Buehlmann,** American marketing communications professional living and working in Germany; **Jim Holtje,** corporate communications professional with international experience; **Wendy Foster**, author, co-author of multiple *German For Dummies* books, teacher of German, French and ESL

# *Writing to Brazil*

Brazil is a huge country with a multi-faceted culture that pulls its diverse peoples together, but the middle class that runs the business world is small and relatively concentrated, though growing. As a result everyone knows everyone, and personal relationships are crucially important. You need to make contact gracefully, maintain relationships, and understand expectations and attitude.

In order to do this, you must be on the scene. Write a brief letter saying that you're coming to Sao Paulo, for example, establish why you're contacting the person, what you want, and definitely anything in common you can find. A vague general exploratory conversation doesn't work. People make plans more spontaneously, so trying to set a meeting up weeks in advance may not work. Neither does showing up on someone's doorstep.

You're likely to find Brazilians polite, warm and friendly but they're also very shrewd in evaluating your potential value. Brazilians themselves have an acute consciousness of class and more subtly, race. They are keyed in to status markers like where someone went to school and brands. They have their own elaborate system that gives them a social map of their own networks.

To find a place in that network, do your homework and look for a contact. Don't expect to transact business quickly. Quick deals do not happen. Work on the relationship and keep building it.

### Practical tips for email and letters

Brazilians see no meaningful distinction between British and American writing styles. Email is a widely accepted means of communication. The post office works, but not quickly.

People generally prefer getting straight to the point unless a relationship has already been established. Polite, clear and direct are fine, but Mariana Esteves notes that 'pragmatism and straightforward writing can sound like giving orders.' She recommends using softer language.

For a letter, opening and closing phrases in Portuguese are usually welcome. *Prezado* is equivalent to *Dear,* as in *Prezado Sr. (or Sra.) Silva.*

When reaching out to a large Brazilian business present mutual advantage early. Try to open with a compliment that relates to the person's work. If you're introducing yourself because you want to import children's clothing, for example, you can say 'I saw beautiful examples of your work in XXX and would like to talk to you about importing them to my store in London. I'm arriving on YYY. . . . ' Or, 'I hear you are the top company in Brazil for . . . .'

A cold call letter may or may not succeed. Look for connections. 'The content of a letter is less important than how you established the contact – who introduces you and how,' Leni Silverstein says. Reference your contact or anything else you have in common immediately.

To begin a dialogue with writing, have the material or prospectus translated into Portuguese and attach it to your letter.

A formal ending may be *Desde ja agrudeco* (Thanking you in advance*),* and finally, *Atenciosamente (*Yours sincerely*).* If you write anything in Portuguese be sure to use the proper accent marks.

### Mistakes to avoid

When communicating with Brazilian business people:

- ✔ Read between the lines: Brazilians dislike saying 'no' directly, so be on the alert.

✔ Don't expect speedy action with business formalities like registration; Brazilian law is cumbersome, inefficient and time-consuming.

✔ Take care in telling someone the people you already talked to because the person may be 'out of network' and not a friend.

✔ Don't make jokes when writing or speaking; Brazilians love humour but their jokes are often risqué.

### Cultural issues

Business and networking in Brazil blends personal relations. 'Networking is more about having a beer and talking about sports and general subjects than going straight to the point,' Mariana Esteves says. 'Relationships have to be built and then business will grow, but not before that.'

The younger generation is more casual than the older ones in some ways, but you should still conduct business formally.

Leni Silverstein suggests two courtesies that can help in Brazil – or any country foreign to you:

✔ Get a mobile phone with a Brazilian telephone number, so you have a local number.

✔ If you are comfortable reading Portuguese (or another language), you may write in English and invite the other person to respond in his or her own language, a gesture that is highly appreciated.

*Contributors:* **Leni Silverstein,** Anthropology PhD and independent consultant with Strategies for Development, a non-profit engaged in international gender and women's health issues; **Mariana Esteves**, International Relations Consultant affiliated with US-Brazil Connect, which brings together Brazilian and American students.

# Part VI
# The Part of Tens

Enjoy an additional Part of Tens chapter online at
www.dummies.com/extras/managingyour
investmentportfoliouk

## In this part . . .

- ✔ Improve, elevate and inspire. Master the art of business writing and change the face of your business for the better.

- ✔ Select the most relevant material for your target audience in order to capture and engage.

- ✔ Tweet your way to the top: Learn about Twitter and how to create a Twitter program. Find out how you can use this digital platform within your business for job hunting or establishing expertise.

# Chapter 15

# Ten Ways to Advance Your Career with Writing

## In This Chapter

▶ Using writing to improve relationships

▶ Elevating your value to employers, present and future

▶ Inspiring yourself with clearer goals and pathways

*G*ood writing helps you succeed. Despite the business world's growing need for effective communications, good writers are ever more difficult to find. Therefore they stand out. This chapter gives you ten specific ways to use your writing skill to advantage.

## Use Everything You Write to Build Your Professional Image

Messages that are well thought out, written, edited and proofed do more than accomplish your immediate goals. Over time, they add up to a powerful tool for creating the professional image you want. Granted, most people aren't conscious of why they find you credible, authoritative and convincing. But they credit you with all these qualities and more.

To capture this respect, use your best writing efforts on every message, not just the important ones like proposals and applications. Plan even the simplest email and draft it with attention to the person who'll read it and your purpose in writing. Review and rewrite as needed, and proofread meticulously. Be sure it's clear, concise, and to the point.

This approach applies even when you're messaging friends and peers. Work and play increasingly blend and overlap; your buddies may be sources of referrals, recommendations and connections. Maintaining good English when you text is harder, but try to be clear and unambiguous at least.

## Write a Great Elevator Speech – and Use It

Introducing yourself well at meetings, industry events, and public occasions can open doors magically. To craft an effective 15-second pitch, focus closely in on your own value to the people you want to meet. Think about what makes you special or unique in your field. Chapter 10 takes you through the entire process.

This mini-speech should say who you are, what you do, and why the person you're talking to should care. Most successful business people invest considerable thought in a strong message that sounds natural and memorable. They see their messages as works in progress, worthy of constant fine-tuning.

After you own a message you like, take it on the road. Find out where prospects, investors, collaborators, or anyone else you want to connect with get together. In-person networking is irreplaceable, despite all the new communication channels. If you're under 35, you may see few of your cohorts showing up and are likely to find yourself welcomed with open arms.

## Write a Long-Range Career Plan for Yourself

If you don't know where you want to be next year, or in five years, or ten, use the power of writing to catalyze your planning.

First write down what you'd most like to achieve in your chosen timeframe. Then look at where you are now, and write down the steps that can get you where you want to go. You may for example need to meet specific people, acquire training, take on certain assignments, or find intermediary jobs that qualify you.

A big advantage of planning this way is that you recognize opportunities you ordinarily overlook. You can also make better decisions because you know what contributes to your goal and what can sidetrack you.

 Writing it all down is essential. Otherwise, your thoughts revolve around the same old paths, and moving ahead just seems overwhelming. Expect to make adjustments along the way as you refine your journey.

# Write an Ad for Your Dream Job

Another good way to channel your thinking about the future is to create an ad for your ultimate job. Put yourself in the employer's place and figure out what he is looking for. Describe the job in detail and list every relevant responsibility, credential and personal quality you can think of. Going through this process shows you how well you currently match up and what you need to work on.

Go a step further and write a cover letter as if you were applying for the job right now. Highlight the experience and capabilities that match up. Thinking this through clarifies what you want and the opportunities to look for. Flip to Chapter 7 for more insights into compelling cover letters, and Chapter 9 for ideas on how to distill your essential value.

# Go Out of Your Way to Thank People

 The busier people feel, the more they forget to be polite, let alone appreciative. One of the easiest ways to make a good impression is simply to say thank you, in writing, when someone does you a good turn. She may have given you a referral or reference, introduced you to someone or tipped you off to an opportunity. Or she may have interviewed you for a job.

A graceful thank you helps you stand out. It establishes general good feeling, gives you an edge and puts you in line for more favors.

To write a good thank you, think about what the other person values hearing. Be specific. For example: 'Your virtual introduction helped me understand the profession better, and also, how to prepare myself for it.' For extra points, try hand-written notes. People really appreciate them. See Chapter 7 for more ideas.

# Take Notes to Control the Conversation

Write things down. Later, you may be the only person who knows what actually happened. People forget quickly when they have a lot going on.

Most people duck the role of note-taker at meetings, but it holds interesting potential. Use your notes to articulate the main points and future actions in a form suitable for sharing – an outline with bullets or numbered points is often sufficient. Your written notes make you the one who recaps what occurred and what decisions were made. Taking this action role brings you kudos and puts you in the loop for new information.

Taking notes on an everyday basis also pays dividends. An assistant manager I once worked with routinely used a notebook to jot down a line or two for every reasonably important conversation and event. She was able to flip through her notes and say, 'Actually, that document came in on January 17th' or 'We talked about that on April 3rd and you agreed to do it this way.' She was hard to argue with. But take care not to use this tactic on your boss too much.

# Use Messages to Stay in Touch and Build Relationships

Many written messages today help you interact with people you don't yet know – and may never meet. Consciously use business email and correspondence to personalize your messages, as appropriate.

Get personal gradually. A first message should be fairly formal. If your correspondent mentions a vacation or a personal milestone, perhaps inquire about that in subsequent correspondence. Or fall back on the weather, as you do in face-to-face conversation.

Take care when interacting with other cultures, however. Most expect more formality than you may be accustomed to, but may see relationships as prerequisite to business. So write with formality but be sensitive to the other person's cues – like moving to a first name basis, for example, or inquiring about the family. Chapters 13 and 14 offer a number of suggestions.

Also use writing to maintain contacts and connections after you establish them. Actively build a network of colleagues, peers, friends, former co-workers and even supervisors. You'll forge unexpected strengths.

# Write First-Rate Blog Posts, Comments and Tweets

A growing number of employers and recruiters look to the Internet for their hiring these days. They're interested in people who show the ability to think and articulate their ideas well, use good judgment and are comfortable with social media and other online tools.

See everything you post as a chance to showcase your skills. Your online presence lets people evaluate you almost as if they're eavesdropping.

Take care with your conversations, comments, and tweets. (See Chapter 11 and 16 for specific advice.) Avoid criticizing anyone else or exhibiting bad temper or hasty judgment. Above all, take care with your writing! Don't come across as semi-literate and careless. Think your ideas through. Express them well. Edit out misspellings, bad grammar and anything that reveals you to be less than the person you want to be.

Nothing is ever really erased. At least one website is devoted to tweets that were deleted by the important people who wrote them!

# Know How to Explain Your Value

Always be prepared to tell other people what you contribute, the value of your department's work, and your organization's goals and/or accomplishments. Think your message through and write it down, even if you expect to deliver it verbally when called for.

When applying for jobs, you must be able to articulate your value to your prospective employer. Today keeping a job is often as much of a challenge as getting a new one. Chances are pretty good that a current or new supervisor may ask you to explain your work, which probably means justifying your salary when budget cuts loom. Know the answer by working it out in writing.

Tackle the challenge similarly when explaining your department's work. And write up your best understanding of your organization's goals beyond the obvious one of making money. Think about how the company plans to do that: Expand? Cut costs? Improve service? Raise public perception?

When you align with company goals you do a better job – and you may well be noticed. To better engage employees with their 'mission' is a big driver for most organizations.

# Profile Your Supervisor for a Better Relationship

Creating a written, detailed profile of the person you report to can show you how to communicate with him better, ask for what you need and perform to higher expectations. The process, which I describe in detail in Chapter 3, also helps you better support the boss and make him look good – always an underlying part of any job.

Create a list of applicable factors, such as: management style; communication style; how he makes decisions (Ideas? Statistics? Impact on people); values and priorities (Efficiency? Teaming? Bottom line? New technology?)

Think also about his hot buttons, positioning in the company, biggest problems, ambitions, what he cares about, what keeps him up at night. You may be surprised at how much you know and can intuit, and how much the information helps you when you want something or wish to contribute more and be recognized. More than once, I've seen people turn an entire relationship around after creating a profile because they better understood the boss and acted on this knowledge.

# Chapter 16

# Ten Ways to Tweet Strategically

*In This Chapter*

▶ Designing a program to accomplish your goals

▶ Contributing material that's valuable to others

▶ Tweeting for jobs, reputation, and more

*T*witter, the social media mini-blog site that relays 140-character messages among its users, is a serious medium of communication despite all the dull 'chatter' that characterizes much of it. Last I checked the community had nearly 200 million monthly active users sending out an average of 58 million tweets daily. You may want to be part of this platform for any number of reasons, ranging from job-hunting to establishing expertise.

Making a Twitter account influential and professionally useful requires a real commitment on several levels. For your tweets to make an impact, the social media gurus say you need to send out five to 20 of them per day. You need to spend some time identifying who and what is out there, and choose people you want to follow. And you need to look at Twitter strategically, integrating it with all your other outreach, both online and offline.

The following ten essentials come from a writer's perspective. You can up your tweet savvy with *Twitter For Dummies* by Laura Fitton, Michael Gruen and Leslie Poston.

# Plan Your Twitter Program

Random tweeting produces random results. Consciously build a Twitter program that aligns with and complements your website, blog, video, other social media investments, and traditional media too (your print materials and presentations, for example).

Plan an overall strategic framework based on what you want to accomplish. Do you want to establish yourself as an authority in your field? Build a following? Draw people to your website or blog? Find a job? Connect with like-minded people – or influential ones? Defining your goals for any communication initiative – and especially Twitter – helps you decide who you want to reach and guides you to the best content for your purpose (see Chapter 11 for more on goal setting and writing guidelines for social media).

# Decide Who You Want to Be

Unlike formal media such as résumés or even websites, Twitter gives you the opportunity to show off your personality and individuality. But don't go freewheeling. Try for carefully spontaneous. Make an active decision about how to represent yourself.

Humor is great if you're good at it, and occasional sharing of personal information makes you real to your followers. But determine in advance how you want others to perceive you and what is appropriate to your goals. If you're aiming for a job in banking, don't share your romantic adventures or tell everyone that you made a fool of yourself at a party last night. If you want a copywriting job, you may want to show off your creativity. Set your own guidelines and stick to them. You're branding yourself.

There's never an advantage to demonstrating bad temper, a mean spirit, or sarcastic turn of mind – no matter how terrific it feels for 10 seconds. Negative or nasty comments don't play well online, and are apt to be widely circulated. And never forget that once 'published,' your short-sighted remarks (or images) may live forever to embarrass or even undermine you. I can think of many public officials in a position to reinforce this advice.

 If you recognize yourself as someone who's regularly tempted to send out angry or ill-considered tweets, use Twitter's scheduled/delayed posting feature, or an app that delays posting until your better angel has a chance to take back the helm.

# Take Pains with Your Bio and Photo

Twitter gives you 160 characters to tell everyone who you are. Use the space well. Try for a lively description that crystallizes your uniqueness, framed by your goals. I tell you how to identify and express your own core value, or that of your business, in Chapter 9. Use Twitter's own Bio Generator to describe yourself in an effective way for this medium. And, do whatever it takes to provide a good photo of yourself as you want to be seen, particularly if you're on the hunt for a job or clients. The bio and photo should reinforce your persona, which I talk about in the preceding tip.

# Listen to Your Target Audiences

Just as you hesitate to plunge into a party conversation before listening to what's already going on, take time to acquaint yourself with what people of interest to you are saying to each other on Twitter.

Notice the tone of the conversation as well as the content. Look for niches with which you're comfortable – questions you can answer, for example, or a subject you can productively comment upon. When you become part of a good exchange, keep it going. If you can build relationships tweet by tweet, you're successful.

# Aim to Be Useful

Never waste those 140 characters on trivialities that only your mother, perhaps, finds interesting. Share substance: news, ideas, tips based on your expertise, insights into events, a snippet from a good lecture you heard, links to something of interest, re-tweets of other people's messages you find worthwhile and believe others will appreciate. Some experienced Twitter users send such re-Tweets out once every three or so tweets, but invent your own guidelines. Whether to use Twitter's re-tweet feature to send your own messages out multiple times is more complicated. The premise is that you capture a different audience each time, but you also risk annoying your audience.

Remember that valued tweets are not necessarily about you. Mine your knowledge base, observe the conversations underway, stay up-to-date with your field, or with the world. `Alltop.com` is a good resource to keep current with what's happening.

# Avoid Blatant Self-Promotion

Don't sound like you're selling something. It's fine to call attention to a new blog post, event, workshop, article, book, product, or service improvement. But resist the temptation to promote yourself or your organization every time you tweet. You'll quickly be discounted as a self-seeker, contrary to the best spirit of the web and of Twitter.

Some savvy tweeters follow a rule of thumb: self-promote one out of four times, max.

That said, you cannot always predict what information may be welcomed. When you travel, for example, tweeting your location can draw useful advice and suggestions. And people may appreciate knowing where you are. I know more than one case in which a traveller tweeted from a remote location where the unexpected took place, and he was recruited as an on-site reporter and photographer for major media.

# Use Twitter for Surveys and Questions

Big companies are looking to Twitter to accomplish research that would otherwise be very expensive, and you can do that too.

Never before has soliciting opinions and knowledge been so quick, easy and cheap. Surveys and crowdsourcing are great ways to use the medium. Want to test-run your new website copy? Or a contest idea? Invite your network to visit your site and comment. Need an idea for employee recognition? Or advice on which logo to adopt? Put out the word. You can also ask your followers for resources and information when you want input. But don't ask questions you can easily answer yourself with Google's help, or request advice so often that you bore people.

# Write Tweets as the Ultimate Self-Edit Test

Writing well in 140 characters isn't easy, but authors are starting to write stories one tweet at a time, chefs are writing recipes to that character count, and employers are writing job descriptions on Twitter.

A good tweet usually requires good editing. Drill down to your message's core and then express that in the most economical way you can. But don't edit out the life and color – work to focus your meaning and limit its scope.

Experienced tweeters limit themselves to 120 characters to allow for easy re-tweeting. Use `bitly.com` to reduce the space needed to communicate links and URLs. As for abbreviations, what can I say? They're inevitable. But aim to be easily understood.

# Tweet at Optimal Times

Would you believe, studies have already been done on how to tweet in tune with your personal biological clock and likely reaction from recipients?

Tweeting early in the day, like 8 or 9 a.m., is most likely to produce upbeat enthusiastic messages, according to a two-year study conducted by Twitter itself and published in the magazine *Science*. That's on weekdays – on weekends, cheeriness peaks a bit later. So you're likely to tweet in an upbeat manner in the morning, and also, to read positive tweets from other people then.

Tweets are most likely to be re-tweeted when posted between 3 and 6 p.m. because people are tired then and prefer relying on other people's tweets. That comes from a HubSpot study. And at 10 and 11 p.m., people tend to send more emotional tweets, according to the Twitter study authors, so you may want to avoid tweeting when you're tired.

Of course, you can write all your tweets when you're in a good mood, according to your personal biological clock, and use a social media distribution service to feed them out over the day.

# Treat Twitter as a Serious Job-Hunting Tool

A growing number of employers use Twitter as a recruitment tool. They find it cheaper, quicker, and more selective than traditional methods. Some regularly follow Twitter conversations that relate to their industries, watching for people with good judgment, expertise, and best of all, a following that indicates they are respected. Others place employment ads on Twitter (to find out how to uncover these posts, and many additional in-depth insights, get hold of *Job Searching with Social Media For Dummies* by Joshua Waldman).

If you're in job-search mode, take special care to create good, useful, steady tweets that show off your best persona. Actively use Twitter along with other social media to showcase how conversant you are with these tools, because this know-how is a plus for many jobs these days. You may need to hone your tweet-skills to supply your résumé in this mini-format.

And check out Vine, Twitter's six-second video app program (vine.co or vine.twitter.com). Anecdotes about brilliant use of this format to score great jobs are tantalizing.

# Index

## • A •

abbreviations, avoiding, 303
About Us website page, 283–284
abstract words, 36, 60–61, 85
academic writing, 15
action verbs, 62–64, 89–91, 220
actor's trick, 236
ad for dream job, 339
adjectives, minimizing, 95–97
adverbs and -ly words, 81, 82,
   85–86, 95–97
Alltop.com, 348
Amemiya, Kaz (contributor), 324
'and' starting sentences, 115
anecdotes. See storytelling
Anglo-Saxon words, 59
animated intros to websites, 287
apostrophe, preposition pruning
   with, 86
Apps, Judy (Voice and Speaking
   Skills For Dummies), 229
Arnold, John (Web Marketing
   All-in-One For Dummies), 283
audience. See also cultural
   differences; global writing;
   relationship building
   as already known, 10
   benefits of understanding, 16
   for business proposals, 188
   connecting instantly to, 33–34
   of cover letters, 153–154
   defining, 25, 27–29
   demographics, 25, 138
   for elevator speech, 225, 227
   for email, 136–138
   factors affecting perception by,
      27–28
   framing content for, 29–30
   generations described, 26–27
   groups and strangers, 30–31
   highlighting benefits, not
      features, 35–36
   imagining your readers, 31–32
   making them care, 33–38
   message length for, 30
   for online media, 256–258
   personality/communication style,
      138
   psychographics, 27, 138
   reading level matched to, 50
   for sales letters, 170–171
   seeing through their eyes, 28–29
   simpatico factor for, 28
   as starting point, 12
   Twitter, 347
   for websites, 275–277
   WIIFM (what's-in-it-for-me)
      strategy, 34–35
audience-plus-goal structure
   for online communication, 19
   planning messages using, 12–14
   for presentations, 17–18
   for thank-you notes, 160–161
Austin-Buehlmann, Leesha
   (contributor), 331
authentic tone, 40

## • B •

Baby Boomers, 26
Becker, Michael (Web Marketing
   All-in-One For Dummies), 283
benefits
   as email focus, 138–140, 141–142
   features versus, 35–36, 261
   giving evidence of, 38
big vision stories, 214

bio for Twitter, 347
Birley, Shane (*Blogging For Dummies*), 289
bitly.com, 349
*Blogging For Dummies* (Gardner and Birley), 289
blogs. *See also* online media
  buttons, icons and links on, 273
  for career advancement, 341–342
  categories and tagging for, 295
  choosing a subject, 290–291
  creating, 288–295
  ease of creating, 270
  further information, 289
  good writing needed for, 270
  headlines and subheads for, 272, 293–294
  interactive strategies for, 263
  keywords for, 271–272
  length of posts, 293
  minimizing scrolling in, 272
  numbered lists for, 105–106
  planning, 289–290
  self-contained pages for, 272–273
  tone for, 292–293
  total number of, 10
  websites compared to, 270
  writing style for, 271–273
  writing tips for, 292–294
*Body Language For Dummies* (Kuhnke), 25
bold type, 2, 68, 147
bottom line, starting with, 34
boxes, 71
Brazil, writing to, 331–333
British English, 300–301
Buffet, Warren (financier), 181–182
building relationships. *See* relationship building
bulleted lists
  in email, 146–147
  giving bullet points meaning, 108
  narrative form versus, 108
  number of bullets, 106–107, 146
  in online media, 266

parallel structure in, 107, 146
punctuation and formatting, 108
in résumés, limitations of, 219
usefulness of, 106
bumpy road stories, 213
business documents. *See also* business proposals
business plans, 193–194
core strategies for, 195–196
executive summary, 178–182
headlines in, 196–198
importance of, 177
persuasive, 198–199
reports, 59, 182–187
tone for, 195–196
business plans, 193–194
business proposals
  big-picture review of, 189–190
  cover letters, 24, 152, 154–155
  formal (RFPs), 187–190
  goals for, 24
  growing need for, 187
  imagining your readers, 32
  informal, 190–193
  online-media related, 253
  presentation tips for, 188–189
  SMART mantra for, 190
  thank-you notes, 162
'but' starting sentences, 115
buttons on websites and blogs, 273

# • C •

call to action on websites, 282–283
capitals, shouting suggested by, 68
captions, 71
career advancement. *See also* promoting yourself
  building your image for, 337–338
  dream job ad for, 339
  elevator speeches for, 338
  explaining your value for, 342
  long-range plan for, 338–339
  note-taking for talking points, 340
  online media for, 341–342

relationship building for, 340–341
supervisor profile for, 342–343
thank-you notes for, 339–340
Carucci, John (*Digital SLR Video and Filmmaking For Dummies*), 240
categories for blogs, 295
Center for Plain Language, 97
China, writing to, 315–317
choppy sentences, fixing, 54, 80
chunking information, 262, 272
clarity. *See also* simplicity
  as basic writing premise, 47–48
  comparisons promoting, 64
  concrete nouns for, 60–62
  ease of reading aided by, 49
  email lead sentences, 132–134
  in legal writing, 97
  numbered lists for, 105
  in online media message, 259
  paragraphing for, 101
  requirements for, 48–49
  in résumés, 219–220
  short words for, 58–59
clichés, 95
closing
  elevator speech, 228
  email, 142–143
  in global writing, 309
  letters of record, 167
  presentations, 232
colloquialisms, avoiding, 303
colors, 69, 173
columns, width of, 68–69
commas, read-aloud test for, 109–111
company names on websites, 279
comparisons, 64–66
complaints, written, 163–165
complicated sentences, 54–56
Conaway, Wayne A. (*Kiss, Bow or Shake Hands*), 304
concrete words, 36–38, 60–62, 216
congratulatory notes, 163
Contact page of websites, 285

content
  assessing success of, 78–79
  big-picture review of, 117–118, 189–190
  cover letters, 151
  email, 132–134, 138–142
  framing for your audience, 29–30
  letters of introduction, 168–169
  letters of record, 166–167
  online media driven by, 250
  user-generated, 263
contractions, 45, 56, 302
conversational tone
  analyzing, 58
  for business proposals, 188
  for email, 144
  illusion of, 56, 57–58
  for online media, 58
  read-aloud test for, 80–81
  reader-friendliness of, 48
  techniques for, 56–57
  for websites and blogs, 273
core message or value statement
  aligning stories with, 216–217
  boilerplate statement, 211
  in business plans, 194
  crafting, 202–204
  defined, 17
  for elevator speeches, 225–226
  explaining your value, 342
  finding true value, 204–206
  as organization touchstone, 202, 211–212, 219
  personal, 17, 209–210
  putting it to work, 211–212
  questions to ask customers, 206
  questions to ask your team and yourself, 207
  stating in business terms, 208–209
  storytelling to illustrate, 214
  for your department, 210–211
correspondence. *See* email; letters
*Cover Letters For Dummies* (Kennedy), 156

cover letters
  brainstorming content of, 151
  business proposal, 24, 152, 154–155
  further information, 156
  goals for, 23–24, 151
  importance of writing well, 150
  job application, 152
  lead sentences, 152
  to multiple audience, 153–154
  planning, 151–152, 154
  résumé, 23, 152
  saving something special for, 154–155
  short notes, 153
  tone of, 155–156
credibility, online, 259–261
cultural differences
  Brazil, 331, 333
  China, 315, 316–317
  in formality, 40, 44–45, 300–301
  France, 320, 321–322
  Germany, 329, 330–331
  importance of, 19–20, 299
  India, 325, 326
  Japan, 323, 324
  media preferences, 305
  Mexico, 327, 328–329
  in native English, 300–301
  for online media, 266
  in pronoun usage, 113
  Russia, 318, 319
  in saying no, 309
  short words for bridging, 59
  working week and hours, 304

### • D •

demographics, audience, 25, 138
department core value statement, 210–211
dialogue in storytelling, 216
Dickinson, Marty (*Web Marketing All-in-One For Dummies*), 283
digital media. *See* online media

*Digital SLR Video and Filmmaking For Dummies* (Carucci), 240
*Digital Video For Dummies* (Underdahl), 240
discovery stories, 213
drafting documents
  list for, 105–108
  pause before editing, 78
  portion of time spent on, 22
  reports, 186–187
  subheads, 102–103
  tweets, 349
dream job ad, 339

### • E •

editing. *See also* grammatical correctness; organizing your document
  assessing content success, 78–79
  assessing language effectiveness, 79–81
  avoiding up-down-up inflection, 80, 81–82, 83
  big-picture review, 117–118, 189–190
  business proposals, 189
  choppy sentences, 54, 80
  clichés, 95
  distance needed for, 77–78
  for global English, 303
  jargon, 93–95
  long sentences, 54–56, 80
  macro and micro levels of, 78
  methods of, 74–76
  modifier minimization, 95–97
  monotonous rhythm, 55, 80
  non-contributing words, 87–89
  overly suffixed wording, 81, 82–86, 303
  paragraphing, 100–101
  passive forms, 62–64, 89–93
  pause between drafting and, 78
  portion of time spent on, 22, 77
  preposition pruning, 81, 86

process of, 74
proofreading, 74, 119–120, 189, 288
for readability, 52–53, 80
read-aloud test for, 14, 80–81, 104, 109–111
repeated words, 81
'show, don't tell' principle for, 96
tweets, 349
video, 242
when to stop, 122
writing compared to, 74
writing improvement guide for, 120–121
writing inseparable from, 73
elevator speech
audience definition for, 225
for career advancement, 338
closing with a question, 228
core value statement for, 225–226
encouraging follow-up questions, 228
goal definition for, 224–225
introducing yourself, 228–229
as an oral tweet, 224
origin of name, 223–224
practicing, 226
for relationship building, 224–225
representing your organization, 228
strategies for developing, 227
tailoring to the audience, 227
time length for, 224
writing down, 226
email
audience analysis for, 136–138
benefits as content focus, 138–140, 141–142
bold type in, 147
to Brazil, 332
bulleted and numbered lists in, 146–147
to China, 315–316
closing, 142–143
Contact page of websites, 285

conventions in this book, 2
to France, 320–321
to Germany, 329–330
global writing tips, 305, 307–309
goals for, 134–135
good writing's value for, 126–127
to groups, 139, 221–222
importance of, 16, 125, 128
inappropriate uses to avoid, 148
increasing amount of, 126
to India, 325–326
to Japan, 323
lead sentences, 132–134
length of, 144
as letters, 149
to Mexico, 327–328
middle section, 140–142
number sent daily, 10
promotions, 221–222
to Russia, 318
salutations, 131–132
short words and sentences for, 59, 144–145
signature block, 148
style of, 144
subheads for, 145–146
subject line, 129–131
time to send, 133
tone for, 139
unrelated or poorly written, 126
wide reach of, 126, 128
emotions. *See also* tone
benefits speaking to, 35–36
as contagious, 39
negative, avoiding displaying, 42–43, 156–157, 292–293
overcoming a blah mood, 43
responding to readers', 31–32
English, global. *See* cultural differences; global writing
*English Grammar For Dummies* (Woods), 109
*English Grammar Workbook For Dummies* (Woods), 109
-*ent* words, 81, 82, 85–86, 303

Esteves, Mariana (contributor), 333
examples, making specific, 36–37
exclamation points in email, 139
executive summary, 178–182
expertise, video for sharing,
    239–240

● *F* ●

Facebook, interactivity for, 263
false assumptions about writing,
    2–3
features, benefits versus, 35–36,
    261
Flesch, Rudolph (readability
    expert), 52
Flesch Readability Index, 49–50, 52
focus, transitions reinforcing, 104
Fog Index of readability, 52
fonts or typefaces
    background colors for, 69
    choosing, 67–68
    dropped or reversed-out, 69
    for letters, 173
    point size, 68, 287
    for presentations, 234
    for websites, 287
formality
    in corporate hierarchy, 40
    corporate hierarchy affecting, 41
    cultural differences in, 40, 44,
        300–301
    decreasing in business, 40
    less in online media, 264
    matching to the audience, 39–40
formatting. *See also* visual
        elements
    bulleted lists, 108
    letters, 173
    résumés, 220
Foster, Wendy (contributor), 331
France, writing to, 320–322

● *G* ●

Gardner, Susannah (*Blogging For
    Dummies*), 289
Generation X, 26
Generation Y, 26–27
Germany, writing to, 329–331
GistOut.com, 65
global writing. *See also* cultural
    differences
    to Brazil, 331–333
    to China, 315–317
    English as language of, 299
    to France, 320–322
    to Germany, 329–331
    to India, 325–326
    Internet presence, 312
    to Japan, 322–324
    to Mexico, 327–329
    monitoring assumptions for,
        304–305
    regulations and red tape in,
        306–307
    relationship building in, 301,
        305–306
    to Russia, 317–319
    tips for global English, 302–303,
        314
    variations in English, 300–301
    websites, 310–312
goals
    as already known, 10
    audience-plus-goal structure,
        12–14, 17–18, 19, 160–161
    business proposal, 24
    complaint letter, 164
    cover letter, 23–24, 151
    defining, 23–24
    elevator speech, 224–225
    email, 134–135
    'just enough', 77
    long-range career, 338–339
    needed for every message, 24
    online media, 254–255
    over-arching versus immediate, 12

presentation, 230
relationship building, 43–44
sales letter, 170
as starting point, 12
website, 274–275
grammatical correctness
comma usage, 109–111
computer tools for, 121
further information, 109
goals in this book, 109
journalist's guidelines, 116–117
noun/pronoun matching, 112–113
'and' or 'but' starting sentences,
115
readability aided by, 48
taking liberties with, 57
'which' versus 'that', 113–114
'who' versus 'that', 114
'who' versus 'whom', 114–115
graphics. *See* visual elements
groups
elevator speech audience, 225
email to, 139, 221–222
introducing yourself to, 167–169
visualizing individuals in, 31
Gunning, Robert (readability
expert), 52

• *H* •

handwritten notes, 163
hard copy, marking up, 75
headlines. *See also* subheads
for blogs, 293–294
in business documents, 196–198
for executive summaries, 182
fonts for, 67–68
hooking readers, 70–71
for letters, 173
online profiles, 220
for websites and blogs, 272
Holtje, Jim (contributor), 331
home page of website, 278–282
'however', using correctly, 111
humor, 266, 303, 311, 346

hyperbole, avoiding, 37
hyphen, preposition pruning
with, 86
hypnotherapist's trick, 236

• *I* •

'I'
for website and blog copy, 273
'you' instead of, 45–46, 171
icons, 5, 71, 273
idioms, avoiding, 300, 303
I-like-you trick, 236
imagining your readers, 31–32
inactive forms. *See* passive forms
inbound marketing, 290
India, writing to, 325–326
indirect constructions, 63–64, 303
inflection, avoiding up-down-up,
80, 81–82, 83
informality. *See* formality
informational interviews, 157–160,
161
-*ing* words, 81, 82, 83
interactivity, 19, 57, 262–263
international audiences. *See*
cultural differences; global
writing
Internet presence, global view of,
312
interviews
informational, 157–160, 161
talking points for, 244–245
thank-you notes for, 162
video scripting for, 243
introducing yourself, 167–169,
228–229, 238–239
-*ion* words, 81, 82, 84, 303
italics, 2, 68
-*ize* words, 81, 82, 85

• *J* •

Japan, writing to, 322–324
jargon, 93–95

job applications
  cover letters for, 152
  imagining your readers, 32
  thank-you notes for interviews, 162
  writing your dream job ad, 339
job hunting, Twitter for, 350–351
*Job Searching with Social Media For Dummies* (Waldman), 350
journalists, grammar guidelines of, 116–117

## • *K* •

Kamdar, Parthiv R. (contributor), 326
Kennedy, Joyce Lain (*Cover Letters For Dummies*), 156
Kent, Peter (*Search Engine Optimization For Dummies*), 250
keywords for websites and blogs, 271–272
*Kiss, Bow or Shake Hands* (Morrison and Conaway), 304
Kuhnke, Elizabeth
  *Body Language For Dummies*, 25
  *Persuasion and Influence For Dummies*, 198
Kushner, Malcolm (*Presentations For Dummies*), 229

## • *L* •

Lawless, Laura K. (contributor), 322
lead sentences
  cover letters, 152
  email, 132–134
  in global writing, 307–308
  online profiles, 221
  request letters, 158
  sales letters, 171
  video scripting, 242

legal writing, clarity in, 97
length of messages
  appropriate, 77
  blog posts, 293
  email, 144
  sales letters, 172
letterhead, 173
letters. *See also* email
  to Brazil, 332
  to China, 315–316
  complaints, 163–165
  cover, 23–24, 150–156
  email as, 149
  formatting, 173
  to France, 320–321
  to Germany, 329–330
  global variations in, 305
  global writing tips, 307–309
  handwritten, 163
  to India, 325–326
  of introduction, 167–169
  to Japan, 323
  making requests, 157–160
  to Mexico, 327–328
  networking with, 157–163
  privacy of, 149–150
  of record, 165–167
  to Russia, 318
  sales, 169–172
  signing, 173
  thank-you notes, 160–162, 339–340
lighting for video, 243
lists. *See* bulleted lists; numbered lists
logic
  paragraphing for, 100–101
  transitions establishing, 103–104
logo, 173
long sentences, fixing, 54–56, 80
Lopuck, Lisa (*Web Design For Dummies*), 274
Lowe, Doug (*PowerPoint For Dummies*), 234

Lurie, Ian (*Web Marketing All-in-One For Dummies*), 283
-*ly* words, 81, 82, 85–86

## • *M* •

macro-level editing, 78
margins, 68–69
*Marketing For Dummies* (Mortimer), 276
marking up print-outs, 75
Mehrabian, Albert (psychologist), 38
metaphors, 64, 303
Mexico, writing to, 327–329
micro-level editing, 78
Microsoft Word, 49, 50, 51, 121
modifiers, minimizing, 95–97
monotonous rhythm, 55, 80
Morrison, Terri (*Kiss, Bow or Shake Hands*), 304
Mortimer, Ruth (*Marketing For Dummies*), 276
music on websites, 287

## • *N* •

networking messages
  handwritten, 163
  importance of writing well, 157
  making requests, 157–160
  thank-you notes, 160–162, 339–340
non-linear strategies for online media, 261–262
note-taking for talking points, 340
not-for-profit organizations, 218, 252–253
nouns
  concrete, 60–62
  matching pronouns to, 112–113
numbered lists, 105–106, 108, 147.
  *See also* bulleted lists

## • *O* •

online media. *See also specific kinds*
  attracting desired audiences, 256–258
  avoiding hype, 261
  business proposals related to, 253
  career advancement using, 341–342
  changes created by, 11, 18, 249, 251
  clarifying your message, 259
  competition in, 18
  content driving, 250
  conversational tone for, 58
  credibility for, 259–261
  digital writing checklist, 265
  giving evidence for claims, 261
  global nature of, 266
  goals for, 254–255
  good writing needed for, 249–250, 251–252
  imagining your readers, 32
  interactivity for, 19, 57, 262–263
  non-linear strategies for, 261–262
  for not-for-profit organizations, 252–253
  profiles for, 263–268
  program development for, 254–258
  readability targets for, 51
  relationship building, 257–258
  search engine optimization, 250, 258
  share-it outlook for, 258–259
  simplicity for, 264–266
  supporting skimming and speed reading, 262, 265–266
  trial-and-error approach to, 255–256
  unlimited opportunities for, 11, 18–19, 252
  user-generated content for, 263
  word-of-mouth promotion, 257
  writing, 220–221

onscreen editing, 75–76
organizing your document
   audience-plus-goal structure,
      12–14, 17–18, 19, 160–161
   blog structure, 292
   at the editing stage, 100
   email, 140–142, 145–146
   letters of record, 166
   lists for, 105–108
   for online media, 261–262
   paragraphing for logic, 100–101
   reports, 185
   subheads for, 102–103, 145–146
   transitions, 101, 103–104, 199
   website structure, 276–278
-ous words, 81, 82, 85–86
overview statement for résumés,
   219

## • P •

paragraphs
   inserting breaks in, 100–101
   number of sentences in, 100, 101
   short, in global English, 302
   transitions between, 101, 103–104
   for websites and blogs, 272
parallel structure in lists, 107, 146
passive forms
   action verbs for fixing, 62–64,
      89–91
   avoiding in global English, 303
   minimizing, 57
   non-contributing words in, 87–88
   'there is' and 'there are', 63, 91–92
   to be verbs, 90–91
   to have verbs, 92
   using deliberately, 92–93
   Word's tool for assessing, 50
personal core value statement, 17,
   209–210
personality, reader's, 138
personalizing messages
   making requests, 158–160
   for relationship building, 44–45
persuasion, 48, 198–199
Persuasion and Influence For
   Dummies (Kuhnke), 198
photo for Twitter, 347
phrases. See words and phrases
Piancone, Sandro (contributor),
   327, 329
PLAIN (Plain Language Association
   International), 97
plan-draft-edit principle, 22–23
planning. See also organizing your
   document
   blogs, 289–290
   business plans, 193–194
   cover letters, 151–152, 154
   defining goals, 23–24
   defining your audience, 25, 27–29
   framing for your audience, 29–30
   generation considerations, 26–27
   imagining your readers, 31–32
   importance of, 21–22
   letters of record, 166
   long-range career plan, 338–339
   making people care, 33–38
   messages to groups and
      strangers, 30–31
   portion of time spent on, 22
   presentations, 230–232
   relationship building, 43–46
   starting with what you know, 12
   tone of voice, 38–43
   Twitter program, 346
point size for text, 68, 287
positioning statement on websites,
   280–282
PowerPoint, 233, 234–235
PowerPoint For Dummies (Lowe),
   234
prepositions, 81, 86, 115–116
present tense verbs, 90–91
presentations
   closing, 232
   delivering, 235–237
   further information, 229
   getting over fear, 229

goal definition for, 230
middle section, 231–232
opening, 231
planning, 230–232
software for, 233, 234–235
theme for, 230–231
tips for relaxing, 236
visuals for, 233–235
writing, 232–233
*Presentations For Dummies*
(Kushner), 229
print media, readability targets
for, 51
printer's proofs, 75
printing press invention, 11
print-outs, marking up, 75
professional image, building,
337–338
profiles, online, 263–268
promoting your organization
core message for, 17, 202–204,
206, 207, 208–209
elevator speech for, 228
email for, 221–222
representing your department,
210–211
storytelling for, 214, 218
true value for, 204–206
promoting yourself. *See also*
business proposals; career
advancement; cover letters
being the person you want to
present, 24
core value statements for, 17
elevator speech for, 223–229, 338
email for, 221–222
framing content for your
audience, 29–30
in online media, 260, 348
online profiles for, 220–221
promotional materials, global, 310
pronouns, matching to nouns,
112–113
proof marks, 75

proofreading. *See also* editing;
grammatical correctness
business proposals, 189
editing compared to, 74
getting help for, 119
process of, 74
tips for, 119–120
websites, 288
proposals. *See* business proposals
psychographics, audience, 27, 138
pullouts, 71
punctuation
in bulleted lists, 108
exclamation points in email, 139
for preposition pruning, 86
read-aloud test for commas,
109–111

• *Q* •

questions to ask
for big-picture review, 189–190
for blog creation, 289
for business plans, 193
closing an elevator speech, 228
for core message, 206, 207
for executive summaries, 180
for reports, 184
for video interviews, 243
for website creation, 274, 276–277
what's-in-it-for-them viewpoint,
168
WIIFM (what's-in-it-for-me)
strategy, 34–35

• *R* •

readability
clear and simple style for, 48–49
matching to the audience, 50
online media targets, 51
print media targets, 51
research results, 52
tips for increasing, 52–53
tools for assessing, 49–50, 51, 80

read-aloud test, 14, 80–81, 104, 109–111
reader. *See* audience
reader-friendliness
conversational tone for, 48
*-ion* words reducing, 84
words and phrases for, 59–60
relationship building
as constant goal, 43–44
cross-cultural, 301, 305–306
elevator speech for, 224–225
messages for, 340–341
in online media, 257–258
personalizing messages for, 44–45
as reward of good writing, 15
supervisor profile for, 342–343
using 'you' not 'I' for, 45–46
Remember icon, 5
repeated words, fixing, 81
reports
determining what matters, 183–184
drafting, 186–187
importance of, 183
organizing, 185
questions for starting, 184
quick tricks for starting, 179–180
reasons for writing, 183
time required for, 186
Request for Proposals (RFPs), 187–190. *See also* business proposals
requests, letters making, 157–160
respectful tone, 41–42
résumés
cover letters for, 23, 152
formatting, 220
overview statement for, 219
tips for effective, 219–220
rhythm
conversational tone using, 56
fixing choppy sentences, 54, 80
fixing long sentences, 54–56, 80
monotonous, 55, 80
natural cadence, 53

varying sentence length for, 53
for writing improvement, 53
run-on sentences, 110
Russia, writing to, 317–319

• *S* •

sales letters, 169–172
salutations, 131–132, 307
sans-serif fonts, 67
Schmitt, Jean-Philippe (contributor), 322
scripting video. *See* video scripting
search engine optimization (SEO), 250, 258
*Search Engine Optimization For Dummies* (Kent), 250
self-promotion. *See* promoting yourself
selling proposition. *See* core message or value statement
senses, engaging in storytelling, 216
sentences. *See also* lead sentences
in bulleted lists, 107
choppy, fixing, 54, 80
ending with prepositions, 115–116
long, fixing, 54–56, 80
number per paragraph, 100, 101
'and' or 'but' starting, 115
run-on, 110
short, for email, 145
short, for résumés, 219–220
short, in global English, 302
varying length of, 53, 56
sequence
numbered lists for, 105
transitions establishing, 104, 199
serif fonts, 67
Services page of websites, 284
share-it outlook for online media, 258–259
sharing expertise, video for, 239–240

short words
  concrete nouns, 60–62
  for email, 144–145
  in global English, 302
  relying on, 58–60, 80
  for résumés, 219–220
  for storytelling, 216
  for video, 242
'show, don't tell' principle, 96, 216
sidebars, 71
signature block, email, 148
signature for letters, 173
Silverstein, Leni (contributor), 333
similes, 64
simplicity. *See also* clarity
  as basic writing premise, 47–48
  for business proposals, 188
  for conversational tone, 56
  ease of reading aided by, 49
  font choices for, 68
  for online media, 264–266
  requirements for, 48–49
  in storytelling, 216
  in use of colors, 69
  in website design, 287
Singh, Sewa (contributor), 326
slang, avoiding, 303
SMART mantra, 190
social media. *See* online media;
  Twitter
sound quality for video, 243
spam, 148
speeches. *See* writing the spoken
  word
storytelling
  basic types of stories, 213–214
  building your story, 214–215
  in business proposals, 188
  core message illustrated by, 214
  framing for your audience, 28
  hard-wired response to, 212
  as human connector, 17
  ideas made real by, 36
  opening presentations, 231
  power of, 212–213

  starting point for, 214–215
  tips for writing stories, 215–217
  truthfulness in, 214
  uses for, 217–218
strangers, writing to, 30–32, 139
strategic writing, 10
structuring. *See* organizing your
  document; planning
style of communication, reader's,
  138
style of writing
  clear and simple, 47–49
  conversational, 48, 56–58
  email, 144
  grammatically correct, 48
  persuasive, 48
  readability guidelines, 49–53, 80
  rhythm, 53–56
  texting and instant messaging, 88
subheads. *See also* headlines
  for blogs, 294
  for business documents, 197–198
  for email, 145–146
  fonts for, 67–68
  hooking readers, 70–71
  for letters, 173
  for websites and blogs, 272
subject line of email, 129–131
subject of writing
  as already known, 10
  for blogs, 290–291
  real and relevant substance, 14
  as starting point, 12
success stories, 214
suffixes, overused, 81, 82–86, 303
supervisor profile, 342–343
support materials, global, 309
sympathy notes, 163

## • *T* •

tagging blog posts, 295
taglines on websites, 279
talking points, 18, 244–245, 340
telephone messages, 245–246

testimonials, 206, 285–286
Testimonials page of websites, 285–286
text-style messages, 88, 264, 266–267
thank-you notes, 160–162, 339–340
'that', 'which' and 'who' versus, 113–114
theme for presentations, 230–231
'there is' and 'there are', avoiding, 63, 91–92
Tip icon, 5
*to be* verbs, 90–91
*to have* verbs, 92
tone
  appropriate, 39–40
  authentic, 40
  for blogs, 292–293
  for business documents, 195–196
  for business proposals, 188–189, 192–193
  for complaint letters, 164–165
  conversational, 48, 56–58, 80–81, 144
  for cover letters, 155–156
  for email, 139
  factors affecting, 38–39
  formal versus informal, 39–40, 41, 44, 264
  importance of, 38
  letters of record, 167
  negative, avoiding, 42–43, 156–157, 292–293
  overcoming a blah mood, 43
  read-aloud test for, 14, 80–81
  respectful, 41–42
  transitions reinforcing, 104
Track Changes tool, 76
transitions, 101, 103–104, 199
translation, investing in, 305
Try It icon, 5
Twitter. *See also* online media
  being useful, 348
  bio and photo for, 347
  for career advancement, 341–342
  commitment to, 345

editing for, 349
interactive strategies for, 263
job hunting using, 350–351
listening to target audiences, 347
number of active users, 10
planning your program, 346
representing yourself on, 346–347
self-promotion on, 348
six-second video app, 351
surveys and questions using, 349
timing tweets, 350
tweets per day sent, 10
writing tweets, 266–267
typefaces. *See* fonts or typefaces

**• U •**

Underdahl, Keith (*Digital Video For Dummies*), 240
up-down-up inflection, avoiding, 80, 81–82, 83

**• V •**

value proposition. *See* core message or value statement
verbs. *See also* passive forms
  action, 62–64, 89–91, 220
  present tense, 90–91
  *to be*, 90–91
  *to have*, 92
video for websites, 288
video scripting
  further information, 240
  for introducing yourself, 238–239
  planning the visuals, 237–238
  production essentials, 241–242, 243
  for sharing expertise, 239–240
  writing the script, 240, 241–243
vine.co or vine.twitter.com, 351
visual elements. *See also* fonts or typefaces
  About Us page photo, 284
  breaking up type blocks with, 37

colors, 69, 173
effective graphics, 70
email, 145–147
of letters, 173
margins and columns, 68–69
for presentations, 233–235
sidebars, boxes and lists, 70–71
value and credibility shown by,
66
for websites, 272, 284, 286–288
white space, 67, 69, 173, 272, 287
visualizing individuals when
writing to groups, 31
voice. *See* tone
*Voice and Speaking Skills For
Dummies* (Apps), 229

## • *W* •

Waldman, Joshua (*Job Searching
with Social Media For
Dummies*), 350
warmth, for conversational tone,
56
Warning! icon, 5
'we', for website and blog copy, 273
*Web Design For Dummies* (Lopuck),
274
*Web Marketing All-in-One For
Dummies* (Arnold, Becker,
Dickinson and Lurie), 283
websites. *See also* online media
About Us page, 283–284
audiences for, 275–277
blogs compared to, 270
building, 273–288
buttons, icons and links on, 273
call to action on, 282–283
company names and taglines on,
279
Contact page, 285
conventions in this book, 2
further information, 274
globalizing yours, 310–312
goal definition for, 274–275

good writing needed for, 270
headlines and subheads for, 272
home page, 278–282
increasing ease of creating, 270
interactive strategies for, 263
keywords for, 271–272
minimizing scrolling in, 272, 288
planning, 273–274
positioning statement, 280–282
proofreading, 288
reviewing existing sites, 274
self-contained pages for, 272–273
Services page, 284
structuring, 276–278
Testimonials page, 285–286
total number of, 10
writing style for, 271–273
what's-in-it-for-me (WIIFM)
strategy, 34–35
what's-in-it-for-them viewpoint,
168, 171
'which', 'that' versus, 113–114
white space
importance of, 67
for letters, 173
right-justified text for, 69
for websites and blogs, 272, 287
'who'
'that' versus, 114
'whom' versus, 114–115
Woods, Geraldine
*English Grammar For Dummies*,
109
*English Grammar Workbook For
Dummies*, 109
Word (Microsoft), 49, 50, 51, 121
wordiness
'just enough' goal, 77
modifier minimization, 95–97
non-contributing words, 87–89
overly suffixed wording, 81,
82–86, 303
preposition pruning, 81, 86
up-down-up inflection, 80,
81–82, 83

words and phrases. *See also* passive forms; wordiness
  action verbs, 62–63, 89–91
  adverbs and adjectives, 95–97
  'and' or 'but' starting sentences, 115
  assessing language effectiveness, 79–81
  clichés, 95
  concise use of, 77
  for conversational tone, 56
  'however' usage, 111
  jargon, 93–95
  non-contributing words (list), 89
  noun/pronoun matching, 112–113
  prepositions, 81, 86, 115–116
  reader-friendly, 59–60
  real and concrete, 60–62
  repeated, fixing, 81
  short, relying on, 58–60, 80, 144–145, 216, 242, 302
  suffixes, overused, 81, 82–86, 303
  for transitions, 103–104
  varying length of, 59
  'which' versus 'that', 113–114
  'who' versus 'that', 114
  'who' versus 'whom', 114–115
working week and hours, 304

writing improvement guide, creating, 120–121
writing the spoken word. *See also* presentations
  elevator speech, 223–229, 338
  numbered lists for, 106
  for practical purposes, 243–246
  rules for, 223
  talking points, 18, 244–245, 340
  telephone messages, 245–246
  video scripting, 237–243

**• X •**

Xunyu, Weng (contributor), 317

**• Y •**

'you', framing messages with, 45–46, 171, 273

**• Z •**

Zarella, Dan (researcher), 133
Zoninsein, Manuela (contributor), 317

# About the Author

**Natalie Canavor** is a nationally known expert on business writing whose mission is to help people communicate better so they can get what they want—whether that means a job, a promotion or a successful business.

She has earned her living as a national magazine editor, business writer, communications consultant and public relations director, winning more than 100 national and international awards along the way. At every step she noticed that in the business, nonprofit and government worlds alike, good writers are valued and rewarded. But ineffective communicators often miss their best opportunities and fall short of their career dreams.

Today, Natalie creates practical writing workshops for businesspeople, writers and professionals in every walk of life. She uses a learning framework based on what works. Her unconventional approach meshes the best strategies from many writing venues: feature articles and columns, video scripts, websites, presentations, print and online marketing materials and copywriting. She finds that given a planning structure and set of down-to-earth techniques, most people can dramatically improve their own writing.

Natalie is the author of *Business Writing in the Digital Age* (Sage Publications), a textbook for advanced and graduate-level students of business and public relations. And with Claire Meirowitz, she co-authored *The Truth About the New Rules of Business Writing* (Financial Times Press), a quick guide to better writing.

She is also an adjunct professor at NYU, where she leads advanced writing seminars for Master's degree candidates in public relations and corporate communications. For five years she wrote a column on professional writing techniques for the International Association of Business Communicators.

Natalie is happy to consult with organizations that see the value of raising the bar on writing, and travels to present custom workshops for businesses, associations and other groups. Find her at: Natalie@businesswritingnow.com.

# Publisher's Acknowledgements

We're proud of this book; please send us your comments at http://dummies.custhelp.com. For other comments, please contact our Customer Care Department within the U.S. at 877-762-2974, outside the U.S. at (001) 317-572-3993, or fax 317-572-4002.

Some of the people who helped bring this book to market include the following:

### Acquisitions, Editorial, and Vertical Websites

**Project Editor:** Jo Jones

**Commissioning Editor:** Claire Ruston

**Assistant Editor:** Ben Kemble

**Development Editors:** Brian Kramer

**Technical Reviewer:** Pamela Jones

**Proofreader:** Melanie Assinder-Smith

**Production Manager:** Daniel Mersey

**Publisher:** Miles Kendall

**Cover Photos:** ©iStockphoto.com/ shironosov

### Composition Services

**Sr. Project Coordinator:** Kristie Rees

**Layout and Graphics:** Jennifer Creasey, Joyce Haughey, Jennifer Mayberry

**Proofreaders:** Lindsay Amones, Jessica Kramer, Susan Moritz

**Indexer:** Steve Rath

### Special Help

**Brand Reviewer:** Carrie Burchfield